THE CEREMONIAL ORDER OF THE CLINIC

Cardiff Papers in Qualitative Research

About the Series

The Cardiff School of Social Sciences at Cardiff University is well known for the breadth and quality of its empirical research in various major areas of sociology and social policy. In particular, it enjoys an international reputation for research using qualitative methodology, including qualitative approaches to data collection and analysis.

This series publishes original sociological research that reflects the tradition of qualitative and ethnographic inquiry developed at Cardiff in recent years. The series includes monographs reporting on empirical research, collections of papers reporting on particular themes and other monographs or edited collections on methodological developments and issues.

Classics in Medical Sociology
An important new initiative featuring revised editions of influential titles in medical sociology.

Also available:
Aspects of Illness: Second edition
Robert Dingwall

The Ceremonial Order of the Clinic

Parents, doctors and medical bureaucracies

P.M. STRONG
Late of the London School of Hygiene and Tropical Medicine

Edited by
ROBERT DINGWALL
University of Nottingham

Ashgate

Aldershot • Burlington USA • Singapore • Sydney

Published by
Ashgate Publishing Limited
Gower House
Croft Road
Aldershot
Hants GU11 3HR
England

Ashgate Publishing Company
131 Main Street
Burlington, VT 05401-5600 USA

Ashgate website: http://www.ashgate.com

British Library Cataloguing in Publication Data
Strong, Philip
    The ceremonial order of the clinic. - (Cardiff papers in
    qualitative research)
    1.Medicine - Practice 2.Organizational sociology
    I.Title
    610.6'8

Library of Congress Cataloging-in-Publication Data
Strong, P.M.
    The ceremonial order of the clinic : parents, doctors, and medical bureaucracies / P.M.
    Strong, with an introduction by Robert Dingwall.
        p. ; cm. -- (Cardiff papers in qualitative research)
    Originally published: London ; Boston : Routledge & Kegan Paul, 1979. (International
    library of sociology) With new intro.
    Includes bibliographical references.
    ISBN 0-7546-1746-7
    1.Physician and patient. 2.Sick children--Family relationships. 3.Parent and child. 4.
    Pediatric clinics--Sociological aspects. 5.Social interaction. I.Title. II. Series
    [DNLM: 1.Child Care. 2.Communication. 3.Interpersonal Relations. 4.Parent-Child
    Relations. 5.Physician-Patient Relations. W 62 S924c 1979a]
    RJ47.7 .S78 2001
    610.69'6--dc21
                                                                2001022936
ISBN 0 7546 1746 7

Printed and bound in Great Britain by Antony Rowe Ltd.,
Chippenham, Wiltshire.

Contents

Foreword to 2001 Edition

Robert Dingwall

Philip Strong died suddenly on 11 July 1995 at the age of 49. Although he was widely recognized as perhaps the most original, creative and intellectually gifted British medical sociologist of his generation, this reputation was based as much on the vivacity of his conference presentations as on a body of published work. Few sociologists outside this specialty had taken note of his challenges to many of their orthodoxies. For a younger generation, he has become a semi-mythical figure, one talked about with great respect by those who knew and worked with him but whose specific contribution remains obscure. In part this results from the accidents of publication histories and of fate. Philip Strong's papers were widely scattered, often in other people's collections and thus relatively inaccessible to electronic search tools. His contribution to the launch version of the Open University's influential course U205, *Health and Disease*, was obscured by the conventions of collective authorship then in force at that institution. His book (Strong and Robinson 1990) on the impact of the 'Griffiths' reforms of NHS management suffered the usual marginalization accorded by medical sociologists to books on nursing - their unthinking reproduction of the hierarchies of esteem in health care is a curious phenomenon. At the time of his death, a projected study of AIDS and the social order was no more than a set of uncollated drafts and notes. *The Ceremonial Order of the Clinic*, his one sole-authored book, appeared only in an experimental and user-unfriendly print format in a short production run.

There has, though, to be a stronger justification for republishing this work than the fact that my own copy has become dog-eared from the fingers of several generations of PhD students, that numerous libraries have seen copies vanish from their shelves and that many of the new health studies libraries developed since 1979 would like to acquire a copy. The enduring importance of *The Ceremonial Order* lies in its continuing relevance to core questions about what it takes to do sociology in a rigorous fashion. This book is not just about encounters between doctors, parents and their disabled children in the health systems of a Scottish and an American city during the early 1970s. It is also Strong's manifesto for a way of doing sociology. Indeed, one of the refrains of the book is the reproof of sociologists, even its hero, Erving Goffman, whose conclusions do not clearly arise from their data and who do not order them in a coherent fashion. Strong may have been one of the pioneers of the study of reality as a social construction but he was in no way a social constructionist in the post-modern sense. For him, the social construction of reality was an objectively observable phenomenon, where the creative powers and improvisational skills of human beings ran into the cultural and organizational frames that made intersubjective understanding possible. In the, slightly dated, language of one of his favourite quotes from Goffman (1972, p.3), his was not the study of men and their moments but of moments and their men. Interaction works because parties recognize the constraints of the enduring frames that are constitutive of their encounter and can improvise within them to achieve their own local and immediate ends. One of the objectives that Strong set for sociology was the study of such enduring features, the specification of their components and the exploration of their histories.

Intellectually, *The Ceremonial Order* comes out of a particular conjunction in British sociology. Strong draws on three main traditions. Most obviously, there is a running debate with Goffman. Few sociologists have managed to get inside Goffman's thinking with such success - it is uncanny how much of Strong's [published as Strong and Davis (1977) but originating in conference papers from the early 1970s] writing on 'role formats' prefigures Goffman's (1975) own writing on 'frames' in *Frame Analysis*. [In later discussion of the themes of *The Ceremonial Order*, Strong (1988) eventually abandoned his own terminology in favour of Goffman's.] Strong is both fascinated by and exasperated with Goffman. He is fascinated by the richness of Goffman's conceptual thought and the way in which he draws on a huge range of literary and historical materials to exemplify and develop this. At the same time, he is obviously frustrated by the lack of systematic evidence for so much of this thought, particularly by Goffman's concentration on the exotic rather than the everyday.

In this, Strong clearly draws more deeply than the citations indicate on ethnomethodology. Although he emphasises his disagreements with ethnomethodology and conversation analysis (then still known as conversational analysis), his concern with the mundane sets him apart from many contemporary qualitative sociologists in the deviance tradition with which he had been associated. Strong's respect for doctors, and his acknowledgement that medicine may be life and death to the rest of us but is also legitimately a routine job of work to its practitioners, are still capable of shaming the superficial critiques of many medical sociologists. Similarly, although he is sceptical about the claim that the only hard data are those on tape, his attention to language and the details of talk mark a quite new turn in ethnography. Strong clearly associates himself with the ethnomethodological critique of interview data and with the primacy of direct observation of behaviour as the basis for understanding the construction of social order. However, that behaviour is not to be rendered at second hand through redescriptions of the observations. Strong gives the reader the talk as near-verbatim as a hand-note can render and then discusses what can be done with it.

Analysis must be carried out with the same rigour. One of the virtues of *The Ceremonial Order* is the clarity with which analytic processes are described. Strong explains in some detail just how to do a constant comparative analysis and analytic induction. The case for his discovery of the bureaucratic format is assembled out of a series of comparisons, between different settings, different tasks, different countries. It is extended by his wholly original use of a deductive approach to test the validity of his claims on part of the data set placed to one side for that purpose rather than included in the original induction. A few of his students have attempted something similar and a similar argument was made by Strauss in some of his later thinking on grounded theory but the post-modernist dismissal of concerns for validity testing has led to the neglect of the possible role for hypothetico-deductive logic in qualitative research.

In distancing himself from ethnomethodology and, more particularly, conversation analysis, Strong may have followed Goffman more closely than hindsight would consider appropriate. Goffman himself had a celebrated love-hate relationship with these ideas and his own position shifted considerably between 'Replies and Responses', cited by Strong as a 1975 working paper and published as part of *Forms of Talk* in 1981, and 'Felicity's Condition' (Goffman 1983). It is arguable that Strong might have had a more positive relationship with the 'institutional talk' movement within conversation analysis, which emerged during the 1990s. His observations on the way in which doctors delivered 'bad news', for example, anticipate the more detailed specifications published by Maynard (e.g. 1996) and others. By this time, however, his own interests had tended to follow those of Goffman himself into the moral order of interaction. This is anticipated in the final chapter of *The Ceremonial Order*, where Strong reflects on the origins of the bureaucratic frame. In 'Replies and Responses' Goffman drew a distinction between structurally and morally adequate interaction. He argued that conversation analysts were only interested in the former - what constituted a structurally adequate next turn - rather than the latter, which addressed the question of the substantive content of the next turn. This argument was extended, but in a way more sympathetic to conversation analysis, in 'Felicity's Condition', where it was formulated as the question of what can we say in the next turn without disconfirming others' working assumptions of our sanity.

At the end of the book, Strong begins a reflection on the sort of society within which the bureaucratic format comes to dominate so many service encounters between citizens and the state. He sees its generalization in fairly traditional terms as the result of the development of welfare states and the extension of the moral neutrality of nineteenth century bourgeois medicine to all classes. The charity format of moral investigation disappears in the face of this advance (see also Strong 1988). This is linked to a discussion of the third protagonist in the book, Talcott Parsons. Although Strong is less dismissive of Parsons's contributions than were many of his contemporaries, he criticises Parsons throughout for the formal approach to role analysis that he had inspired and for the lack of explicit evidential support from his own observations for the propositions set out his classic exposition of the sick role. At the end, however, Strong notes that Parsons was the first to comment on medical gentility, the overwhelmingly polite character of medical encounters. He still has some scepticism about Parsons's explanation of this phenomenon but uses this to launch a discussion of the interdependence of bureaucratic medicine and working-class participation in the political process.

1979, the year in which *The Ceremonial Order* was originally published, was, of course, also the year in which Margaret Thatcher was elected Prime Minister on the basis of a critique of the post-war welfare state that Strong saw as fundamental to the bureaucratic format. The search for a different kind of medical practice has continued to preoccupy governments through the subsequent twenty years and is as prominent in the new Labour agenda as it was under the Conservative administrations of the 1980s and early 1990s. Although, as *The Ceremonial Order* indicates, the bureaucratic format is remarkably resilient, it has come under increasing pressure to move more towards the private format and a more consumerist medicine without confronting the extent to which the private format is incompatible with the cost control and standardization inherent in tax or insurer-funded health care. Strong's attempt to understand this phenomenon led him in a rather different direction to many of his contemporaries. For him, the attack on collectivism merited a serious attempt to understand its intellectual roots rather than a simple rejectionist response. If the British working-class had consistently voted for a more marketized society, this could not be dismissed as a simple matter of false consciousness. There was some deeper story of dissatisfaction that required a more systematic understanding of the culture of liberal capitalism. The work associated with the AIDS project reflected this concern with the roots of order and the desire to understand how liberal society could function. In terms of medical encounters, the issue remains, of understanding how the increasing affluence and continuing embourgeoisement of advanced societies generates discontent with standardized goods and services, even where, as Strong noted, many of the distinctions may be largely or entirely spurious.

Editor's Acknowledgements

The text was prepared from the original and copy edited by Edward Dingwall and I should like to thank him for his sterling efforts. Pam Watson revised the index to reflect the new pagination. This work was supported by funding from the London School of Hygiene and Tropical Medicine, organized by Nick Black. A few original typographical errors have been silently corrected, one footnote has been altered to make it clearer to a new readership and the bibliography has been revised to take account of the publication of materials cited as 'unpublished' or 'in press', where these can be identified. The whole project has been sanctioned and supported throughout by Philip Strong's partner and literary executor, Anne Murcott, and I am most grateful to her for constant advice, encouragement and assistance.

Preface

This is a book about the meetings that doctors have with parents when a child is sick or needs medical inspection. (Here and there therapists too will make an appearance.) It says nothing about the medicine involved in all this and very little about people's feelings, opinions or perceptions. These things are interesting but they are not my interest here. My concern is with ceremonies: with the social form of the occasion and the sorts of identity tacitly claimed by each party and conferred upon the other.

One way of seeing it is as a study of 'the doctor-patient relationship'. Of course parents are not patients, meetings are not the only part of a relationship, and doctors can meet with patients in a variety of ways, not just one. All of these qualifications will get a mention. Nevertheless, the phrase is worth hanging on to until something more precise - if rather more academic - appears later on.

Research always takes place somewhere, so these are particular meetings between doctors and parents circumscribed by time and place. Most of them occur or occurred in a Scottish city over three and a half years in the 1970s, the rest took place over three weeks in an American city of much the same size. Narrower still - and three weeks seems narrow enough - these are primarily meetings in the outpatient (or ambulatory) clinics of two hospitals, though a few other kinds of encounter are mentioned.

So now my title seems grandiose and even the sub-title is inflated. (Would 'Three Weeks in Another Town' be better?) Nevertheless there may be something in this exaggeration, though justification will have to wait.

Sticking to the meetings - and I shall do this most of the time - the point of my description is this: here are over a thousand separate occasions on which parents met doctors and met them in all kinds of different circumstances, and yet the manner of their meeting, the ceremonial order of the occasion, was pretty much the same no matter how other things might vary. One can go further. The outward form of their relationship took just the one shape, give or take a few minor alterations, in all of the Scottish consultations and in most of the American ones too.

So here we have something fairly powerful, a manner of meeting, a mode of being doctor or parent, which was used across a great range of contingencies and particularities; this mode - the 'bureaucratic format' - is my main topic and I shall try to describe its nature, its origins, the methods by which it was sustained and the actual fit between this outward show and the matters which it clothed.

In doing all this I have several aims, some modest, others less so. One is to comment on medical work with children and their parents, another is to reflect more generally on medical consultations, for although paediatrics is one small segment of the clinical world its methods and dilemmas may well have their counterparts in other areas of medicine. There may also be something for sociologists. Medical consultations are merely one in a myriad of those occasions and events which sociologists study, and the frames or formats used therein may be of little interest save to specialists in the field of service relationships. Nevertheless, since the master of ceremony, Erving Goffman himself, has paid little attention to the study of any one order, the careful delineation of a form may still have something to say about formats in general and the structures which shape our daily lives.

Acknowledgements

Unlike most modern products, sociology is normally presented as the work of named individuals. Washing machines and cars may come to us with the names of their makers attached, but we know that this is the name of an organization, not of an individual. Our own machine is merely one of thousands like it, in whose production thousands are typically engaged. Further, the manner in which this work-force is best coordinated is a topic of constant public and theoretical concern. Sociology, however, is often seen, even by its members, as a craft where the quality of any individual piece of manufacture i.e. predominantly fixed by the skills of the craftsmen and the intellectual tools with which he or she works. It is to these features and not to the organization of the craft that attention is typically directed. We focus on the paradigm involved, which itself can hardly be said to produce things, and on the specific arguments, which are seen as representing the qualities of the individual worker.

Moreover, even if we do inquire into the way this piece of research came to be undertaken or that article written, we experience great difficulty. For such information is rarely given to us. We are presented merely with a finished product whose most striking clue to its production is the name of the author(s). The nearest that we normally get to discovering the conditions under which this product originated is a brief section, such as this, called 'acknowledgments' and the address of an institution in small print on the fly-leaf. Occasionally a book may be found to be part of a series of such works, all carried out at a particular institution. But such information gives no clue as to how the work came into being. The main focus still rests upon the author.

Such neglect is fostered by the craft nature of the discipline. Not only do we 'see' authorship in others' work but we experience it in our own. For, as members of a cottage industry, we are typically in control of some important aspects of our own production. We can often determine the topic, the rate at which we work and the occasions of our labour. Such personal control, particularly when contrasted with its absence in many other kinds of work, can conceal some of the important constraints that bind us. Although we can often exercise some choice as to what we will produce, in practice almost all of us have to choose from a very limited range of topics because of the conditions of our employment as teachers or researchers. Teachers find it hard to do field-work while researchers, though they are certainly allowed, even pushed into the field, often have little choice as to the specific pasture or how long and in what fashion they may graze.

At the same time, this individualization of the product conceals not merely the constraints that bind the individual producer but the essential contribution made by others. For intellectual goods are above all the products of *conversation* and in this respect are co-authored by one's colleagues and friends and those entrepreneurs who create the intellectual and organizational climate in which one works.

Clearly, one can do little in an acknowledgments section to repair this gross omission. I have taken a long time to produce this book and am indebted to a great many people, many of whose contributions must remain unacknowledged for there is little space in which to mention them and little enough awareness on my own part of the role which they have played. My first thanks must go to those who persuaded me to move from teaching to research and also to the SSRC (UK) which actually funded the project on which this book is based, as part of a programme grant to the Institute of Medical Sociology on 'Objectives and Needs in Systems of Social and Medical Care'.

To all of my colleagues on the programme and at the Institute I owe a great deal but particularly to Alan Davis who not only gathered the data with me but has been a source of invaluable ideas and conversation over many years. Various drafts of the manuscript were typed several times by Jeanette Thorn with speed, accuracy and amazing good will. It was then read by Mildred Blaxter, Alex Campbell, Robert Dingwall, Gordon Horobin, Raymond Illsley, David May and Ross Mitchell, many of whose comments I more or less grudgingly accepted. I am also indebted to the medical staff of the various hospitals and clinics who put up for so long with such an intrusion – as did the parents and their children. Since I have substituted letters for names and invented new ones where these appear in quotations, I cannot mention anyone directly but I would, in particular, like to thank Dr C, Dr I, Dr O and Dr N for all the help they gave me. Finally I owe an enormous amount to the advice, support and long-suffering nature of Gordon Horobin, Raymond Illsley and Angela Weight.

1 Introduction

One of the most striking features of modern life is the constant invention, application and modification of modes of formal organization. So endemic is this practice that we have a special name for those social entities that are most susceptible to this process. 'Organizations' are called after the techniques they most dramatically embody. Many of us work within formal organizations and all of us routinely encounter their representatives in our daily lives. However, although the social technology of the modern organization is as important as the industrial technology around which it is also based, it receives rather less publicity. Inventing the petrol engine has more status somehow than designing General Motors, if possibly smaller rewards. This is not to say that such matters are ignored, merely that the attention which is paid them is usually partial or specialist. Since this is so, the bureaucratization of medicine and its effects in the doctor-patient relationship, or more generally staff-patient relationships, have received little attention. Much effort has been expended on examining some of the minutiae of these relationships, surprisingly little has gone on examining the context in which they occur. Without an understanding of that context and of the forces that produce it, many suggested reforms of medical practice will prove futile. This book does not itself set out to suggest such reforms. My aim is simply to provide information for their discussion.

Before considering my arguments in any detail it may prove useful to reflect on quite why the bureaucratic context of medical work has been ignored. First, much everyday discussion of organizations is often merely critical rather than analytic. In popular usage 'bureaucracy' and 'bureaucratic' have pejorative meanings rather than the purely technical ones that are standard in sociology. 'Official' is a rather more neutral term but it shades off into officious and officialdom, just as formal organizational procedures become red tape. Even 'organization', which has a largely technical meaning, has developed shades of menace, as in The Organization, and facelessness, as in The Organization Man. In this lay version, bureaucracies and bureaucrats are impersonal entities against which individual human beings struggle as best they can. It was somewhat in this fashion that Stimson and

Webb's (1975) sample of patients told each other stories of their 'triumphs' over doctors. Similarly, the staff in this study had their moans about the bureaucracies of which they were a part, but here 'the bureaucrats' turned out to be someone other than themselves; the real villains were the administrators or the booking and record staff.

The discussion in which such terms are used and stories told is rarely systematic. A less critical and more descriptive view of organizations may be found in novels, television and films. Nevertheless, with a few notable exceptions, for example 'Something Happened' by Joseph Heller, or the films of Olmi, routine organizational life is largely ignored. The demands of television for an endless supply of material have indeed generated series that are based within organizations such as police departments, aircraft factories, prisons, motels and hospitals, and this genre has recently spread to popular novels and films. However, with a few possible exceptions such as the early programmes of 'Z-Cars', the organizations are merely a backdrop for dramatic incident. Their creators focus on bank robberies rather than petty theft, on staff's romances, not on their alienation. Moreover, just as the daily workings of these entities are ignored, so too there is a similar absence of popular works about the history of organizations. Most general readers of history are more interested in the personal and biographical; in kings, queens and politicians. The only organizations which receive much written attention are military ones and those such as ITT which have been implicated in major political scandals.

There is, however, one popular form which does describe the daily practice of organizations, the documentary, and it is this which most closely approximates my intention here. Filmed documentary has one powerful advantage. The audience are shown the data with a vividness unmatched by any other form of presentation. However, such a method is analytically weak. As Galbraith has remarked, a picture may sometimes be worth a thousand words, but the reverse is often just as true. Ideally one should join the two methods and in a more perfect world a book such as this would be accompanied by a film of some of the typical events that it describes.

For most people reflection upon organizations is a thing of the moment. For some it is their daily bread, and here at least we may find systematic analyses of the mysteries of organizational action. However, these too have their own particular biases. The central weakness of much academic discussion of these matters is the polar opposite of that found in popular thought. Whereas the latter over-emphasizes individuals, scholarly debate commonly removes them altogether. The triumph of cog over machine, the drama of the operating table, the love between nurse and doctor; all these disappear. In their place stands the autonomous organization, independent of human will and action and vested with its own purposes and acts. In their concern to define and study organizations precisely, these writers have laid their entire stress on those formal procedures which separate organizations from other social entities and in doing so have reified bureaucracies, have turned them into things set totally apart from those who work within them (Bittner, 1965).

This reification is partly the product of the typical aims of such research. Managers and administrators and those whom they sponsor, whether directly or indirectly, to engage in research are all largely preoccupied with the efficiency of organizational functioning. Monitoring and evaluation are the key tasks and organizational modification the end. However, these concerns would seem to have a differential effect upon the students of bureaucracy. Academic outsiders tend to reify the organizations which they study, but those involved in daily struggle within them are prone to a somewhat different fault. In this second version, and it is this which dominates the discussion of medical work with patients, the central concept in understanding bureaucracies is 'communication' (Ley and Spelman, 1967; Fletcher, 1973; Bennett, 1976; Byrne and Long, 1976). Whereas in the academic model the organization is reduced to a series of formal procedures, here these aspects disappear and emphasis is placed upon relationships between individuals. In this it has something in common with the lay tradition mentioned earlier. However, unlike this, its principal stress is on consensus not conflict, on reaching understanding not on achieving victory. The lay tradition emphasizes intensely personal feelings and interests, with the organization a mere locale for their expression, but these exist in the communications model only in so far as they are held to be organizationally relevant. Politically, the model is espoused by the liberal and counter-posed to what are seen as old-fashioned formality and unquestionable hierarchy; and in many ways it presents a critical, reforming approach to professional work. At the same time, it upholds and undoubtedly stems from that central ethic of the profession which emphasizes service to the individual client.

This emphasis on individuals leads to a stress on personalities, perceptions and individual style. Staff are instructed to inspect their own actions, to be nicer and more understanding towards their patients. Harsh, intolerant action is condemned, and so is the unthinking and routine. Staff are also exhorted to learn more about the different personal and cultural backgrounds of their clients, and there may also be pressure for professional recruitment to reflect this diversity. At the same time such analysts are sensitive to the problems, opinions, satisfactions and dissatisfactions of their patients. Interview studies of patients are a favourite vehicle for combining both these approaches. On the one hand they may reveal something of their background and expectations; on the other hand they give them a chance to express their opinions on the service they have received. Finally, great awareness is displayed of the many possible misunderstandings that may occur between staff and patients. The research that is done here pays special attention to how staff and patients actually talk to each other. Its emphasis is on listening more carefully to what people say, using a language they will understand, and so on.

The principal reform that is urged by such writers is better education. They seek the modification of the medical school curriculum and may even themselves provide means for re-education. Byrne and Long (1976) not only organize conferences at which general practitioners may learn new communications skills, but also provide a home tutor in these. There is much that is beneficial in such an approach and yet, as Freidson notes, it suffers from the faults of all individualist thought:

> In considering how the members of the profession work its leaders typically see solutions to the problem of poor or unethical work in recruiting better-motivated and more capable entrants to school, in improving their professional education and in generally 'raising standards'. All these devices are predicated on the aim of changing the quality of *individuals,* the assumption being first that social pathologies connected with medical care, like illnesses connected with mankind, are 'caused' by the characteristics of the individual providing the care rather than by the environment in which those individuals provide care, and second that they are best treated by treating the individual rather than the environment (Freidson, 1970b, p.6).

In other words, the communications approach, by emphasizing the individual, renders the organization itself transparent; its actual workings, organizational procedures and resources, the social settings and roles of the participants, all of these are simply assumed. At the same time, despite this atomization of individual members, organizational purposes are still present but in covert and thus uninspected form. Individuals are viewed not in their own terms, not in the light of their actual interests, commitments, resources and constraints, but solely as regards the official goals of the organization. Thus 'communication' is used in a very special sense. It does not refer to all the myriad ways in which doctor and patient both present their behaviour and read that of the other as each attempt to make sense of and to control the situation, but simply means seeing that illness is efficiently diagnosed and patients properly informed about their illnesses.

Similarly, although there is a search for disharmony and an attempt to put it right, such matters are regarded as purely surface features, for there is a basic assumption that the interests of staff and patients are one and the same. Patients want to be cured, staff wish to cure them. Most conflict or dissatisfaction is viewed as a product of misunderstanding or mistaken technique and not of anything more fundamental.

My own position emphasizes the structural context in which individual action occurs. If one wishes to explain behaviour or seeks to modify it, it is as important to look to the system as it is to the individuals who work within it. At the same time I take a rather more pessimistic view of organizations than is held by those who write within the communications tradition. As I shall argue, there are fundamental and irreconcilable conflicts inherent within medical consultations, and these occur, not just between staff and parents, but even within the various things that any one individual may want or have to do. We seek to solve these dilemmas as best we can and may at various times try out a variety of solutions, but each entails its own problems and none is more than provisional - though some may prove more satisfactory than others.

Medical Role-relationships

My own aim is to render the transparent apparent, to set the business of diagnosis, treatment and their discussion within an organizational framework. There are various ways in which this might be done and mine is only one of these and a highly restricted one at that. My concern is with the consultation itself and more specifically with its overt social form. The question I have asked of each consultation is: what kind of social occasion is this? When we ask this question normally, we refer to something rather special and out of the ordinary. A 'social occasion' is seen as more formal, more public and more artificial than everyday events. To be at one is to be on display and thus hopefully on one's best behaviour. One needs to know in advance just what the rules are: what one should wear; what may and may not be said; and to whom one may talk and when. And yet, seen from another perspective, all social intercourse shares these qualities, if to a less self-conscious degree. Whenever we talk to someone we are in one sense on display. Judgments about our character and competence are routinely made by others as we in turn judge them. The smallest detail of speech, tone, posture or dress can serve as evidence in this, and may accordingly be adjusted to suit the occasion. Thus, all social life has an artificial, rule-governed and ceremonial aspect (and may thus be seen as artfully constructed), though many of our calculations are so routine that they pass unnoticed even by ourselves. It is this ceremony that I am principally concerned with and, in a phrase, my topic is the 'ritual' aspect of medical consultations.[1]

As we shall see, there are special sets of rules that make medical consultations distinct social occasions, rules that are clearly informed by the location of the action within a bureaucratic setting. In claiming that this occasion has a distinct form, I do not deny that there are important differences between one consultation and another. Some recent researchers who have observed medical consultations have emphasized the differences between doctors. Byrne and Long (1976) have noted distinct personal styles with respect to the role that doctors let patients play in the consultation. At a more microscopic level, Bloor (1976a, 1976b) has demonstrated that in one condition at least, tonsillitis, different consultants use very different criteria and search procedures in their decision-making. Consultations will also differ according to the patient, the medical condition, and the particular setting in which the patient is seen. The research reported here was done in collaboration with Alan Davis, whose own work (1978) has focussed on the distinct variation produced by the different tasks which different clinics set for the doctor. Yet, despite all this variation it still makes sense to talk of a general form, or rather forms, which medical consultations hold in common, something over and above these other differences, and which distinguishes them from, say, taking one's car to a garage or buying groceries at a supermarket.[2]

These forms, as I argued earlier, have received relatively little empirical attention. The two studies worthy of note are those of Parsons (1951) and Stimson and Webb (1975). Parsons's study was in fact carried out in the 1930s but it was not written up until many years later. It utilized the classic sociological concept for expressing the differences between social occasions, the theatrical metaphor of role. In this, each person is seen as having a repertoire of different parts, some of which are common to all, others of which are more specialist. Parsons described two roles in medical consultations, the role of the patient - the 'sick role' - and the corresponding role of the doctor; the two together equalling the 'doctor-patient role relationship'. His analysis has been extremely influential but since it is highly complex, being in fact part of a much wider attempt to explain all social life, it will not be considered in detail here.[3]

Suffice it to say that there are several parallels between the analysis presented in this book and that of Parsons. Both models emphasize the doctor's technical authority over the patient, and the impersonality and neutrality of medical interaction. At the same time Parsons's analysis has serious flaws. Although it was derived from both observation and interview, the research itself is not specified and no data are presented to warrant the assertions made, a drawback which is all the more considerable given the very high level of generality at which Parsons writes. He also assumes that there is only the one role-relationship between doctor and patient, that the social form is always the same. This, as will be shown later, is a gross mistake and one which arises in part from the ahistorical nature of the analysis. Parsons fails to link his description of the rules of doctor-patient interaction to the specific structural, ideological and organizational context. There is little sense in his work that doctors are doing a job under specific sets of conditions which severely constrain the work they perform.

The general model of interaction which Parsons uses, that of role analysis, is severely defective. In one sense role theorists have taken the theatrical analogy too far. They write as if there were detailed, pre-ordained scripts which players learnt off by heart and then repeated, word for word, on relevant occasions. They omit the sense in which social occasions are continuously constructed by their participants. There are indeed rules to be followed but there are often many different ways in which this may be done, and one rule may conflict with another. Moreover, rules are used as well as followed, but role theorists omit the conflictual and strategic aspects of interaction. For Parsons, moral neutrality, medical control and impersonality are simply written into the script. He fails to see that achieving them and using them for whatever purposes one has presents serious and complex problems to the participants.

Although many of Stimson and Webb's conclusions about the form of the occasion are in some respects similar to those reached by Parsons, they are more adequately demonstrated and are set in a far more convincing general model of interaction, that provided by Goffman.[4] However, just as Parsons's main interest was the formulation of a general theory of society and not the study of consultations, so for Stimson and Webb the social form of medical relationships is a backdrop to their principal theme. Their main story concerns the patients, not the social form, and they are interested in patients' expectations of a medical consultation, their strategies during it, and their consequent behaviour and opinions. Therefore they do not set out to provide a detailed model of the doctor-patient role-relationship, while their relatively brief reflections upon it are based on only a limited amount of data: they observed fifty consultations in two group practices run by general practitioners.

There is therefore scope for a detailed study of the social forms of medical consultations. Such forms I shall call 'role formats', although I will not stick unswervingly to this terminology and to avoid the endless repetition of the term I shall substitute phrases such as 'mode', 'model' or 'framework' on occasion. In the consultations reported on here, there were four types of role format in use, which I have named the 'bureaucratic', 'charity', 'clinical' and 'private' modes respectively.[5]

With these formats I am concerned, almost exclusively, with doctor-parent interaction. By and large the matters to be considered here do not directly involve children. At first, it may seem odd for a study of medical work with children to exclude any systematic consideration of the children themselves or of adults' relationship with them. If this study were of a ward or concentrated entirely on therapists' work with children, then such puzzlement would indeed be justified. In such studies children played a central part in the interaction; and, as Alan Davis and I (1976a) have shown, medical work took on a special shape to accommodate this.[6] But in outpatient clinics things were different. In all but two cases, the child had an adult representative, someone who could act on his or her behalf, someone who in fact took over most of the patient role within the consultation. It was the parents or guardians who owned, managed and worried about the children's future; and it was to them, as the children's representatives, that talk was normally addressed. For almost all children, even the older ones, were routinely and smoothly excluded from the bulk of the action within most consultations; the adults present, both staff and parents, used a wide range of devices to this end.

Thus, the reason for my exclusion of children from this book is that they themselves were largely excluded from the consultations. Quite how this exclusion was managed will be considered in chapter 8. For the moment I shall merely note its occurrence.

My topic, then, is the formats used between doctors and parents; and of the various modes that were in use I have selected just one, the bureaucratic format, as the principal object for analysis because it was by far the most commonly observed form. Despite the striking differences between the principles that underlay the Scottish and American medical services, this one mode was found in almost all settings. It was in universal, though not always sole use in the Scottish hospital, and was the most frequent mode in the American hospital. Even in clinics where other formats were used, it was still the typical mode.

Note that in calling it the bureaucratic format I am not suggesting that it has all the characteristics which are popularly ascribed to bureaucracies. The particular form that I describe here is subtle and complex, and one that might not spring immediately to mind if one was asked to speculate on the shape that medical bureaucracy might take in consultations. For this reason, the greater part of the book is devoted to an explication of its various rules and their use in differing circumstances. Only at the end do I suggest reasons for their existence and discuss how far my analysis may be generalized to other medical work.

Note also that although the bureaucratic mode will receive most of my attention, I shall at times pay close regard to certain aspects of the other formats. My aim is not to engage in any systematic study of these other modes, for I have little enough data on some of them; rather it is to bring out the special nature of the bureaucratic format by highlighting particularly striking differences from other modes. My analyses of the latter are meant to serve as signposts to the bureaucratic format, not as detailed maps to their own interior.

The Concept of Role Format

Before proceeding to outline the research on which this analysis is based, it may be useful to outline my underlying theoretical stance and to spell out in a little more detail just what is meant by role format, though non-sociologists may prefer to skip this section.

Given my concern with the ceremonial aspects of medical interaction, I am heavily dependent on the work of the leading analyst of everyday ritual, Erving Goffman (1961, 1963, 1970, 1971a, 1971b, 1972, 1975a, 1975b).

However, the central concept in this monograph, that of role format, is not to be found in Goffman's own writings, but is one of my own invention. Goffman has produced so many new concepts in his time that I thought I might try my own hand at this game and besides, despite his great proliferation of conceptual aids, none of the relevant terms which he offers quite fits my own purposes, though what I myself have to suggest is merely an offshoot or close relative of Goffman's own classifications. The fundamentals of Goffman's analysis are described by Gonos in the following fashion:

> Everyday life is seen to be made up of more or less well-delineated 'worlds', realms of special meaning within which a particular language of reality is binding. The world is a mode of experience fleshed out by adherence to the rules of a frame or occasion ... a frame is described by the stable rules of its operation, whatever the circumstances of any particular enactment. In other words, frames are not to be thought of as empirical in the way that situations are (Gonos, 1977, p.857).

> What guides conduct in this structuralist world is not a set of shady core values or the influence of others who are co-present, but the individual's place within the formal social organization of a concrete social activity, or to put it differently, one's place with respect to the social relations of production of a ritual world (Gonos, 1977, p.862).

Grasping Goffman's own classification of these frames is a rather difficult task, since he has written voluminously in and around the area but has never supplied any ordered guide to his own work. New terms and new ideas are continually appearing and the relation of any one to any other is a matter for some speculation. Moreover, he himself has not been interested in depicting the particularities of any individual social forms, save those of games and of the theatre, both of which are rather special kinds of frame set apart from the more serious business of daily life.

Three broad distinctions between types of frame can, however, be discerned in Goffman's work. The first of these is a division of frames into two fundamental classes, those which are seen as applying to 'natural' events and those which are used for 'social' phenomena (Goffman, 1975a). Among social frames there is in turn a crucial distinction between 'focussed' and 'unfocussed' gatherings, that is between those which apply when people are merely in one another's presence and those which regulate occasions when there is a single focus of cognitive and visual attention. These latter occasions are termed 'encounters' or 'situated activity systems' (Goffman, 1961). Finally Goffman distinguishes between different types of encounter, between those which are merely one-off affairs and those which develop an institutionalized form:

> When the runs of a situated system are repeated with any frequency, fairly well-developed *situated roles* seem to emerge: action comes to be divided into manageable bundles, each a set of acts that can be compatibly performed by a single participant. In addition to this role formation, there is a tendency for role differentiation to occur, so that the package of activity that the members of one class perform is different from, though dependent upon, the set performed by members of another category. These kinds of roles, it may be added, differ from roles in general, not only because they are realized and encompassed in a face-to-face situation but also because the pattern of which they are a part can be confidently identified as a concrete, self-compensating system (Goffman, 1961, p.96).

With this final distinction we have at last a unit of analysis which is appropriate to the interaction considered in this study. Medical consultations are clearly institutionalized activity systems, encounters that are repeated over and over again, though not always by the same participants or in the same settings. Moreover there is, as I shall show, a complex division of labour which sustains a joint version of reality across such a wide diversity of individual circumstances that the frame can, with some truth, be seen as self-compensating.

Goffman's own attempt to encompass the ceremonial order of such frames, the notion of 'situated role', is clearly inadequate, and represents a partial throwback to the traditional versions of role theory. He writes as if there was only one situated role for each participant in an activity system, thus repeating the classic mistake of assuming that there was only one role for each and every status. This was certainly not true of the medical consultations discussed here where a variety of frames were in use; for the precise way in which an activity is framed is historically situated and changes according to different circumstance. The definitions of reality embodied in a particular frame are both shaped by and enforce a particular balance of power. Indeed, political dispute is precisely centred around the proper content of frames: what is or is not the correct way of doing this or that activity. To presume that for every activity there is one and only one frame is to re-enter that timeless, unchanging and apolitical world of functionalism from which sociology has spent so much effort trying to escape. Roles are not situated in quite this sense.[7]

Aside from these political considerations, there is also a point which concerns the priority of individuals or frames in frame analysis. By itself, a concept such as situated role gives undue prominence to one individual's share in any particular ceremonial order and detracts from the sense in which an institutionalized order forms a coherent whole. What is needed then is a concept which refers to the entire ceremonial order and it is this which I have termed 'role format'. Situated roles still have a place in this analysis but they are merely components of a larger unity.

It should not be thought that the notion of a role format means a narrow determinism, with each and every action constrained to fit a particular social order. Far from it. Although such a concept helps to capture the heavily structured nature of social life it is also meant to avoid the over-determinism typical of traditional role analysis. A role format supplies merely a guideline for the overt form of events, not a detailed prescription; indeed, more than one role format may be used in an encounter. Further, since role formats are concerned primarily with the outer show, with overt and not covert behaviour, all manner of things may be done so long as they are decently clothed. Thus, although such forms are based on and originate in a particular balance of interests and resources, they can in fact accommodate quite wide variation within these. They constitute a resource to which all kinds of problem may be brought for solution, so long, that is, as the participants agree. In essence, role formats are not structures which totally determine action but are instead routinized, culturally available solutions which members 'use' to solve whatever problems they have at hand.[8]

All this is not to say that we are free to do whatever we like. In any particular encounter, actions are constrained by the following circumstances: by the interests and resources of the participants; by the range of role formats available to them; by the identities and actions that these permit; by the extent to which other participants share a common interest in the use of particular role formats; by one's relative ability to enforce an agreed practical meaning of the constituent rules of a format; and finally, by the extent to which participants are accountable to outsiders for their actions, are visible by the same and are in some way dependent upon them. As these features vary so the participants in some encounters may be relatively free to do what they like, while in others they may be severely constrained. The encounters to be considered here fall into the latter category, but even here there was still considerable flexibility compared with the rigid prescription of action as formulated in traditional role studies.

A Description of the Research

The data on which my analysis is based were gathered over a three-and-a-half-year period in some of the paediatric services of two cities of roughly comparable size, one Scottish and the other American. The Scottish city formed the principal location. Within these two cities, the paediatric and therapy services of the two children's hospitals were the main objects of attention, but study was also given to the children's clinics run by the city and state authorities. During the study 1,120 consultations were observed between staff, patients and parents, all but 100 of these within the Scottish settings. Apart from this, observation was also carried out at a number of consultations where only staff and child patients were present. Almost all of these occurred in the ward-round at an intensive care unit for newborn babies in the maternity hospital in the Scottish city.

The principal method of data-collection was that of verbatim note-taking. Two researchers gathered the data, Alan Davis and myself. Typically we stood or sat to one side of the consultation, often with medical students, and made a written record of what was said and done. (In only one setting did this not apply: in the American city children's clinic accounts of the cases were written up from memory immediately afterwards.) All these written notes were then taped and transcribed. Apart from this observational data, interviews were carried out with those staff who had been studied most intensively. Doctors often engaged in informal discussion about the work of clinics in the intervals between consultations, sometimes with the researchers, and sometimes with other staff or students. This too was noted, taped and transcribed.

The extent to which particular conditions, settings, patients, parents and staff were studied varied considerably. Nevertheless, the data were sufficiently extensive to allow a wide range of internal comparisons to be made in testing the universality of the rules under investigation. Further details of the settings and of the data are given in chapter 2. At this point the following features of the data seem worthy of particular attention.

First, one setting, the Scottish neurological clinic, was studied continuously over a three-year period. This provided an opportunity to study the relationship between doctors, patients and parents as it developed over time, in contrast to the purely cross-sectional data available from the other settings. At the extreme, one child was observed 12 times in the neurological clinic, and three others were seen on nine separate occasions. Three years is by no means the limit of a patient career in an outpatient department, for many will require medical attention all their lives. Nevertheless, this period of observation provided a useful insight into the more long-term relationships and the way they developed.

A second relevant feature of consultations was the great variation in their length. Some lasted no more than a minute, a few took over an hour. A great range of medical conditions was also seen. (This is discussed more fully in chapter 2.) A fourth source of variation lay in the number of staff observed. In all, the work of 40 doctors and 12 therapists was studied, although the number of staff considered in any detail was rather less. In essence, this book is about the work of 9 Scottish doctors, 5 Scottish therapists and 4 American doctors, but even though far fewer data were gathered on other staff, these have none the less provided a useful check on the main body. Fifth, just as there was considerable variation in the types of patient and parent observed in most settings, so too an attempt was made to study a variety of doctors in any one setting or type of setting. Thus, at one extreme five Scottish local authority doctors were studied.

Some data were also gathered on the same patient in different settings. This formed a sixth type of comparison, though very few such cases were seen. In all, 27 children were observed in more than one Scottish setting, 21 of these in just two locales and the remaining six in three others. The great majority of these cases were patients at the neurological clinic who were also being treated in one of the therapy departments, or else children who were receiving simultaneous treatment at both occupational therapy and physiotherapy. Turning to the number of settings involved in the study, observations were made in 24 types of locale, though only a few of these were studied in detail. Once again the American data inflate this number considerably. In the principal area of study, the Scottish city, only 9 types of locale were studied.

The American data, though small by comparison and stretched across a wide range of staff and settings, nevertheless provided a valuable series of comparisons, for there are major differences between the Scottish and

American medical systems and these provided two contrasting sets of possible variables.

Such a list demonstrates the considerable width and depth of the data. However, the following negative features should in justice also be noted. First, interview data were gathered only from the doctors, not from the parents or children, though a separate interview study with the parents of 40 children from the neurological clinic was carried out by Heather Gibson. (This had as its main focus a somewhat more specialized topic, the medical experience of handicapped children.) Second, the outpatient work of only two children's hospitals was examined, and one of these in only the briefest of detail. Third, the data are almost exclusively concerned with paediatricians and therapists. Yet there are many other medical specialities to be found in children's hospitals, specialities which may well have different traditions or different technical constraints. Fourth, the range of specialisms within paediatrics itself was by no means covered. Fifth, as a result of these last two omissions certain extremes to be found in medical work are not present. The severe problems presented by handicap were certainly studied in detail; but very high technology medicine as found, say, in specialist paediatric cardiology units is not represented (see Hilliard *et al.,* 1977). Nor, on the other hand, is the most heavily routinized work considered, such as routine decision-making concerning adeno-tonsillectomy (see Bloor, 1976a, 1976b).

Four Pre-emptive Manoeuvres

Finally, some doubts may arise concerning the adequacy of my procedures for gathering and analysing the data on which this study is based. Does observation alter people's behaviour so radically that such accounts are worthless? Can such data be quantified and, if not, what value are they? Is it possible to grasp the meaning of action in any adequate fashion given what we all know about ambiguity, indexicality, self-deception and error? Are there any coherent procedures for the generation and testing of hypotheses in qualitative data? Such worries may be of no concern. In which case, read on. For the more cynical or technically-minded some discussion of my answer to these questions may be found in an appendix.

But not everything can be so readily assigned to oblivion, for some prior comments must be made concerning the fairness of my account. The first concerns my terminology. Words such as 'bourgeois' or 'bureaucratic' are intended in a technical, sociological sense and should not be read as condemning the phenomena which they describe. Likewise, my choice of names for the other formats is not meant to convey any particular approval or disapproval of their nature. The bureaucratic format is so called simply because it displays many of the classical features ascribed by sociologists to bureaucracies, while its use was so nearly universal within the medical bureaucracies that were studied that this name seemed more appropriate than any other.

Second, some of the methods used to demonstrate the existence, nature and scope of the rules of the bureaucratic format lead to a concentration on the extreme and the atypical. Thus, it should not be assumed that the quotations I provide are totally representative of the general run of behaviour in clinics; and in this sense the book is misleading. But this emphasis on the abnormal is not a mere pandering to exotica. For my purpose, which is the demonstration of the existence of certain rules, it is the unusual which very often has the greatest technical relevance. As I have argued in the appendix, it may be the only means by which the nature of the rules may be brought home fully to the reader.

Some unease may arise through my constant contrasting of overt and covert action. The comparison of what we say in private with what we say in public is commonly used to make a moral point, to reveal the hypocrisy of the speaker and the occasion; but such debunking is far from my intention. It is central to my argument that people necessarily say one thing here and another thing there, that types of discourse are appropriate to the occasion. In consequence they should not be judged by standards imported from different contexts. I am not arguing that there should be one standard for all occasions, or that staff or parents were hypocrites and liars. One may quarrel with the exclusion of particular matters from a particular ceremonial order, but to assert that any exclusion is in principle bad is to ignore the reality of the way all social interaction is actually conducted. Social life depends upon a tacit agreement to concentrate on some things and ignore others.[9] My emphasis on the ceremonial order of consultations serves merely to display the complex social rules which any competent participant is normally obliged to observe. Similarly, in comparing overt and covert action, I aim simply to reveal what is and is not said and to show the difficulties that are caused by the inclusion or exclusion of particular topics.

This mere exposition may at times seem to 'expose' those whom I have studied, and this is particularly true of the medical staff; for while I have extensive data on the public actions of both doctors and parents my data on their more private thoughts or deeds are asymmetrical. I have considerable evidence of the more covert feelings and actions of staff, but far less which concerns those of parents. Although more data on the latter would obviously have been desirable, their absence presents no major technical difficulties. My principal topic is the overt order, while since it is staff who principally control the interaction, their covert actions are of greater analytical significance than those of parents. Although this asymmetry does not seriously threaten the credibility of the argument, it may at times serve to show staff in rather a poor light. Whereas I can quote doctors who said one thing to parents but said the opposite as soon as they had left the clinic, I cannot do the same for parents, although no doubt they regularly behaved in a similar fashion. To those who are offended by any of this I apologize.

2 Medical Systems and Settings

Summary descriptions of institutions and rapid surveys of the sources of one's data normally engender a creeping paralysis in the unfortunate reader. Here, alas, there seems no way round it. Without some mention of my data I have no warrant for my analysis; without a sketch of the various clinics and the medical systems of which they were a part the reader will make little sense of what I have to say.

The description of the settings has in fact a treble purpose. It serves to familiarize the reader with the background to my story, so that the individual scenes described later become somewhat easier to visualize. But it is also an essential part of the telling of that story, for one of my main themes, the use of the bureaucratic format across a wide variety of circumstances, can be appreciated only if one has some knowledge of those circumstances. At the same time, some background knowledge of organizational structure and setting is essential when considering the origins of both the bureaucratic format and of the other formats mentioned here.

A General Comparison Between the Scottish and American Systems

I shall begin the task of scene-setting with the broadest possible brush and contrast the Scottish and American health systems, or at least those aspects of them which are most relevant to my purposes.[1] Although I have relatively little data on the services for children in the American city, the very striking differences in the system of which it was a part may bring some of the essential features of the NHS into much sharper focus. I shall describe first the Scottish services.

Broadly speaking, the aim of the Scottish health system was to provide services for the entire population, and it was in fact used by almost all of that population. Four main principles are crucial to an understanding of its workings. First, it was a self-consciously organized system which was planned, in certain vital respects, as an ordered whole in which each part had its special place. Thus the Scottish city had just one children's hospital, which in principle handled all the serious medical conditions affecting any child in the city (apart that is from infectious diseases, which were seen at another hospital which had isolation facilities). Certain services did overlap in some respects, such as the well-baby clinics and the general practitioners. There were also some demarcation disputes: for example, as between occupational therapy and physiotherapy, and between paediatrics and orthopaedics. Nevertheless, there were key structuring principles which maintained an order between all the various parts:

a) Patients 'belonged' to the general practitioner with whom they were registered. Local authority doctors had no authority to prescribe or treat and could refer patients to hospital only via general practitioners. Each time they saw a patient, hospital doctors were obliged to send a letter to the general practitioner describing what they had done.

b) Doctors were crucially divided between generalists, who worked in general practice, and specialists who worked in hospitals. Since the former had only a general training and had limited technical resources they were obliged to refer their more serious or difficult cases to hospitals.

c) Patient access to the system was heavily controlled. Patients could have one and only one general practitioner (though in a group practice they might well be treated by more than one of the partners). Only general practitioners could refer patients to hospital. Self-referral was not allowed, except to 'Casualty'. Similarly within the hospital, referral, both as between departments and as between different hospitals, was controlled by staff. Patients did, however, have the right to ask for a second opinion.

d) There was an elaborate body of governing committees at both local and national level which mediated disputes between sections and which was responsible for the formulation of policy and the provision of finance.

The second principle for understanding the Scottish system is that the means of financing the service were provided almost entirely by the state, and that finance was conceived of at an organizational level rather than in terms of individual transactions between professional and patient. Although all employed citizens paid a 'contribution' to the health services as a separate tax upon their income, and although part of the local property tax, 'rates', went to finance the local authority health department, nevertheless the greater part of health expenditure came directly out of central government funds. Just as crucially, the accounting systems normally took no notice of individual medical transactions. That is, it was not just that medicine was 'free' but that there was no 'fee-for-service' paid either by the state or by insurance companies. (This avoided the enormous paperwork commonly associated with this method.) Doctors' income was fixed not by their patients but by national criteria negotiated through their professional association.

Third, the services were available to all those domiciled in the country, and were routinely used by all but a tiny fraction of the population. The clinics that were observed treated the children of academics and American oil-workers, local businessmen and local aristocracy, as well as those of farm-labourers and tinkers, the unskilled and the unemployed.

Finally, although the majority of services were simply there and available to anyone who turned up, a few were enforced upon the population as far as was possible. The hospital obstetricians and paediatricians had worked closely with the city health department in trying to monitor and control every pregnancy and every young child in the city. All confinements were hospital confinements. All newborn babies could therefore be screened at birth and all were followed up at clinics - or at least the attempt was made. Where they did not appear health visitors pursued them in their homes, and central registers were kept of children who needed special attention. Great pride was taken in the efficiency and effectiveness of these operations, and great upset was caused if a child with a clear impairment slipped through the net.[2]

By contrast the American system was based, not on an ordered division of labour but on its opposite, a free market philosophy. Different medical units were in open competition with each other. Although there was only one children's hospital in the city, there were several other hospitals which had children's wards and there was considerable competition between these to attract the more lucrative patients. In those specialisms where it was particularly strong, the children's hospital also competed with hospitals in other areas of the state and indeed across the whole region of the United States in which it was situated.

At the same time, there was no such clear division between generalists and specialists, between individual practitioners and hospitals as was found in the Scottish system. Thus, there was no distinction between primary and secondary levels of care, and patients could refer themselves to hospital if they so chose. In consequence, although the American children's hospital was in some ways more specialized than its Scottish counterpart (concentrating heavily on orthopaedics) it also saw patients who would have been treated entirely by their general practitioner if they had been in Scotland. At the same time, many individual practitioners were specialists themselves and either had important technical facilities of their own, or else, or in addition, used those of local hospitals. Thus, there was a tradition of hospitals being staffed by individual practitioners - called 'attendings'. Hospitals in this classic version were little more than locales with technical facilities to which individual practitioners brought their patients when necessary. Where other types of specialist were required this was an individual deal between the private patient, the doctor and the other specialist.

The range of choice available to patients was therefore extremely wide compared to that in Scotland, at least in theory. In practice, of course, only the rich could exercise this freedom with ease. As Roth (1977) has argued even the middle classes in America are beginning to be restricted to set health service organizations through the increasing use of pre-paid schemes such as Kaiser-Permanente. For the poor there was little choice, and for them many of the services rendered by general practitioners in Scotland were filled, after a fashion, by the casualty departments of the large city hospitals (Roth, 1975). Since the main organizing principle was financial, there were many sick children in whom the various private organizations had little interest, since their parents had no money. Only the rich were worth competing for. In consequence a variety of agencies attempted to fill some of the gaps. One of the other hospitals in the city had a large research grant to study neonates, and ran a free baby clinic to attract subjects. A local ethnic organization also ran a children's clinic, as did the city itself.

These other services did more than fill gaps. They also added a further element of competition. The complex in which this worked is best seen by examining one service, the Crippled Children's Service, which was jointly funded by federal and state government for the benefit of the poor. Normally, this money was given direct to the state government to run its own service. However, in this particular instance the greater part of the funds went to the children's hospital studied here, even though it was a private institution. In return it agreed to offer its services to the local poor. The government service therefore provided clinics only in the more distant parts of the state. In this respect it had lost out to the powerful private hospital and faced yet further threats elsewhere. For example, one of its clinics was under pressure from another hospital in which it was temporarily located. If this hospital saw the patients directly and cut out the state service, then it would receive the federal and state money instead. In other words, the various medical units such as practitioners or hospitals competed, not simply for the fees of individual patients, but for income from any source whatsoever, whether city, state or federal schemes. Thus the financing of what were 'private' institutions often contained a very large proportion of public money.

This welter of competing institutions was not without various forms of regulation. At one level there were federal and state laws. (The poverty of the state medical department meant that its principal function was a licensing one - approving this or that hospital or clinic - though in fact it had never yet withdrawn a licence.) At another level the insurance companies, the principal means through which the better-off paid for their medicine, were taking an increasing interest in the efficiency or at least the cost of medical services. The children's hospital had begun to modify various of its practices in line with pressure from these companies. There was also some internal ordering of the market in progress. At the suggestion of the local medical school a cartel had recently been formed by the various hospitals in order to remove the more extravagant results of competition such as the duplication of cardiac surgery units. Finally, the last few years had seen a trend towards the creation of a full-time body of hospital staff, although the extent to which this had occurred varied. There was only one 'attending' left on the paediatric side of the children's hospital, but rather more on the orthopaedic side.

Despite these various attempts at rationalization, the system was still fundamentally competitive. This produced several important contrasts with the Scottish system, as regards both the public style of individual organizations and the quality of care at both individual and community levels.

Since each American organization was in the marketplace, each tried to establish a distinct public image and each displayed the certificates which warranted it a proper institution in a prominent public place. In one way or another each organization had a product to sell, even if the rewards were sometimes political and not economic. The city children's clinic, for instance, was decorated with large photographs showing members of different ethnic groups going about their daily rounds, shopping, eating and talking. The style of these images was morally uplifting. Apparently the community was one and the city fathers cared. The main city hospital, again a public institution, had a large board in its entrance hall on which were numbered the babies born that day and the inpatients currently in residence. (How many had just died was not announced.) The children's hospital, a private institution, was also decorated with photographs, wistful or joyous children in this case. It too stressed its own special qualities. It had its own flag; visitors were shown round on guided tours; and brochures told of its special qualities:

> City Children's Hospital is widely recognized throughout the state and the nation as an outstanding medical facility.... Unlike most other children's hospitals, patients are received from birth and continue through age 21 so that the effects of growth and maturation, both in the physical and psychosocial sense, takes place with continuity in the total care and management of the child.

Its Public Relations Department stressed the loving care of the staff, and the pioneering advances they had made. The theme of 'service' was a central one, and the hospital's official goals were spelled out for its customers and backers in the following terms: 'care and treatment for children without restriction to race, colour, creed, sex, national origin or financial status.'

By contrast, the various institutions in the Scottish city had a faceless character. They did not issue prospectuses or state their goals for all to see. That each organization cared for all, regardless of race, colour, creed or income bracket might have been assumed, but it was not stated. The children's hospital had a sign outside which gave its name but that was all. It was apparently just a children's hospital, much like one might find anywhere else in the country. There was no literature which proclaimed its strengths or special nature, and no photographs or certificates hung on the walls. Similarly, although the Scottish city authorities took great pride in their health services, such pride was not made visible in the iconography of their clinics.[3]

The two services also differed in the quality of the care which they provided. This was not so much a question of technical expertise as of organization. So far as could be ascertained, there were few significant differences in the technical experience of the staff or the quality of their work, although the American children's hospital, as one of the centres of excellence in the United States, offered more advanced orthopaedic care. Many of the Scottish doctors had worked for a time in hospitals in the United States and, although there was not a reverse flow of similar proportions (only one of the American doctors having worked in Britain), the research of some of the Scottish doctors was known and esteemed by their American equivalents.

If the differences in technical competence were relatively minor there were still significant differences in the coherence, continuity and distribution of care between the two services. In the American system patients were not necessarily attached to any one practitioner and might receive treatment for the same condition from a variety of individual doctors, clinics and hospitals. Moreover, there was no linked record system between these different agents and agencies. The hospital only sent routine reports on what they had done when a private practitioner had referred a patient, while not all such practitioners gave their records to hospital staff. Doctors at one city hospital complained that private obstetricians sometimes delivered a baby at the hospital and then left, taking the records with them. By contrast in the Scottish system, not only was each patient registered with one general practitioner through whom both local authority doctors and hospital specialists worked, but there were systematic procedures for the exchange of essential information. The local health authority was, for example, routinely sent the discharge notes of all the babies who had been kept in the Special Nursery and it maintained At Risk and Handicap registers drawn both from their own staff's work and from the hospital records.[4]

The systems also differed in the continuity of care offered by the hospital service. Given the large turnover of junior staff, both the American and Scottish hospitals faced problems here; but the Scottish hospital made much more systematic attempts to provide continuity of care for at least some patients. Certain clinics, the special clinics, were run just by one doctor, while in the general clinics, the doctor in charge, normally a consultant, tended to reserve the more long-term cases for himself. Moreover, it was hospital policy to continue to see many of the more severely handicapped cases long after it was medically necessary to do so. Many retarded children were, for instance, seen at six-monthly and then yearly intervals. In most of the American hospital clinics, such continuity of care was not so readily available for any except the wealthy, though some doctors made an exception with the occasional patient.

The overall coverage of the two systems also differed. In the American system, many fell through the net or were excluded, and no one organization had any responsibility for the entire community. In contrast to this, in the Scottish medical system there was not only a doctor allocated to every patient but, as has been noted, certain services were pressed on clients regardless of whether they had asked for them. As a result medical care was more generally spread throughout the population and some impairments in children were spotted much earlier than in the American system. This emphasis on the health of the total population was reflected even in the kinds of research done by some of the Scottish doctors. Just as there were great efforts to ensure that some services reached the total population, so too the funnelling of every patient into just the one agency meant that research into the characteristics of the total population was a relatively easy as well as a necessary task.

Finally, it may be noted that the different methods of financing health care affected not just the distribution of service but the mechanics of consultation. In the Scottish settings, since anyone was financially eligible and the transaction itself was not a unit of account, patients simply checked in at the appointments desk, had their consultation and left. By contrast, to attend an American clinic was a complex procedure in which one's financial as well as medical health was examined in detail. The American doctors did not deal directly with finance themselves, but such concerns permeated their work. The hospital social workers spent most of their time on financial matters and the doctors were obliged to consider how far any proposed action was covered by a particular insurance policy or state scheme.

Despite these considerable differences in the mode of organization, there were nevertheless some important similarities between the two systems. In both, specialist paediatrics was a recent creation. In the Scottish city there had been no full-time professor before the War, the chair being held part-time by a general practitioner. Similarly, the chief paediatrician at the American children's hospital had fifteen years previously been the sole paediatrician on staff, and then only as a joint appointment with the main city hospital. Despite these recent origins, the discipline had undergone tremendous changes. Whereas the post-War battle had been to get general paediatrics recognized as a proper medical subject, the discipline was now fragmenting into a series of specialisms and at the hospital level at least had become increasingly research-oriented. So quickly had this change occurred that one of the older Scottish staff referred to himself as 'the first and last paediatrician'.

There were also strong similarities as regards sexual and professional stratification. In both services the more prestigious occupations were filled almost entirely by men. All the staff doctors in the American children's hospital were men, as were all the paediatricians in the Scottish hospital at Consultant or Senior Registrar level, with only one exception. On the other hand, all the therapists and nurses in both institutions were women, as were all the doctors that were observed in both the Scottish local authority clinics and the American city children's clinics. The social status of doctors was also similar. There was a greater surface informality in the American hospital - at least downwards - in that doctors commonly called therapists and social workers by their Christian names, a practice not normally observed in the Scottish settings. It was also true that some therapists and nurses had achieved a more specialist status in the American hospital. Nevertheless in certain fundamental ways they remained firmly under doctors' control, just as in the

Scottish hospital. Therapists, for example, could obtain patients only through a doctor's referral, and overall charge of the American therapy departments was vested in a doctor.

In both systems, hospitals depended heavily on trainee labour. In both the children's hospitals the majority of doctors held only temporary posts and were undergoing some kind of training or aiming at some qualification. Indeed, many of the junior doctors would eventually leave hospital medicine altogether. Thus a great deal of work was done under supervision, sometimes real, sometimes nominal.

Despite this similarity there were also some important differences here. Scottish medical students began practising medicine two years later than their American equivalents and also finished their training at a rather later stage. Moreover, in the American hospital there was no equivalent of the Senior Registrar level, that is of doctors in their middle to late thirties. These Senior Registrars formed an important resource in the Scottish hospitals, situated as they were between the permanent staff and the relatively untrained junior staff, the registrars and housemen, who were the equivalent of the American interns and residents. This greater use of untrained staff in the American hospital may account for the wider range of questions and tests that were asked of and given to new patients there, as compared with the more focussed proceedings in the Scottish hospital. However, here as elsewhere, some may also discern financial motives (Janeway, 1974).

Keeping this rather crude summary of the two systems in mind, we may consider the particular settings that were studied and the types of case that were seen.

The Scottish Clinics

In this, the major part of the study, nine different types of setting were observed, the bulk of them in the children's hospital. All of the clinics were run either by paediatricians or by therapists and, since some of the hospital doctors also taught in the local medical school, their students formed an audience in several of the settings. I shall consider each locale in turn.

The neurological clinic (children's hospital)

This was a special clinic run by a senior registrar. It had been created to give more time to handicapping conditions, and the cases seen here included cerebral palsy, epilepsy, breath-holding attacks, spina bifida, general retardation, muscular dystrophy, storage diseases, speech delay, speech problems, dwarfism and 'autism'. Certain important handicapping conditions were not seen at this clinic; for example, Down's syndrome (mongolism) and cystic fibrosis. The time actually spent with patients varied widely. Return patients where everything was under control, as in some epilepsy cases, might get only three minutes. Conversely, the most serious and complex chronic cases could take up to an hour, if a new case, or half an hour as a repeat.

This setting was observed for a three-year period, 113 clinics being attended in all. During this time, two doctors, Dr I and Dr J, ran the clinic, one doctor being observed in 82 clinics, the other doctor in 31. In all, 218 different children were observed in a total of 517 consultations.

The general medical clinics (children's hospital)

Each consultant paediatrician ran a general clinic which took cases from across the whole range of paediatric work. These included the standard child fare of chest complaints, allergies, urine infections in girls, hyperactivity, headaches, 'failure to thrive', convulsions, enuresis/encopresis, abdominal migraine/growing pains, and examination for adoption, as well as a variety of other problems such as congenital deformities, handicap, metabolic disorders, rickets, worms, and various odd and anomalous conditions. The clinics of two consultants, Dr G and Dr H, were observed, one on six occasions and with 51 cases, and the other on three occasions and with 16 cases. The average time spent by the first doctor on new cases was eleven minutes, and on old cases six minutes, though there was wide variation in the time spent on individual cases. Such figures are impossible to calculate for the second doctor, since he ran his consultations in a different way. These clinics were the main centre for outpatient teaching and training in paediatrics. Each consultant therefore worked with assistants, often a registrar who saw cases in side-rooms, as well as with an audience of medical students.

Physiotherapy (children's hospital)

This was a long-established department with three staff and attached students, which took a wide variety of cases of physical handicap on an outpatient basis. These were seen weekly or fortnightly for half an hour at a time.

Inpatients were also treated, some on a daily basis. In all, 29 cases and 59 treatment sessions were observed here.

Occupational therapy (children's hospital)

This was a new department with two staff. Like physiotherapy it did both in- and outpatient work with handicapped children, but it also took some psychiatric cases; 27 cases were observed on 58 occasions.

The orthoptic clinic (children's hospital)

This clinic worked closely with the department of ophthalmology and was mainly involved in the treatment of squint. It was staffed by one therapist, and 29 cases were seen at seven sessions. These lasted an average of fifteen minutes. This was the only one of the Scottish therapy departments in which parents stayed during treatment.

Paediatric ward-rounds (maternity hospital)

All babies received a standard examination from a paediatrician at between 12 and 24 hours after birth. They were then checked briefly every day. There were no home confinements in the city, all births taking place in either the maternity hospital or in one of the various small maternity 'homes'. Mothers and babies in the hospital were either at risk in some way, though normally only very marginally so, or else medical staff themselves. Babies were normally kept by the mother's bedside and most beds were on open or Nightingale wards, though there were a variety of side-rooms which contained from one to five beds. The ward-round was also an important vehicle for training medical and nursing students. Four such rounds were observed, in which 21 standard examinations were seen and 154 other brief consultations. The ward-round was the principal responsibility of one doctor, Dr K, though another doctor was observed with a few babies.

Special nursery ward-round (maternity hospital)

Newborn babies who were in any way problematic were admitted to the Special Nursery. Some babies were kept in overnight if they appeared 'jittery', while other more serious cases might spend several weeks there. At the time of the study roughly 40 babies were in the nursery at any one time. There was a daily ward-round by paediatric staff, which lasted about an hour and on which only the more serious cases were dealt with in detail. Six ward-rounds were observed over a period of a fortnight.

Special nursery follow-up clinic (maternity hospital)

All the children admitted to the Special Nursery were seen at the follow-up clinic at the ages of 10 and 18 months, although the more problematic cases might be seen both earlier and more often. The clinic was staffed by a paediatric senior registrar, Dr F, who carried out a brief assessment of the child, the cases lasting between five and ten minutes. Most children were discharged. Just one doctor was seen here over four clinics and 27 cases. This clinic was also an important centre for teaching. Observation at this and the general medical clinics was normally limited to occasions when only a few students were present.

Local authority well-baby clinics

The health department of the city authorities ran baby clinics located throughout the city and staffed by their own doctors. Any mother could bring her baby to such a clinic as an alternative to visiting her general practitioner. These clinics also carried out regular weighing and immunization of babies. In addition there was a screening programme providing developmental assessment at 6 and 12 months for the entire age-group in the city. An average of four such assessments was scheduled for each session of the clinic. Five doctors, A, B, C, D and E, were observed in seven different locations, and in these 18 clinic sessions and 112 consultations were observed.

The American Study

The data in this study were far less extensive, although a roughly comparable range of locales was observed.

The children's hospital

This was a private foundation and had originally served 'crippled children' only. It now had a paediatric wing where a wide variety of conditions was seen. Two main types of clinic were observed. The first of these was somewhat similar to those in the Scottish city and included neurological, developmental and general paediatric clinics. In all, five clinics of this type were visited and a total of 12 sessions and 22 consultations observed, though this latter figure relates only to cases where all or a majority of the total consultation was seen. Four hospital staff doctors, Dr O, Dr P, Dr Q, Dr T, and five junior doctors - interns and residents - were involved in these cases. In the second type of clinic, the 'amphitheatre clinic', a great many specialities were simultaneously involved. All the other settings were based on the principle of one clinic, one speciality. In amphitheatre clinics, which handled multiply-handicapping conditions such as cerebral palsy and spina bifida, all the specialists deemed relevant attended. A total of four amphitheatre clinics, involving 18 consultations, were observed. The work of three therapy departments (occupational, speech and physiotherapy) was also briefly seen, with the observation of four sessions in all.

The city children's clinic

The city authorities ran a children's clinic catering for children up to school age. It was lavishly equipped and considered to be better than many such clinics in comparable cities. Since most of its clientele did not have a general practitioner of their own, the clinic was the main medical service for the children of the poor. There was no total population screening programme. For those who did turn up (and there was apparently a low attendance rate), there was a set programme of assessment and immunization with six checks during the first year of a baby's life and once a year after that till school age. This clinic was attended over a two-day period, and four doctors (including Dr S) and approximately 30 cases were observed.

The state clinics

The state health department licensed city-run clinics and provided certain specialist services for the poor in areas where these were not available from other institutions. Thus, although its headquarters were in the same city as the children's hospital it ran no clinics there. Two state clinics were visited in other cities, both sited in rooms provided by a local hospital. One of these was run by the 'Crippled Children's Service', while the other was a developmental clinic which, like its counterpart in the American children's hospital, included psychiatric as well as paediatric aspects of development, a conjunction not found in the Scottish clinics. In the state developmental clinic one doctor, Dr R, and two cases were observed, while in the Crippled Children's clinic, eight cases attended by three doctors and one physiotherapist were seen.

Variations Within and Between the Settings

The bare list of the clinics that were attended and the numbers of cases that were seen gives little indication of what went on there. To put some flesh on these dry bones, I must describe, if only briefly, the kind of work that went on, the people involved, and the various others who were present.

Perhaps the most crucial feature of any consultation was the type of condition presented by the patient and the particular stage in its medical treatment at which the consultation occurred.[5] Conditions may be distinguished along a number of dimensions as regards the medical work which they entail. They differ widely as to the ease with which they may be diagnosed; the extent to which the doctor is reliant upon patients or parents for information; their seriousness; the ease with which they can be treated; the length of time which treatment, if any, may take; the accuracy with which their prognosis can be foretold; the extent to which patients, parents or others are in some way the 'cause' of the condition; the degree to which treatment involves other departments and services; and the extent to which staff are dependent on patients' or parents' co-operation in their treatment.

Different cases combine these matters in different ways. At one extreme in this study there was a case of worms, where the diagnosis was immediate and drug therapy was simple, quick and effective. At the other extreme stood conditions like cerebral palsy. In its most severe form, therapy was non-existent; aetiology, diagnosis and prognosis might all be uncertain; a whole range of medical and social services might be involved; and the potential effects, both on the child and on its family, were of the most appalling magnitude. In between these polar types there were all manner of possible variations.

A second important variation in medical work concerns the mode of referral. Where clients were self-referred then a central task for both doctors and parents was the presentation and discovery of a relevant medical problem. By contrast, old patients or patients referred by another doctor came with a problem that had already been certified as relevant. Finally, there were some patients who in one sense were not patients at all. In several settings screening was a central medical activity. This was typically done to a formal agenda, unlike most other sorts of medical investigation, and was not occasioned by a current medical problem. It was a systematic search for problems initiated by the profession rather than by the clientele, and a search which normally proved fruitless, for most of those screened were passed as normal.

Settings also differed widely in the extent to which staff had a mandate for treatment or diagnosis. In some Scottish settings (for example, the local authority clinics and the special nursery follow-up clinic) doctors had no such mandate; their job was solely assessment and diagnosis. Where treatment was required the patients had to be passed on to other clinics for, just as some clinics specialized in diagnosis, others specialized in treatment. At the extreme here were the therapy clinics where diagnosis was the principal responsibility of the doctor, and therapists merely elaborated on the initial diagnosis for the purposes of treatment. (This at least was the form of the thing if not always the practice.)

Since clinics differed systematically in their mix of conditions, their referral procedures and their mandate, their atmosphere showed significant variation (Davis and Strong, 1976b). For example, although screening could potentially threaten the normality of any child, this had most effect in the special nursery follow-up clinic, since all the children there had been defined as problematic at birth. By contrast, in the American city and Scottish local authority clinics, screening was a routine and normally jolly affair. Clinics also showed systematic differences in the extent to which doctors, patients and parents could get to know each other. In those clinics where a high proportion of children were discharged, as in the screening clinics or the general paediatric clinics, everything was geared to a rapid turnover of clientele. Others by contrast, like the neurological clinic, saw a much smaller number of patients, more intensively and over a longer period of time.

A further important source of variation lay in the kind of adult representative who accompanied a child. Normally this was the mother, and it was also normal for the mother to be the child's sole representative. This occurred in roughly 900 of the consultations. In all, only 67 couples were observed in a total of 107 occasions. Only 14 fathers were seen alone with a child. Grandmothers were a slightly more frequent representative; they accompanied 18 different children at a total of 30 consultations. Apart from this, mothers were accompanied by grandmothers on five occasions, and by grandfathers on another three occasions. Many more fathers and grandparents accompanied mother and child to the clinic but did not actually enter the consulting room. Apart from relatives, foster-parents and social workers might also act as representatives for a child; 17 foster-mothers were observed on 25 different occasions, and house-mothers from local children's homes brought children on another 25 occasions. Sometimes social workers also accompanied a child, though never by themselves. They were present overall at 12 consultations.

The extent to which both parents rather than just mothers were present varied significantly according to the severity of the child's condition. Thus the Scottish neurological clinic had by far the highest proportion of cases in which both parents came with the child. Out of 218 cases that were observed here, 52 (26 per cent) had both parents present in at least one consultation. In the total number of consultations (518) a slightly smaller proportion of couples were present (96 or 19 per cent). By contrast, in the eight Scottish general medical clinics there were only four couples present in 67 consultations (6 per cent of the total). Even this might be considered relatively high, for not one couple attended any of the 112 Scottish local authority clinic consultations or brought along their child to any of the Scottish therapy sessions. The same was also true of the American city children's clinic. Although insufficient numbers of cases were observed in any one American hospital clinic to permit such generalization, six out of the total of 55 cases seen in the hospital were accompanied by both of their parents (11 per cent). In both hospitals middle-class children were more likely to be accompanied by both their parents than working-class children, as were children who lived some distance away compared with those resident in the city.

Some clinics also differed in the class and ethnic background of the parents. In the Scottish clinics, almost all patients belonged to the same ethnic group; for there were no immigrant minorities in the city of any size, unless English and American residents count as such. Moreover there was only one Scottish setting, the local authority clinics, in which there was any distinct class bias in the nature of the clientele at any one clinic - a product of the residential location of the different clinics. In contrast, certain of the American services were specifically for the poor; and even within the children's hospital, private patients were seen by some, though not all, doctors in their own room rather than in the general clinics. Further, the American city had a large black and Puerto Rican population, with both groups living largely in semi-ghetto conditions. The Puerto Ricans in particular formed a distinct cultural minority and many had little grasp of English.

Having discussed the kinds of adult who accompanied children, we may now consider the staff. At the same time I shall also comment on the rooms in which the consultations took place, for the kind of staff who were present strongly influenced the design of the setting. At one extreme were some of the American private consultations and the Scottish local authority clinics. In both of these each child and parent was seen by one doctor in a large room with no one else present, apart from the researcher. The doctor sat behind a desk and patients were shown in one by one as their turn came. At the opposite end of the spectrum there were a variety of settings in which consultations took place in the presence of many other people, sometimes patients, sometimes staff, sometimes both, some of whom had rights to intervene in the action. For instance, in some of the therapy departments several children were treated at the same time by different therapists in just the one large room.

In the amphitheatre clinics in the American hospital, consultations took place on a floodlit stage in front of a large audience of doctors, therapists, nurses, social workers, interns and residents, who sat in tiered seats in semi-darkness. Although one doctor typically controlled the occasion, there might be two or three staff on the stage all playing a part. Members of the audience might also join in: by calling out comments and questions, by being asked their opinions, or by coming on to the stage themselves.

In the paediatric ward-round at the Scottish maternity hospital the majority of mothers were in large Nightingale wards and the doctor was often accompanied by a group of medical students or trainee nurses. Doctors conversed with the mothers at the bedside, normally without the use of screens, so that most of what happened was both audible and visible to the other mothers in the ward. Such rounds were watched with keen interest by this audience, who joined in on occasion with jokes and comments.

In between these extremes there were many consultations which took place in a single room, but where there was an audience of nurses and students of variable size. In the Scottish children's hospital, general paediatric clinics were located in a suite of three rooms. In the middle and larger room the consultant sat behind a wide desk. To one side of this desk there were chairs placed for the child and family, to the other side there were one or more rows of chairs for medical students, of whom up to seven or eight might be present during term. In the side-rooms, which were much smaller in size, the junior doctors saw their patients. In some instances these doctors consulted with the senior doctor present before finishing a case. Patients were booked for different times in the afternoon and waited upon their arrival in a special area at the far end of a corridor. When their turn came they were shown into the appropriate room by nursing staff, who also showed them out when their appointment had finished. The Scottish neurological clinic was also based on such a suite of rooms, but the doctor occupied only the large room and the audience was far smaller. A nurse was usually present during the consultations, as was a secretary for a planned assessment centre. Students attended on occasion; but here as elsewhere in the Scottish hospital they played a passive role in the consultations. Only on the ward-round at the maternity hospital did they play any active part in the examination of the patients.

By contrast, in the American children's hospital the outpatient or ambulatory clinic consisted of a long corridor on which were located a dozen small, windowless cubicles, each with an examination couch and two chairs. In the middle and on one side of the corridor there was a large room out of which all the doctors and students worked. This room contained all the 'files' or 'charts' of the clinic cases, as well as chairs, coffee and a bank of phones for dictating notes. This served as a private room for the discussion of cases. There was no door on this room and although there were doors on the cubicles these were kept open most of the time, as they were claustrophobic when kept shut. All the patients were booked for the same time, and those who arrived first were shown immediately into the vacant cubicles. The rest of the patients and their parents waited in easy chairs at the far end of the corridor. Interns and residents 'worked up' the patients in the cubicles and then left to consult with their 'chief'. Since a chief might have to advise up to six or seven of the more junior doctors, though the latter gave considerable help to each other, the patients often had to wait for considerable periods of time. The layout and practice of the American city children's clinic was very similar, except that here it was nurses, not interns and residents, who did the work-up. In summary, the difference between the two outpatient departments was that in the Scottish hospitals the patient was brought to the doctor, whereas in the American hospitals the doctor came to the patient.

Some consideration must be given to the activities of the nursing staff in these various settings, for they had an important facilitative role. Whereas therapists worked by themselves, doctors in the hospital clinics were aided by nurses who performed a variety of minor but important tasks. One job common to all settings was that of gatekeeper. Nurses regulated the flow of patients to the doctor and monitored them in the waiting area. They checked appointments against lists, told doctors when patients had arrived, warned them when parents had got fed up with waiting, and accompanied patients when they left. They also handled incoming phone calls, telephoned other departments, fixed admissions, checked on patients who were attending other clinics, and handled relations with the appointments and records staff. They might also regulate visitors to the clinic, such as other doctors, students and researchers.

Nurses might also play an important role in the preparation and examination of patients. They weighed and measured children, took urine samples, checked that the records were available, took patients to X-ray, calmed children during examination, and generally helped out in any of a great number of problems that might arise. They sometimes, for example, stepped in to clear up a misunderstanding between doctor and patient. These duties were taken rather further in the American settings. In the ambulatory clinics at the hospital, the nurses performed various psychological tests, and in the city children's clinic they did the entire work-up. In both systems they also prepared each clinic for the day's work, generally arriving before the doctors and reading through the records to see what might be needed, and what eventualities might occur. They laid out the seating and trolleys and saw that all the files were present.

Where there were several doctors working in a clinic, nurses could have a crucial role in ordering the whole occasion. In one of the Scottish general clinics this role was taken by the consultant but in the other, as in the American clinics, the nurse on duty took charge. She reminded interns when they had left a patient sitting in a cubicle for thirty minutes, advised the more junior doctors on what cases they would find easy or interesting, and generally made sure that things were running smoothly.

Although nurses had fewer medical responsibilities in the Scottish clinics, they had by and large more say in doctors' actual interaction with the patients. In the American hospital the division of labour between juniors and chiefs and the tiny space in the cubicles meant that the American nurses, when they were not administering tests or weighing patients, spent much of their time in the duty room. Scottish nurses, however, spent long periods in the same room with the doctor and their role was more like that of a personal secretary. A skilled nurse knew what each doctor liked and disliked. One wanted his desk prepared just so, the telephone in exactly this position and the files in that. Another did not mind about his desk but had his own special arrangements about how patients should be prepared. Each doctor had his own set sequences of action and special signals to indicate what was to be done. The nurse who knew these could move swiftly to the doctor's aid almost before he had moved, turning off the lights for an eye-examination or holding a child during a physical. In such ways Scottish doctors became heavily dependent on the nursing staff; and the absence of a regular nurse was cursed by every doctor, for things kept on going wrong and nothing was in its right place: 'It just isn't the same when Staff's not here.'

Some nurses tried to aid doctors in yet another way. They stood and talked in the corridor to old patients, and commiserated with them when they had to wait a long time. They chatted away as they prepared a child for the clinic or guided parents to another part of the hospital. In doing this they gleaned a good deal of background information about the parents and their lives. Such detail was obviously of major interest to the nursing staff but little use of it was made by doctors. Nurses often wished to chat about a particularly striking case, to grieve, enthuse, moan or gossip. Doctors rarely did, but pressed on to the next case. In consequence nurses only occasionally reported what they had uncovered and then only when the news was of the greatest relevance: that this mother was an alcoholic, or so her grandfather had hinted; or that that mother was very angry with the doctor as she felt the drugs had caused a recent bout of vomiting.

A Moral

The main point of this rapid tour is this: here was a considerable variety of clinics - set in two very different kinds of medical system, one of which encompassed a great range of types of practice - and to these clinics came all kinds and conditions of patients and parents; yet, as I have argued and as I shall go on to demonstrate, the ceremonial order of the consultations was remarkably invariant. To repeat my earlier assertion, not only were there institutionalized role formats, but their number was severely limited and of these, one - the bureaucratic format - was to be found in universal though not sole use in every type of setting observed in the study. In each clinic, most consultations were framed by the bureaucratic format most of the time or, put another way, though they met in all manner of circumstances, doctors and parents routinely transcended the mundane particularities of their meeting and invested themselves and their relationship with much the same ritual form.

Why this one form was chosen rather than any other is a question which must be left to the end of this monograph. For the moment I shall concentrate on its description; a task which requires several chapters, for the rules on which it was based, though relatively simple, required some care in their enactment.

Before I begin, two general points should be borne in mind. Both concern the procedures used by the participants to rise above the actual circumstance of their meeting.

First, even where a rule characterized only one of the parties, its creation and maintenance were the work of both staff and parents: the bureaucratic format was a collaborative effort. Second, although there were a variety of rules within the format all were established by the same fundamental procedure, that of avoidance. Rules were maintained by ignoring those matters which they could not cover. This device, or as Goffman (1961) has termed it, the 'rule of irrelevance', is the basic procedure used to sustain any encounter, wherever it may occur. For present purposes in interaction, any features of the setting that do not fit, any qualities of the participants, any emotions or attitudes and any involvements in other action: all these, if they form no part of the current order, are treated as irrelevant. We make a world and behave, for the moment, as if we could not see the wider worlds from which it was made and in which it is situated. Children when they play a game may turn themselves into soldiers, old clothes into uniforms, and chairs and tables into forts. Similar, if less readily visible transformations occur in any adult encounter.

This magic, if I can use the term for so routine a human accomplishment, is not always made with ease. There are some things which will not disappear if we merely shut our eyes, but require a little work if they are to vanish. My account of each rule is therefore in two main parts. Where the trick was pulled with ease, the rule itself was invisible. In consequence, the demonstration of its existence requires a detailed comparison with other formats in which a different principle held sway. By contrast, where active nullification was required, the work that was necessary to render other matters irrelevant made the operation of the rule and thus the rule itself at least partially apparent.

3 Natural Parenthood

Of the various rules which made up the bureaucratic format the first which I shall examine concerns the identity ascribed to parents. As we shall see, what parents were actually like: whether they really loved a child or not; the degree of competence with which they cared for it; the responsibility which they themselves might bear for a child's condition - none of these things were at issue, at least on the surface, and none of them affected the idealized image which parents were granted.

Thus, although children were represented by others, all was for the best, since their representatives were very special sorts of people. Matters could hardly be otherwise, for the qualities ascribed to parents were seen as entirely natural in origin; they went with the job. Every mother, just because she was a mother, was an ideal mother, someone who naturally wanted and loved her children and cared for them with a wholly natural competence.[1] Likewise, every mother made an ideal representative. Children might not know how to fend for themselves in medical consultations; but there was little to fear, for their mothers were honest, intelligent, reliable and impartial; or so the story ran.

Not only were mothers possessed of these admirable qualities; but their worth was such that their presence alone, along with the child, was a sufficient condition for a proper consultation to take place. On only a handful of occasions, all involving the breaking of bad news, were both parents requested to attend; and even here this request was by no means typical.

If the mother could not be present, though as we have seen she normally was, then either the father or a grandparent would do; but both were normally treated as substitutes for the real thing. Even so they too were idealized in their own fashion and ascribed a suitable measure of virtues.

Given the ideal nature ascribed to mothers and, as will be seen in the next two chapters, the equivalent idealization of staff's competence and motivation, medical consultations within the bureaucratic format were extremely polite affairs. Many formal courtesies were paid to parents, questions were asked in a mild tone of voice, and considerable effort was normally made to respect their feelings. Staff made many apologies: for keeping parents waiting; for delays in getting test results; for misunderstandings; or for making mothers repeat stories which they had already told before. In general there was an air of some gentility, harsh or bad language was avoided, and the best rather than the worst was overtly assumed about those present. There was, of course, some variation in these matters; particular staff on particular occasions were more or less courteous, and sometimes their impatience or irritation were only barcly concealed. Nevertheless the predominant tenor of the proceedings was politeness.

The mechanisms through which parents were idealized form the main body of this chapter. However, before I go on to describe these it may be useful to begin in quite another way: by making a comparison with a separate format in which mothers were vilified rather than sanctified. And to do this I must first describe the nature of idealization and its counterpart a little more closely.

Character Work and the Charity Format

Identity is the central topic on which any ceremonial order legislates, and moral status is a fundamental part of that identity. But since the ceremonial order is a matter of outward show, the moral order which it creates is regularly threatened by the actual facts of the case and by the incidents and upsets that occur in any form of human intercourse. In consequence, the parties to an encounter are presented with a series of constant challenges, either actual or potential, which threaten their moral worth or that of their fellow-participants. The ways in which such challenges are handled may be called 'moral work' (Strong and Davis, 1978), and within this we may distinguish two main types of response. The first, which Goffman (1972) has termed 'face-work', is a kind of running repair: the ascribed identity and moral status of the individual is treated as the true reality and any discrepancies between the two are simply glossed over.

There is another type of moral work, one which may be called 'character-work'. Unlike face-work this is only rarely used in encounters, for it does not concern the maintenance of a smooth surface appearance but involves the uncovering of a person's moral essence, a rather more tricky endeavour. That essence, or the everyday concept of character, refers to an assumed moral core, inherent within individuals and transcending any particular social occasion. Character on this account is what people 'really' are underneath it all. Whereas face-work attempts to preserve the ideal image that a person may present in any one encounter, character-work seeks to go behind this and explore the reality. Face-work is microscopic in focus and serves to smooth the present, while character-work is more explicitly concerned with future behaviour and the effects of the individual on society at large.

Since character-work is exploratory, it varies according to what is uncovered and may take one of two forms when wrong-doing is revealed. In the first of these, which may be termed 'ameliorative', the procedures are those of criticism and exhortation to reform. In the second and stronger type - 'reconstitutive' work - such measures are too late and there is nothing left but to proclaim the individual's fundamental immorality.[2]

Having made all these distinctions we can now put them to some use in considering the 'charity format', a mode whose nature was quite separate from the smooth politeness of the bureaucratic form. The charity format was not at all common; indeed only one doctor in the entire study was observed to use it.[3] Nevertheless, through studying it we may learn much about what was avoided elsewhere.

Whereas face-work was the staple diet of the bureaucratic format, character-work was the standard fare in the charity mode. The doctor who used it, a doctor in the clinic run by the American city, distinguished three types of moral character in mothers.[4] First there were the penitent and eager to learn. Second, there were those who might seem overtly penitent but whose capacity or willingness to make amends was in some doubt. Finally, there were the impenitent or those of revealed bad character. In the 15 consultations all but two mothers were identified as being of the second, rather dubious type, for the standards set to enter the first category were those of the doctor herself. To count as moral and competent and to be treated as such, mothers had to do exactly what she would have done; and she was middle-class, white and medically trained, whereas the mothers were poor and mostly black or Puerto Rican.

The only mother with whom the doctor enjoyed an easy relationship was a young white woman of serious demeanour who engaged in self-criticism. She described how she fed the child, mentioned what she had read about feeding and asked for the doctor's advice in this matter. In all, she enacted the role of a humble but keen medical student. In return the doctor provided her with reassurance and a mass of technical information. But other mothers did not formally ask her advice, nor did they mention any books or articles they had read and thus demonstrate their concern. They were therefore subjected to forceful interrogation, which undercut any of their claims to competence as a mother. Here, for example, is an excerpt from a case in which the presenting problem was nappy rash. All the doctor's remarks were made in a most aggressive fashion:

Dr S: What do you wash her nappies in?
Mother: Ivory Snow.
Dr S: Why do you use Ivory Snow?
Mother: Well, it's supposed to make the nappies softer than other washing powders.
Dr S: How do you know Ivory Snow makes nappies softer?
Mother: (shrugs awkwardly) Well, um ... (she mumbles something about her mother and advertisements).
Dr S: You don't want to believe everything you see in the adverts. It's a business. That's *their* business. *Your* business is your baby.

The doctor then explained that nappy rash was due to ammonia in the urine and that Ivory Snow was too weak. The mother should therefore use an ordinary washing powder.

Mother: I do put vinegar in it.
Dr S: (in amazed tone) Why do you do that?
Mother: Well, I was told.
Dr S: Who told you?
Mother: Well, my mother did.
Dr S: What difference does it make?
Mother: Well, she said ... I thought it ...
Dr S: It doesn't do any good at all.

The doctor then gave an explanation of the chemistry involved.

Since the doctor held that the only rational criteria for behaviour were her own, those who behaved in a different fashion were deemed irrational, and ignorance was seen as a lack of love towards the child and even, on some occasions, as proof of hatred: feeding a two-and-a-half-month baby on solid food was characterized as a 'hostile' action.

Although the doctor denounced many mothers in private, her normal strategy was ameliorative. She urged mothers to repent and was often most rude, but overtly she still had hopes of reform. In one case matters took a different turn; and since the outcome was so exceptional it is worth considering in some detail. The issue on which everything revolved was demeanour. In criminal proceedings the character assigned to the guilty person often rests on the agent's decision as to whether due contrition has been demonstrated (Piliavin and Briar, 1964). In this one case the mother, an unmarried black woman, laughed when describing one of her child's problems, and the doctor instantly switched from ameliorative to reconstitutive work:

> Dr S: Are there any other problems?
> Mother: Well, he chews cigarette ends ... (laughs)...It's very difficult to stop him.
> Dr S: Why are you laughing? Do you think it's funny?
> Mother: No, I don't think it's funny.
> Dr S: Well, why did you laugh then; do you always laugh at this?

Reconstitutive work was quite different from that used with other parents. Apart from calling the mother to account for her demeanour, something that was not done elsewhere - parents were normally given great latitude here - the doctor repeatedly tried to expose contradictions in the mother's story and show that she was lying. In all the other cases in this study there was an overt assumption that mothers were telling the truth. Contradictions were treated as mistakes or surface obscurities and normally went unremarked. But here they were explicitly sought out in order to prove that the mother was truly a bad character. For example:

> Dr S: So you entirely ignore it when he starts chewing cigarettes?
> Mother: No, I don't.
> Dr S: Well, why did you say you did?
> Mother: I didn't.

Apart from trying to prove the mother a liar, the doctor also mocked her intelligence. Whereas in other cases this was never openly questioned by staff, here the doctor jeered at things that the mother had forgotten, and criticized her use of English. For example:

> Mother: It looks so stupid when you see a fine-looking man with his feet turned in like that. I don't want my baby growing up like that. (The child has turned-in feet.)
> Dr S: What do you mean by stupid? Do you think your brains are in your feet?

Finally, the doctor engaged in a wide-ranging search to find other failings in the mother. Unlike her practice in other cases she did not concentrate on merely the one problem and its reform, but treated the initial crime as symptomatic of a much wider range of abuses. Just as face-work could prove that a mother was entirely good, so reconstitutive work could demonstrate her complete iniquity; for it is characteristic of our treatment of those found to be unrepentantly deviant that emphasis is placed, not upon the initial sin, but upon the corrupted character of which the present sin is merely a symptom. Apart from quizzing the mother about her attempts to stop the child chewing cigarettes, the doctor interrogated her for several minutes about where she kept poisons in the house, and asked detailed questions concerning the child's care and the mother's marital and financial status, all of which were put in a hostile and sceptical fashion; her aim being to prove the mother uncaring, promiscuous, work-shy and sponging off the state.

Natural Motherhood

This sketch of the procedures used in the charity format can also tell us much about the bureaucratic mode. For what was raised in one form had to be avoided in the other. The rule that every mother was a good mother meant the systematic exclusion of all those things that were explicitly raised when character-work was done. In the bureaucratic format doctors had to strive to use a polite rather than an aggressive tone; to ignore inconsistencies; to avoid open condemnation; and to stick to the matter in hand rather than search for fault upon fault. And they had to do this whatever their actual feelings about the circumstance of the case.

But staff were also involved in more positive work, for a mother's good character could not always be guaranteed through passing some things by in silence. Certain disreputable topics necessarily intruded into the conversation and on some occasions doctors could not avoid criticism of what mothers had done. Some regularly missed appointments and others were highly incompetent. For some conditions a mother might reasonably be held to be partially or even wholly responsible. In other cases mothers refused to accept the doctor's version of the child, and in yet others they were unable to cope with it, whereas all mothers were supposed to have this capacity. Some mothers lived disreputable lives and on occasion inquiry into these was medically unavoidable.

The wide variety of circumstances in which a more active face-work was necessary meant that doctors' tactics varied to suit these. For example, the paediatrician who did the ward-round at the Scottish maternity hospital called all mothers 'Mrs' regardless of their marital status. But this imposition was not always possible. On some occasions inquiry had to be made into private lives and, since the doctor could not know in advance what would be found, the mother's good character was often maintained by making no overt assumptions at all, by treating any household arrangement as a simple matter of fact:

Dr G: Is there anybody else in the house with you?
Mother: Well, my husband.

Despite this necessary variation in tactics, certain broad medical strategies may be discerned within the bureaucratic format. When criticism had to be done, doctors emphasized the spotless future rather than the murky past. Here, for instance, is a quotation from a Scottish local authority clinic in which a mother was interviewed about her grossly overweight baby, who at six months was covered in rolls of fat and weighed 20 pounds:

Dr B: And you feed him on Farex?
Mother: In the morning and evening.
Dr B: And porridge?
Mother: Aye.
Dr B: Does he get anything else for elevenses?
Mother: Just biscuits.
Dr B: How much porridge does he get?
Mother: Oh, nae much.
Dr B: How much does he get at lunch-time?
Mother: Oh, just mince and tatties.
Dr B: Do you give him anything in mid-afternoon?
Mother: No.
Dr B: And what does he get for his tea?
Mother: Oh, a boiled egg or a scrambled egg.
Dr B: And this is as well as milk?
Mother: Aye.
Dr B: Does he get anything else?
Mother: Aye.... (rest inaudible)
Dr B: Well, I think he's putting on a bit too much weight. Is he fatter than your other children?
Mother: Aye.
Dr B: If I were you I'd miss out the Farex and the porridge at breakfast and the biscuit as well. It's best to do this now because if

children get fat now then they tend to be fatter later on in life. He's supposed to be twice his birthweight now and he's a good bit more than that, isn't he? This is very important. He's putting on a bit too much weight.

If one contrasts this with the case of nappy rash discussed earlier, several important differences emerge. Far from being aggressive the doctor here posed her questions in a neutral fashion, as if they were purely a matter of form, while her advice at the end was given in a breezy and non-pejorative manner. At the same time, the seriousness of the problem and thus of the possible offence was under-played. It might be 'very important', but then he was only putting on 'a bit too much weight'. The most crucial difference lay in the focus of the discussion. The doctor who inquired about feeding asked solely about what the mother did. By contrast, although the other mother's behaviour was mentioned - her use of Ivory Snow and vinegar - the charity doctor's emphasis was upon the beliefs that underlay those practices. Since she indicated by her whole manner that these were incorrect, to ask the mother persistently for the grounds for her action was to ask her to make a fool of herself. Indeed, to conduct any detailed inquiry into the grounds for someone's action is to imply that they have acted incorrectly. The reasons why we act as we do normally go unspoken. They are presumed to be obvious and in good faith and are only revealed when others judge us, or might do so. The result of such inquiry in the American clinic was that the mother became increasingly unwilling to answer the questions, began to mumble and eventually broke off in embarrassment. By contrast, the matter-of-fact inquiry into actions rather than beliefs meant that the Scottish mother responded in a free and open fashion.

Further, when the doctor in this latter case delivered her verdict this was done in a fashion that did not necessarily question the mother's competence. The doctor treated herself as an expert who knew things that the mother did not, but the mother was not cast as a fool. The doctor simply told the mother what the 'best' thing to do was, that it was 'important', and that if she were in the mother's place then this is what she would do: 'If I were you'. She presented the mother as agreeing with the wisdom of what she had said: 'Isn't he?' Her strategy was to spell out what she saw as the correct policy and then to demonstrate that this was the sensible thing that anyone would do, once they knew the facts. The emphasis was not upon the mother's mistake but upon the right thing to do in the future. The charity doctor operated like a policeman for whom ignorance of the law was no excuse. By conducting an interrogation about the past she emphasized the mother's guilt. The Scottish doctor emphasized the mother's future action which, it was overtly assumed, would be correct now that she had learnt what to do. Such a strategy allowed the mother to retain her ideal character. Her competence did not lie in knowing what was the best way of bringing up a healthy baby, that was a matter for the doctor. It rested instead on taking an active interest in her child's health and in following good advice.

Even if mothers did not follow staff's instructions, they could still retain their overt good character within the bureaucratic format. Doctors did not press hard, except where the most serious matters were at stake, and even then they still used the same, future-oriented strategy. The past was written off and parents once more had a chance to prove themselves. This emerges most clearly if we consider the one matter about which all Scottish hospital staff got worked up: failure to attend. The only basic demands made of mothers were that they attend the clinic when asked to do so and, if this should prove impossible, that they give prior warning. For a mother to meet either of these conditions ensured her treatment as entirely competent and moral, regardless of any other circumstances. Part of the reason for this priority lay in the appointments system. Since parents were booked at particular times their non-arrival might leave staff with nothing to do, a major irritant for those with many other demands on their time. And, of course, parents who did not appear not only failed the doctor but they failed their children as well - patients who could not attend on their own behalf.

It would therefore be no surprise if doctors' irritation or anger occasionally surfaced here. One mother, for example, had missed three appointments; at the end of the consultation at which she finally appeared, the doctor commented with heavy sarcasm, 'Thank you very much for bringing her to see us'. And yet what is truly remarkable about this comment is its exceptional nature: it was the most critical statement made to a mother in any of the Scottish clinics. Other staff, and indeed this same doctor on other occasions, behaved in a quite different fashion. They still treated non-attendance as a serious matter, for they routinely asked mothers to provide reasons why they had not come on a previous occasion. On this issue at least they dug up the past. But they did so in a way which removed any overt implication that this was a moral investigation. Not only did they conduct their inquiry politely but, although they called mothers to account, they commonly furnished them with good excuses in doing so. 'Have you moved?' 'Did you lose your appointment card?' 'Have you been ill?' 'Have there been any problems with transport?' Questions such as these both required a reason, and suggested that the answer would indeed be reasonable. In this way, while attention was drawn to a fault, the offence was indicated to be a misdemeanour and the questioning in no way threatened their overt good character.

By such means within the bureaucratic format staff routinely transformed the possible crimes committed by mothers into something that was readily compatible with the ideal that every mother was supposed to he. They did so by skirting around some issues; by minimizing their offence; by providing them with good excuses; and finally by dismissing the past as of no account. In fact, such was the commitment of doctors to the idealization of their clientele that they attempted this even when they got no support from the mothers themselves. So far I have made no mention of the mothers' own cosmetic practices but left the reader to assume that they cooperated readily with staff in this regard. Normally this was indeed so. There were however two exceptions. But even here the doctors tried to demonstrate the mothers' good character and competence. Since these two cases represent the greatest test to which idealization was put, some space must be devoted to them, though I shall examine only one in detail.

In the first of these cases the mother was mentally retarded, and this status was publicly if indirectly displayed. To be retarded is to have grave doubts cast on one's ability to represent or care for a child; and in fact this mother was accompanied by a social worker who treated her in many ways as if she too were a child. She regularly intervened to correct the mother's account and, when she did so, spoke about the mother as if she were not there and able to speak for herself. The mother acquiesced in all this quite willingly and showed no signs of irritation or embarrassment at being interrupted or discussed in this fashion. After each of her own remarks, whether they were questions or replies, she gave a special kind of grin, self-deprecating and self-consciously childish, such as no other parent gave. This grin was a constant and deliberate reminder to her audience that she was formally defined as retarded. Its message was that she was doing her best, that she was trying to be helpful, but that she was retarded and not to be blamed for any mistakes she might make.

The oddity of the mother's behaviour and of the treatment she was accorded is summed up by the manner in which new instructions about the dosage of a drug were given and received. The mother listened to the instructions in a fashion unlike any other adult representative, her whole body overtly tensed in the most extraordinary way and her eyes riveted upon the doctor. The only comparison to be made is with the behaviour of young children during testing, some of whom assumed the same pose of totally committed and forceful concentration. Just as such children would suddenly break off and announce that they could no longer continue, so too this mother, without any warning, blurted out that she could not remember what the doctor had said. He therefore sat beside her and, at the social worker's suggestion, gave her written as well as verbal instructions, two procedures that were never followed in other cases.

Although the doctor treated the mother in a special way, what was equally striking was his consistent attempt to define her as competent. When parents interrupted their children's remarks the conversation normally stayed with them and the child was excluded from then on. Here, however, the doctor reverted to the mother each time with only the slightest acknowledgment, if any, of most of the social worker's comments. Even when the doctor wrote out his instructions and discussed these with the social worker, he still indicated his trust in the mother's competence:

Dr I: If James has just one fit then she (the mother) can still stop the phenobarbitone as he's likely to have one or two anyway. But if he has more, then she should immediately start James on the phenobarbitone again.
SW: How will she know if he has attacks? She may miss them.
Dr I: (to mother) I don't think you miss them very easily, do you? Because you can tell by the way he breathes.
Mother: Yes, he has funny breathing, yes.
Dr I: And you sleep fairly close to him, don't you?
Mother: Yes.
Dr I: (to social worker) So I don't think she would miss many.

Although this case was exceptional, it being the only occasion on which a mother who was actually present at the consultation was herself represented by another adult, there are some interesting parallels with the problems that might arise when both parents were present. For, just as intervention by the social worker could undercut the mother's story, so too one spouse might contradict another. To take one example from many:

Dr J: How about his speech? Is that OK?
Mother: Yes, he uses a lot of words.
Dr J: When did this start?
Mother: Well, he's been saying 'Mammy' and 'Daddy' for a long time.

	And he's been saying more than this for quite ... (pause) ... Well ... (pause) ... this past two months he's been really chatting.
Dr J:	For how long?
Mother:	The past couple of months.
Father:	Oh, it's been longer, surely?
Mother:	No, he only said 'Mammy' and 'Daddy' before.
Father:	No. You think about it. He used to say 'Daddy's car' ... (he gives two further examples) ... He's been saying these for quite a long time.

Such conflict was resolved by the mother being given priority - but at the same time this was done discreetly. Staff did not ask parents to make their minds up, nor did they come down too openly on the mother's side. Such disagreements were treated as private quarrels in which staff had no part to play. They became a sideshow, not a part of the main action; and staff waited until they were finished before resuming their questioning or discussion. The only comment that any doctor actually made on these matters was to lean forward to a young girl, some aspect of whom the parents were disputing at considerable length, and remark, 'They're talking about you.'

In the other case in which a doctor took an advocate role on the mother's behalf despite her rejection of the proffered ideal, the child was neglected (it had recurrent scabies and a skin-rash) and had not been brought to the clinic for some time for consideration of its severe cerebral palsy. As in the previous case, the mother was accompanied to the clinic, this time by a health visitor, though she, unlike the social worker, did not actually enter the consulting room. The good character of the mother was nevertheless clearly in doubt, a possibility that was reinforced by her demeanour. She remained sullen and accusatory throughout the consultation, refusing to co-operate in any display of ideal qualities. She paid no attention to her baby, offered no apologies for her failure to attend, and refused to make any promises for the future. Her manner made it plain that she felt the occasion to be a criminal trial, that she was there against her will, and that she had no hope of justice. As such she refused to defend herself. Nevertheless the doctor acted with continual courtesy; and since she failed to display 'normal' feelings towards her child or to provide reasonable excuses for her behaviour, he himself sought to fill the gap. Since she showed no affection for the child he praised it in extravagant fashion and encouraged her to do the same, likewise offering her a long series of excuses for her failure to attend. Only after a succession of offers and rejections, during which it must be said he grew increasingly irritated, did the doctor abandon his attempts. Even then he did not overtly condemn the mother, but merely said that he would refer her to a social worker to see if she could help.

Normal Mothers and Abnormal Children

So far it may seem that any mother could be easily idealized so long as she was relatively competent, attended regularly and had no competition from husband or social worker. This was indeed true of a large number of cases where discrepant information was readily avoided and little if any repair work was necessary. But whatever the actual qualities of a mother, certain medical conditions posed a serious and sustained threat to the easy achievement of the ideal. Psychiatric cases and those of mental or physical handicap were equally dangerous, if in different ways. Severe handicap was an immediate challenge to a mother's capacity to cope and might also, particularly in the long run, threaten the affection and care that was a child's due. In psychiatric abnormality the parents might be the actual cause of a child's condition and, since the mother was the child's normal manager she must, it followed, bear a large part of the blame. Thus both types of condition created circumstances in which a mother's character might be rewritten or indeed might have to be rewritten if a cure was to be effected. Here then were two serious threats to the image of natural motherhood; how could they be met without using the reconstitutive character-work that marked the charity format? Since these conditions differed in their potential effects, staff adopted different procedures to solve this problem.

As regards psychiatric abnormality, doctors' basic strategy within the bureaucratic format was, as elsewhere, simple avoidance. If the possibility of maternal involvement was not mentioned, then there was no overt risk to the mother's good name. Such a stance was eminently plausible since these were medical and not psychiatric clinics. There were however a large number of conditions which staff felt to have an important psychiatric aspect, or might on occasion be wholly psychological in origin. Asthma, headaches, enuresis, encopresis, breath-holding attacks; in all these cases doctors could have made searching investigations into family life. This was not, however, their practice, even when this aspect was raised by parents themselves. This for instance is an enuresis case:

Mother:　Could it be his nerves?

Dr G: That's certainly part of it.
Mother: Well, he was given an injection at the doctor's. It might be that.
          He's never wet during the day. Could it be his nerves?
Dr G: And he's just seven?
Mother: Seven.

The doctor continues on to other topics.

This example is from a Scottish clinic; and it demonstrates very clearly the standard Scottish practice of not even mentioning the possible psychiatric aspect of such conditions if it could be avoided, let alone investigating this with the mother. In this respect there was an important difference between American and Scottish practice, a difference which would seem to reflect the different status of psychiatric problems within the two cultures. Psychiatric investigation was explicitly linked with paediatric work in two of the specialist American clinics, but in none of the Scottish ones. At coffee- and meal-times some of the American staff discussed themselves, their colleagues and the hospital in psychiatric terms. Such a vocabulary was never used by Scottish staff. Further, while it was only a minority of American staff who engaged in such analysis, all seemed far more ready to talk about psychiatric matters with parents than did their Scottish equivalents. Psychological problems were treated as more everyday affairs, which did not necessarily threaten a parent's good name. Thus, in contrast to the case of enuresis seen by the Scottish doctor here are an American doctor's remarks to the mother of a child with encopresis:

Dr O: It's psychological so your paediatrician is right. There are
          always three things it could be. (He describes two somatic
          possibilities and the reasons why he thinks they do not apply
          here.) Thirdly, it can be a thing between the mother and the
          child. It starts up at around the age of two because that's when
          children learn to control their bowels.... Let me tell you this,
          we're not going to have too much trouble there. He's a normal
          kid. You ought to see some of the kids we have in here, so
          withdrawn, right in themselves. He's really fine. He's a nice,
          normal kid.... We've got to consider the dynamics of the
          situation. It's a battle between you and him. It is with all
          children. At the moment he's on top, but you're OK, because
          he's really a normal kid. It's not a conscious thing, it's
          unconscious, just like you can have headaches when you don't

want to do something. Really, this is a pretty normal problem - well, almost.

This difference between American and Scottish staff must not be exaggerated. American doctors might mention the psychiatric aspects of a condition more openly but they did not investigate them, while they also minimized the parents' contribution to the problem. The condition lay in the child not in the mother. Although the American doctor described the problem as originating in a 'battle' between mother and child, the mother's role as combatant was not considered when he spoke to her. When he described the case to the interns, however, he argued differently: 'You'll find the parents in these sorts of cases are very constricted people.'

Thus, given the different status of psychiatric problems in the two cultures, doctors' typical strategies were much the same. Moreover, it was not always possible for Scottish doctors to avoid all psychiatric matters - some parents over-protected their children and required advice on how to cope with the ensuing problems, and on other occasions children were referred from the department of child psychiatry for neurological assessment - and in both these instances the doctors followed a similar line to that of their American colleagues. The problems were out in the open so they had to be faced; but at the same time the parental contribution to their origin was minimized.

In summary, in both cultures psychiatric problems were typically reified. In the Scottish clinics these things were treated as purely natural in origin, requiring no investigation of the social and thus moral sphere. Where such avoidance was not possible then the problem was reified in another fashion: by locating it within the child and not in any wider familial context. The American doctors were more likely to follow the second of these two approaches, but in doing so they also took great care to avoid besmirching the parents' good name.

Although reification was the normal procedure for handling psychiatric problems, there were a few instances in which the mothers' responsibility for the condition was directly addressed. This produced a major challenge to the principle that every mother was a good mother, a challenge that was met in a highly circuitous but ingenious fashion.

My analysis of this is based on three cases, all of which were seen in the Scottish neurological clinic and in each of which the doctor thought it quite possible that a child was handicapped; but at the same time the child's behaviour was so bizarre and the mother's reaction so extreme that a psychiatric explanation was equally or even more likely.

In such unusual circumstances staff were obliged to investigate the condition of both the child and the mother. Whether or not the child was handicapped could be ascertained by wholly conventional means, though it might take some time, but the investigation of mothers called for special procedures. The difficulty here was that if the mother was involved - and such was the eventual decision in all three cases - then it was essential to get the mother to see herself as part of the problem, but to do this was to engage in reconstitutive work.

The solution to this problem was to do things slowly. Whereas in the charity format mothers were expected to plead guilty on the spot, such instant insight was not demanded in the neurological clinic and parents were allowed to confess over time. Further, no direct accusation of guilt was ever made by staff, for the naming of the offence and the discovery of the offender were left to the mothers themselves. Doctors merely provided the means to this end through ruling out organic conditions and by giving the mothers an opportunity to talk. Although they used social workers and other ancillary staff as their principal vehicle for the achievement of insight, they too played a part, seeing such mothers more frequently and in greater privacy than was the case elsewhere. Such a strategy was slow and often tortuous, in one case taking over three years before it finally succeeded. The difference between the beginning and end of this process can be seen in the following two quotations from one of these cases, one from the first visit and the other from the final consultation at which the child was discharged. In the first quotation the mother defines the problem as entirely within the child:

Dr I: Well, what can you tell me about him?
Mother: Well, basically it's his head-banging and his shyness.... And he's got very violent tempers, he screams and screams. ... And he was very slow to walk. ... He's very loath to co-operate with strangers. We can never leave him with anyone. ... And also he's not been sleeping for two days and nights at a time.
Dr I: Does he ever hurt himself in an outburst?
Mother: Yes, he gets very miserable and very violent. The very violent ones don't last too long. We've tried various ways of handling them, everything we could think of, but with no success.

During the examination the child screams and fights very violently.

Mother: (rather desperately) This is what he gets like.

A little later the child starts to scream and bang his head repeatedly and heavily on the floor. Dr I flinches.

Mother: We've tried everything, we've tried slapping him, cuddling him, putting him to bed ... (She cries.)
Dr I: (soothingly) Don't worry about it. It doesn't matter.

Mother picks the child up from the floor and both sit there, streaming with tears.

Dr I: Would you like to go and talk elsewhere because of the noise? It's far too noisy in here to talk.
Mother: Yes.

They leave - but without the child.
The next excerpt is several clinic visits and a year later:

Dr I: Brian has been without occupational therapy for the last couple of months and seems fine.
Mother: Oh, yes, but I'm continuing to see Mrs Adams (social worker). I find her very understanding and helpful. Also, my doctor's (GP) been very good. He's given me a different drug and I can relax much more now. I just don't worry about things so much and I'm therefore not on their backs all the time and it's better for them.
Dr I: And he's sleeping a lot better now.
Mother: Oh, yes, there's no problem there now, if he wakes up I don't.
Dr I: And the other thing was temper tantrums.
Mother: They're much better now and if he does have one I just walk off and he comes round in his own time.

Through waiting and through giving the mother time to talk, her ideal character had been preserved, despite her admission of at least partial responsibility, and she herself had played a part in the formulation of her guilt and was therefore due praise as well as blame. As in more trivial cases such as the one where the mother had overfed her baby, her guilt was placed firmly in the past. It was the present and the future that counted, and in these she was clearly now a good mother, ideal like any other.

This emphasis upon waiting, allowing mothers to make their own judgments in their own time, was also the standard strategy in cases of severe handicap. But since such cases threatened mothers' ideal nature in a very different way, the strategy was adjusted to suit these special circumstances. In some respects the problem was reversed. In psychiatric cases, staff either avoided the question of the mother's guilt or else were forced to demonstrate it. By contrast, handicap was not a question of guilt but a challenge to a mother's capacity to cope with and love her child.

Such a challenge could not be avoided; indeed, it grew as the years went by and the gross nature of a child's abnormality was revealed. The most severely handicapped babies often looked little different from other babies, regardless of the severity of their condition, and many made no special demands upon a mother. But such a five-year-old might at one extreme be almost literally a monster: grotesque, violent and uncontrollable; or else, at the other extreme, a mere vegetable: immobile, passive and noiseless. In consequence, staff held that very severely handicapped children made demands upon parents which they could not, in the long run, be reasonably expected to meet. The 'natural' duties and feelings of a mother towards her child were predicated on the assumption that that child was normal, and those mothers of grossly abnormal children who could cope no longer did not thereby impugn their good name; indeed for a mother to persist in coping with her child alone was devotion beyond the call of duty, perhaps even foolhardiness.

It might seem that such conditions presented no great threat to a mother's idealization. However, the exception that staff could make so easily was not a matter of everyday routine for mothers. Doctors had seen many such cases and, knowing the difficulties, were only too ready to suspend the rule. But for many mothers, as Voysey (1975) has shown, that rule had a universal application and the gradual realization that they could not cope and did not always love was the most terrible challenge to their sense of self. There was in consequence a major conflict between the viewpoint of staff and that of mothers. Staff felt obliged to inquire whether mothers were coping in order to provide help where necessary, but mothers could read this as reflecting upon their competence. At the same time, many mothers took years to accept fully the nature of their child's handicap. This made any discussion of how they were coping doubly difficult, for staff's discussion of these matters necessarily formulated either the mother or the child as possibly abnormal. In consequence, although for rather different reasons, staff adopted a similar strategy to that used in the investigation of psychiatric abnormality; they waited and they offered mothers the chance to talk, but they did not enforce such talk upon them.

To show how once again such a strategy could effect change without confrontation, I have chosen three extracts from a case that was seen throughout the three years of the study and which posed this dilemma in an extreme form. The child was three years old at the time of the consultation quoted below and suffered from a metabolic disorder which caused gradual deterioration and eventual death. Despite her daughter's grotesque appearance and behaviour, the mother was unwilling to accept that she was abnormal. On this particular visit the child had run amok, screaming and fighting uncontrollably. Eventually she had been slapped hard by the father, a most unusual event in the clinic; and after this incident the doctor tried to raise the general problem of coping:

Dr I: She's always on the go, isn't she? Is she always like this? I mean, is this typical - it's not just this afternoon?
Father/Mother: It's typical.
Dr I: And you can cope?
Father: Yes.
Mother: You get used to it.

Since the parents failed to respond to the doctor's offer, he turned to other issues. Next time, six months later and in the face of similar behaviour, he raised the matter again, using the same non-committal terms. On this occasion he called the child 'quite a handful', and was met by a similar refusal to discuss the topic further. But three years on and five more visits later the picture was very different. The parents enter and are greeted by the doctor.

Dr J: How has she been?
Mother: Oh, much worse since she's been at home. (The child had been in care while the parents were on holiday.) We're having to feed her now ourselves. It's very difficult.
Dr J: And what about her sleep? Is she sleeping now?
Father: No, she didn't get any sleep last night.
Dr J: So, how's she been generally then?
Father: Well, she is much stronger now.
Dr J: Is she more difficult to handle now?
Mother: Yes, very much more difficult.... The nurses said it took two of them to bath her. I mean, how can anyone cope with her? The

main problem that we have been having is with her feeding. You get very frustrated when you can't do it and you end by smacking her. I smacked her across the face the other day and it's just not fair to her. I can well understand why children do get battered. You just lose control. You just get so angry and I get frightened about what I'm going to do to her.

Dr J: Yes, I can understand, I understand how you can feel like that.

This last passage contains several noteworthy features. In such cases doctors typically began the consultation, as here, with an open-ended question as to how the child had been getting on. This allowed mothers, if they so chose, to discuss any problem that had arisen and gave them the chance to control at least part of the agenda. And yet in the case of this child as in many others it took some years before the mother responded to the invitation. Doctors let mothers decide when their normal duties were no longer appropriate. That such a decision had finally been taken is evident here, for the parents' ability to cope was not just a side-issue, one raised gently by the doctor and dropped by the parents, but had become almost the only issue, one that the parents raised at the beginning of the consultation and which dominated it throughout. Note also the mother's emphasis that this was not just a question of their own capacities but of the ability of any adult to cope. Since all could now agree that the child was abnormal her own status as a normal mother was no longer in question. She could thus freely confess to the most violent feelings and actions, for here that confession could be followed immediately by medical absolution. With such an unnatural child the mother's reactions were now only natural.

Thus, simply by waiting, doctors were able to preserve the ideal image of motherhood that was required by the bureaucratic format. The grave threats posed by psychiatric abnormality and mental or physical handicap could be met by letting mothers do the reconstitutive work, at their own pace and in their own words.

The Loving but Incompetent Father

So far I have talked solely about mothers; but other sorts of adult might occasionally represent a child, or at least be present in the consultation, and these too need a mention.

Fathers provide an especially interesting case for examination, despite the relative infrequency of their attendance - for they themselves brought a child to a clinic on only 18 occasions,[5] though they did accompany their wives at a further 107 consultations.

A consideration of the role ascribed to fathers throws some light on a common version of fatherhood in our culture, but may also help us to comprehend that image of the ideal mother that was so central to the bureaucratic format, for the deficiencies that were found in fathers reveal what was merely assumed about mothers. The very naturalness of the qualities with which mothers were overtly endowed meant that there was no need for their discussion. For example, although the children's clinics run by the Scottish and American city authorities both engaged in routine developmental assessment, in no instance were mothers praised for the health and cleanliness of their babies, or for their devotion, or for the speed with which their children had progressed. Just as failure was glossed over, so too was success. In the natural order of things every mother naturally succeeded and their competence and motivation were neither criticized nor commended, but simply assumed.

No such overt assumptions were made about fathers. Their character as human beings was not questioned but their qualities as regards children were strictly limited - or so they were treated. While their capacity for love was not openly doubted, a display of affection was an occasion for some comment: 'She's daddy's girl', or 'He's daddy's boy'. Such remarks were never made about mothers; that every child was mother's child went without saying. Even if father was unusually loving, he was normally treated as incompetent and irrelevant. When mothers attended clinics by themselves almost no reference was made to their husband's existence. Staff did routinely ask about the father's health, age and employment, but the information required was typically minimal and for the record only. Beyond this they made little inquiry. Nor were mothers normally asked what father thought about things or about his relationship to the child, the only exception being cases of handicap; but even here staff were only interested if the father's attitude was of concern to the mother, his own feelings were not normally treated as of importance in themselves. Similarly, just as staff made little reference to fathers, so did the mothers themselves. Not only did staff treat mothers as entirely competent to answer their questions, but mothers typically answered in the same fashion. The following instance was the only occasion on which a mother indicated that her husband and not herself was competent in these matters:

> Dr H: How many (tablets) does he get?
> Mother: Ah! That's my husband's department.

When a couple did attend a clinic together, staff placed fathers in a subordinate position to their spouses. Questions were asked directly to the mothers and, though fathers sometimes added their own comments to which staff might reply, they normally returned to the mother for their next question. Most fathers accepted their fate readily enough; indeed, one even asked permission to be present: 'Is it all right if I watch?' Watching was in fact what most fathers did, along with minding the children while their wives talked to the doctor. In only one instance did a father claim priority for himself, though some, as we have seen, quarrelled with particular statements made by their wives and a few regularly demanded a more equal treatment of their own opinions. The infrequency of such assertion was at least partly due to the subordinate position in which fathers were placed. Staff might not openly intervene to back one side or another when parents disagreed. But, since their attention was directed primarily to the mothers, those fathers who had a lot to say had usually to interrupt a running conversation. The structure of the situation automatically defined them as rude and inconsiderate: a fact which such fathers usually acknowledged with grins and apologies. Moreover, their claims to competence could be readily undercut by mothers, given a medical audience who tacitly validated the mothers' authority.[6]

Having considered the general absence of fathers from clinics and their subordination to their wives when they did attend, one may now turn to those rare occasions when they were a child's sole representative. Since on these occasions at least they could not be excluded from the conversation, such meetings are unusually revealing about the identity which staff ascribed to fathers. First, given the rarity of the event, it typically produced some comment and speculation, as the following quotation illustrates:

> Dr G: Now this (file) is the new patient.
> Nurse: It's the father who's come up with him today.
> Dr G: Uh-huh. I wonder why it's always the father. His father brought
>   him to the GP, so the GP noted. The father brought him here
>   today (pause) ... Father is taking on the maternal role today then.
>   Or rather, I suppose it's all part of the merging of roles that's
>   going on these days ... (pause) ... Mind, they're still not very
>   good at giving histories.

After the consultation:

> Dr G: That young man wasn't too bad. He was a bit vague and a bit glib. He was overdramatizing the situation and he was obviously trying to please me. He said 'Yes' when he wasn't quite sure.... Fathers often want to please you. They tell you what you want to hear. They don't realize the importance of it. They think it's like a chap in the family asking questions about finance; any answer will do.

Fathers then had distinct drawbacks when called upon to act as a child's medical representative. But many mothers were also held to be inadequate and, as has been seen, this did not prevent their idealization. With fathers it was different. Whereas mothers' competence was never openly questioned, this was almost a matter of routine for fathers. Ten out of the thirteen fathers were clearly treated as both substitutes for their wives and rather poor ones at that. The incompetence ascribed to them did not, however, affect their good character. They might not be the ideal representative for a child, but it was also made explicit that this was not a duty to be expected of a father. Staff did not question their character, merely their knowledge of the child.

To begin with, staff routinely inquired about the father's wife. Mothers were not expected to account for the absence of their husbands but fathers were often asked this, either directly, or rather more tactfully the question might be put to the child instead: 'Has mummy come today?' Moreover not only could a consultation not start without such a question, but it could not normally end without a further emphasis on the fact that here was a substitute. Fathers were asked if their wives had any questions that they wanted answering, or else given a message to carry home with them: 'Well, if you could tell your wife that although it may not clear up, not all cases do, but there is a very good chance.'

Apart from such indications of their secondary status, fathers were normally told that staff did not expect too much from them; and when a father did well he might be elaborately praised, whereas mothers never were:

> Dr I: What was the weight at birth?
> Father: 7½ pounds.
> Dr I: Gosh, you've got a good memory! I expect mothers but not fathers to remember. It's 7½ pounds, *you think* (my emphasis).

One father displayed great technical knowledge about his child's condition and was able to describe his medical history in a most sophisticated fashion; but even he was treated as naturally ignorant when it came to discussing the child's present state:

> Dr I: I just want to ask you a few questions about what Ian is doing now. I don't know how you'd manage since I'd have great difficulty in answering them myself, but let's see how you get along.

Male doctors, it seemed, might lack such knowledge of their own children, and they did not normally expect it of other men.

There were three fathers whose competence went unquestioned; of these, two were solely responsible for the care of their child, the only two fathers in this position. Only here it would seem were they treated not as substitutes but as representatives, and granted the wholly ideal character that was given with such ease to any mother.

Grandmothers

Grandmothers might represent a child on occasion, and in many ways they received similar treatment to fathers. They too only performed this task infrequently, though slightly more often than fathers, 18 grandmothers being seen in a total of 30 sessions and with nine different staff members, two of them American. Similarly, they might also accompany mothers to the clinic, though far less frequently than fathers, a total of only six such occasions being noted. In this latter situation they too were accorded a subordinate role, while when they were a child's sole representative they were once again treated as a substitute. Queries were commonly made about the mother's absence, and they were often asked if the mother had any special questions or worries. Just as great affection between father and child was worthy of some comment, so too the love of a grandmother was not that of a mother. Where grandmothers were themselves taking care of a child, their affection and commitment were not simply assumed but were praised or asserted, since such responsibility was beyond the natural order of things.

There were, however, two important ways in which the character of grandmother was rather different from that of a father. Typically their competence was not at issue; and their very claim to this, when coupled with their greater independence, meant that their subordination to the mother could not be so readily assumed. Once again these features were displayed most clearly on those occasions when they alone accompanied the child. As mothers themselves, grandmothers were assumed to know how to look after young children and, as interested parties, they were taken to know a great deal about any child whom they accompanied. Here the staff discuss the normal qualities of grandmothers. Their talk is prompted by the total silence that has greeted the doctor's announcement that the grandchild is likely to be retarded:

Dr J: I don't think they (mother and grandmother) took much of that in.

Nurse: No, and the grandmother seemed worse than the mother, which is unusual.

Dr J: Yes, they've seen more of life if nothing else and they've got more experience of children so they talk more.

In these ways a grandmother might make a better representative than a father. There were, however, problems, for their ability to supply detailed, current information might be as bad as any man's: 'It's a pity the mother's not with her; she (grandmother) won't know much about the case' Nevertheless, grandmothers were still idealized in a fashion quite unlike that of fathers. Overtly their competence was unquestioned and this gave them the opportunity, if they so wished, to criticize the competence of the mother herself. Only one father attacked his wife's capacity to look after their child, and then only on the known medical grounds of her insanity. Several grandmothers however made criticisms of their daughters or daughters-in-law.

Grandmother: Well, I think he's too fat; is he?

Dr A: Well, he certainly seems to be putting on weight pretty quickly. (She then questions her about the baby's feeding and adds....) Well, I should definitely cut down on what you're feeding him, otherwise he'll be very overweight later on and his weight'll be just too much for him to carry about, and it'll be bad for his chest.

Grandmother: Aye, it must be bad for his chest. He gets porridge too. His mother's not very good with him. She never perseveres with the bairn.

Dr A: Well, I should try cutting the Farex out.

Grandmother: She gave him custard yesterday.

Dr A: That's no good either. Strained soup is better.

Grandmother: Yes, I agree.
Dr A: And I should cut out all the cereal.
Grandmother: He's quite content with that.

Such comments show that when a mother was not present her character, far from being assumed, might be a central topic of discussion. This was particularly true when a child was no longer living with its natural parents. Instead of competence, care and affection being placed firmly in the natural order of things, at least for mothers, these were now the subject of detailed investigation by staff and possible denunciation by the child's present guardians. Here for instance is a quotation from an American grandmother who had permanent care of a child:

Dr R: What about her parents?
Grandmother: Her father doesn't love her at all. He doesn't hold her like
               a normal child. He just refers to her as 'the child'.
Dr R: Do the parents live together?
Grandmother: Yes, but neither of them is normal.... She was very odd
               when she was young and then she ran off and married the
               father and he's just the same. They're both very odd. All
               his family are mental in some way.

These last two quotations illustrate a more general rule than any that have so far been considered. As one can now see it was not that mothers were always treated as ideal within the bureaucratic format; such qualities were guaranteed them only so long as they were physically present in the consultation. Rather, whoever was with the child was to be treated as of good character, almost regardless of what they did or said. The grandmother who criticized her daughter's feeding of the child had an oily, ingratiating manner which the doctor disliked intensely. She was also known by the health visitors to have neglected her own children when they were small. Nevertheless, such facts were only mentioned after the consultation. Within it she was still idealized, just as her daughter would have been had she appeared instead. This idealization differed somewhat according to the type of representative, whether they were mother, father or grandmother but in no case was their fundamental integrity overtly doubted.

The Exceptions

Two limiting cases to my argument should be noted. These concern, first, a child's bureaucratic eligibility and, second, some further properties of adequate representatives.

To arrive at a clinic, patients had first to come through the correct organizational channels, and all of the the settings had some form of prior screening in which ancillary staff checked identities, purposes and appointment cards and, in the American settings, investigated finances as well. The patients and parents observed in this study were therefore pre-selected, and the idealization that took place within the consulting room was carried out on those whose bureaucratic fitness had already been certified.

That certification was a necessary condition for idealization can be seen by examining those instances when things went wrong, for not all the patients who reached the doctor met the proper criteria. Some latitude was permitted. Some mothers turned up at the wrong time or in the wrong week but, although they often had to wait a while, all were seen and treated in the normal fashion. There were, however, two cases, both in the Scottish children's hospital, which deviated far more grossly from the standard criteria, and in these no such accommodation was made. In one instance a casualty officer interrupted a clinic as he could not find a doctor to warrant an emergency admission to the hospital. In the other the parents were American and did not realize that Scottish hospital doctors could be seen only through referral from a general practitioner. In both cases there was a child with a medical problem and parents to act as representatives. The standard conditions for a consultation and for the consequent idealization of the parents were thus met. In neither case did a consultation occur, despite the parents' attempts to initiate this. The first doctor talked solely to the casualty officer, ignoring the mother's remarks about her child; she was treated throughout as if she were not physically present. The American parents were talked to, but curtly and about the Scottish medical system, not about their child. To be treated in a proper fashion one had first to come through the proper channels.

The other exception concerned cases where there were serious doubts as to the adequacy of the child's representative. It has already been seen that this adequacy was not a matter of actual character or competence. Whatever the qualities of a mother, the bureaucratic format clothed her in only the seemliest of garments. Fathers and grandmothers too, though plainly substitutes, were nevertheless idealized. But there were limits. The first of these involved the command of English. Those who could not speak it could not be representatives, however admirable their other qualities. Five such cases were seen, all of which ended in chaos and the open expression of frustration by medical staff. The second limit was a less technical matter. Familial substitution for a child's mother could not go beyond fathers or grandmothers, any further was illegitimate and a parental dereliction of duty. In such circumstances the unfortunate substitutes, far from being idealized, could be openly criticized, along with the parents who had sent them. Only two such cases were observed, but they were also the only two occasions on which familial substitution went beyond the normal bounds. In one American hospital clinic the mother had sent a neighbour; while in a Scottish hospital clinic an elder brother aged around 20 made do for the child's parents. Both were treated in a fashion quite unlike that accorded to other representatives within the bureaucratic format. The brother says his parents cannot come because it would mean bringing their baby girl out in cold weather.

> Dr J: Well, I don't think I'll be able to get anything in the way of a good history without them. (This is a referral for suspected epilepsy.) I'll try something.

The doctor asks the child about the fits, but she can remember nothing. The doctor repeats that it is difficult to get a good history under these conditions.

> Brother: (truculently) But you can't bring a baby out in this kind of weather.
> Dr J: Oh, well, I suppose we'll just have to soldier on and do our best.... What was her weight when she was born?
> Brother: I don't know.
> Dr J: And when did she sit up?
> Brother: At the normal stage, I think.
> Dr J: Well, if you don't know there's no point in guessing. When did she walk?
> Brother: (truculently) I don't know.
> Dr J: Oh, well, I think we'll just have to give this up.

In fact this consultation trickled on for some time, though with little more progress being made and with no increase in cordiality.

Limiting cases such as these were exceptional, but they have great analytical value. They show clearly that the ideal character normally ascribed to a child's representative was not simply a matter of staff's personality. It was not the case that some doctors were naturally courteous and automatically idealized every adult who accompanied a child. The vast majority were so transformed, but only in so far as they met certain specifiable criteria. Those who did not were treated in a different fashion. They were not condemned as in the charity format, but they might well be ignored or their inadequacies spelt out and the consultation abandoned or postponed. Idealization was the general rule, but it was not for everybody; and where participants could not be properly idealized the whole encounter was in jeopardy.

4 Collegial Authority

Mothers, and most of the other adults who might normally represent a child, would seem to have done well out of the bureaucratic format. But so far my description has only been partial, for within the format each participant had several contrasting identities. Mothers were not only mothers; they were also subordinates. In regard to their children they were authorities of unblemished character and competence, but as regards medicine and their relationship with staff, they were granted no such authority. Their idealization as naturally loving and able was thus counterposed by an equivalent idealization of their medical ignorance. However much medical knowledge mothers had, or thought they had, they were almost universally treated as technically incompetent. Correspondingly, whatever the actual knowledge or competence of staff, in practice they both assumed and were granted the mantle of expert.

These twin identities form the subject of this chapter. In it I examine, in so far as they can be separated, the procedures through which staff's expertise was idealized and the methods which dramatized the ignorant and subordinate status of the child's representative. The chapter ends with an analysis of those situations which presented the greatest threat to staff's authority, and of the ways in which these challenges were overcome.

Every Doctor a Good Doctor

The idealization of staff's technical competence within the bureaucratic format had two distinctive features. First, this character was given quite unequivocally; expertise was displayed rather than proved. In the Scottish clinics, doctors' status was warranted simply by their being there, dressed in white coats or dark suits, seated behind desks and being spoken to in a deferential manner by other staff. Second, this expertise had a 'collegial' rather than an individual character. Doctors were expert because they belonged to an expert profession. In this version, hospitals and clinics were staffed by a uniform body of professionals, each one competent and all with equal access to a standard body of medical knowledge.

The principal method by which individual staff came to represent this collective wisdom was that of avoidance. Just as mothers' character and competence went uninvestigated and was thus simply assumed to be good, so the staff's actual competence was ignored. Typically no mention was made of their names, mandate, training or special interests. No patient ever asked a member of staff where they had trained, what were their precise qualifications, where they had worked before, how many publications they had got, or how long their studies had taken them. More particularly, no parent ever asked how much experience the doctor had in cases of this type. The unimportance of the doctors' biography was summed up in the manner in which introductions and greetings were typically done. Although doctors greeted mothers by name as they arrived, they rarely named themselves. Naming the mother was more than polite, for it had an important organizational purpose. In doing this, doctors could check that this was indeed the person they thought it was. Naming themselves had no such bureaucratic relevance.

This impersonality extended beyond name and personal history to cover the clinic's remit, the doctor's own powers within it, and the history of the service. For example, because they had no power to prescribe, Scottish local authority doctors referred some mothers to their general practitioner, but they did not normally mention why they did so. Nor did they inform parents as to the origin or purpose of total population screening, the nature of the various sources of data from which they derived their information on parents - such as the 'At Risk' and 'Handicapped' registers which they kept - or the way in which their work was supervised by a superior. Again, just as they did not talk about their own work, so staff did not compare it with that of others. The head of the Scottish physiotherapy department was proud of her policy of 'mat' as opposed to 'plinth' work, but the pros and cons of this issue were never mentioned to parents, nor were any other of the special features of the department. Such reticence was uniform in all the clinics observed. Typically, staff mentioned their particular competence or remit only when parents asked for services that a clinic could not provide, or else when they referred a child to another clinic, and even in these cases they said but little.

This idealization of the character and competence of the staff who ran these clinics was complemented by a similar treatment of those who saw children in other contexts. The assumption of collegial rather than individual expertise required a general rather than a personal anonymity. What parents thought of their general practitioner, of other hospital specialists, of local authority doctors and social workers was almost never mentioned; and this silence was maintained even under the most trying of circumstances. 'Not in front of the patients' was the rule - even where there were major professional demarcation disputes, or where it was staff's job to check on others' work. The only partial exceptionn was the treatment of health visitors. In three instances, Scottish hospital doctors either initiated or concurred in criticism of these relatively low-status staff. By contrast, when hospital staff referred to other kinds of staff, their comments, though uninformative, were often flattering: 'You'll have to see Mr McIntosh (orthopaedic surgeon) about this; he's the expert in these matters.' 'I think you should see Mrs Armstrong (physiotherapist) about this; she's very good with children like this.'

The general avoidance of comment about other professionals is best illustrated by taking one example in detail: the way in which general practitioners were referred to by both staff and parents in hospital clinics. Not all American parents had such a doctor, but Scottish parents certainly did. It was from him that the hospital doctor most commonly received an initial referral, and most parents saw their general practitioner more often and knew him better than they did the hospital or local authority clinic doctor. Moreover, hospital doctors were obliged to write to the general practitioner after each visit, describing what they had done and advising on further treatment if any. General practitioners were therefore involved in almost every case observed in the study, and yet they were almost never a topic of conversation between staff and parents. This was particularly striking given the fact that clinic doctors sometimes disagreed with the diagnosis suggested by the GP, and on some occasions felt the practitioner to be incompetent. Moreover, whereas clinic staff knew, if only by reputation, most of the staff within their own organization, few general practitioners were known to them. They had therefore little to go on besides the referral note itself and this was sometimes both brief and opaque. Was this, for example, a rebellious or prestigious parent rather than a mysterious complaint? 'This is interesting. The GP's written a letter on his own notepaper rather than using the standard referral letter. I don't know why he's done this.'

Despite such doubts, doctors normally made no inquiry into parents' transactions with their general practitioner. They asked neither what he nor the parents had said and they certainly did not inquire into parents' feelings about the relationship. There were only four occasions in which this rule was broken, and then only in part. Each of these involved a major discrepancy between the diagnosis given in the referral letter and that made by the doctor in the clinic; and in each the hospital doctor's version was less serious than that proffered by the general practitioner. Although the three hospital doctors involved did, in these instances, make some inquiry into the previous consultation, they did so in an extremely delicate fashion. They did not point out the discrepancy between their own version and that of the GP, far less did they censure his judgment.

To give an example: in the following instance the general practitioner had suggested a diagnosis of cystic fibrosis, whereas the clinic doctor thought that the problem was a worm. Given the seriousness of the initial diagnosis, the doctor questioned the mother very closely about her consultation with the GP, yet made no overt criticism. In answer to the doctor's first question the mother had revealed the presence of a worm in the child's stool, something that was not mentioned in the referral letter; but the following comments are the only references the doctor made to the GP:

Dr G: Did you tell your doctor about it (the worm)?
Mother: Oh, aye.
Dr G: Uh-huh.... (He asks a series of developmental questions, then returns to the worm.) Your doctor here, you see, says that this has been going on for nine months but you don't think it has.
Mother: Well, I can't really remember.
Dr G: No.

The doctor asks further questions about the child's bowel and chest problems and then returns to the worm.

Dr G: When you saw the worm were you surprised by it?
Mother: Oh, I just felt sick.
Dr G: Yes. Did you think it was a worm right away?
Mother: No, I thought it was slime, but when I saw it wriggling, ugh!
Dr G: And did you actually go to your doctor about it then?
Mother: Well, we were on holiday at the time. We came back on the Monday, I saw the doctor then....
Dr G: What did your doctor say about it?
Mother: Well, he said it was just an earthworm, but I didn't think it was.
Dr G: No, no. All right ... (pause) ... I would think it possible that it's been a worm that's been upsetting him.

Thus, even where some discussion of the general practitioner's actions was necessary it was handled with the greatest delicacy. Even if one finds the lack of staff's reference to general practitioners surprising, it should be noted that it was only a little more frequent among parents. Whatever had passed between them typically went unmentioned. When a clinic doctor gave a diagnosis, some parents commented that this is what their general practitioner had said. More rarely, parents might cite their general practitioner as agreeing with them in order to bolster their own version of events, while three parents criticized the diagnosis that he had suggested. All these cases were again played with great caution by staff. In the following instance a child had been experiencing great pain passing stool and the general practitioner had prescribed a laxative, but on examination the hospital doctor had found a small anal fissure:

Mother: (angrily) The doctor didn't see it.
Dr J: (mildly) Well, it may not have been there then.

In line with this silence over their own and others' competence, staff maintained a similar reticence over what may be termed the 'organizational history' or 'career' of any particular case. Even the healthiest child was examined a good many times in the Scottish city, while those who had illnesses of any consequence were often seen by many different staff, all of whom might play some part in the analysis and treatment of a child's condition. If a child was an inpatient all this was invisible to the parents: just who was involved, who had noticed this and when, was not mentioned. The diagnosis was presented to parents as an accomplished fact. The processes of observation and debate which led up to it were not revealed, nor were the errors that might also have played a part.

One of the most noticeable features of the ward-round on the intensive care unit was the number of mistakes, most of them extremely minor, that were confessed as the round proceeded. It seemed quite routine to make mistakes and there was normally no criticism of those who owned up. Errors were expected, and discussion concentrated on procedures to minimize these in the future. But in clinics errors were never mentioned, unless they were grossly obvious. It was not that staff presented themselves or others as infallible but that such matters were almost never mentioned. Avoidance was the fundamental strategy used by staff to transform their particular capacities and acts into the ideal form suitable for consultations within the bureaucratic format.

That such a strategy was accepted by parents is well brought out in the following two instances, which illustrate just how far the anonymity of such medicine was treated as purely natural. The first quotation comes from the end of a consultation which has lasted half an hour. Only then does the mother reveal that she does not know just who she is talking to:

Dr I: What was Dr Maxwell (child psychiatry) planning for her?
Mother: Well, she said that someone would be seeing her. Someone interested in specific speech delay. Is that you?
Dr I: Well, I'm interested in it, but I don't think it could be me.
Mother: And the other person we'd be seeing is a paediatrician with an interest in coordination.
Dr I: That's me. The other one may be a psychologist.

This quotation has an added interest in that it was the only occasion in which a doctor discussed his particular medical interests; and, as can be seen, it was only due to parental questioning and foreknowledge. In all other cases such matters went unmentioned. Indeed it would appear that some parents, at least overtly, did not only *not* need to know just who the doctor was but they did not even require to know *why* they were there. In the following case and two other instances like this mothers only asked why they had been asked to attend at the very end of a consultation, having already answered all the doctors' questions. It was just assumed that organizational purposes were good ones and one cooperated willy-nilly:

Dr G: Well, that's fine. I'll tell your doctor that he's all right. Everything seems to be fine.
Mother: Well, I don't know what it was all about.
Dr G: Well, it's just that jaundice can affect things later. But I'll write to your GP about it... Goodbye.
Mother: Bye... (leaves).

In this particular case the hospital where the baby was born had arranged for another hospital, one near the mother's new home, to follow the child up, but the mother herself (or so it seemed) had not been informed of this arrangement. It was nevertheless accepted with apparent equanimity. The experts might be anonymous but they knew best.

Expertise in the Private Format

Since the principal method of establishing collegial expertise was to avoid inquiry into, or even mention of, the particular competence of any one member of staff, it is difficult to cite instances which adequately demonstrate the procedure. As with my analysis of mothers' character, I shall therefore rely on a comparison with another format in which the identity ascribed to doctors was of a rather different nature.

My description of the 'private' format, as I shall term it, is, like my earlier description of the charity format, based on only a very limited number of cases. There may well be other ways of doing private medicine, and it seems quite likely that styles of selling will change from time to time. To repeat an earlier caveat, my analysis is not intended to serve as a full description of the phenomenon but aims merely to bring out the contrasting qualities of the bureaucratic format. (At the very end of this monograph I shall discard such caution, but such abandonment is to suit a rather different set of purposes.)

Only six private cases were seen in full detail in the American hospital.[1] All six of these cases shared certain distinctive features, even though they stretched across the work of three clinics and three different doctors. These features were also to be found, at least in part, in two cases in the Scottish neurological clinic, both involving representatives who were relatively unfamiliar with the medical system and had had considerable experience of private medicine. Although the Scottish doctor did not permit a complete switch to a private format, in each case the child's representative made strong attempts to effect such a transition, and these consultations therefore contained a mixture of both formats.

In some respects the private format was similar to that of the bureaucratic mode. However, although doctors were idealized in both, the emphasis in the private format was on the competence of the individual doctor and not on that of the profession as a whole. Doctors within the bureaucratic format were anonymous, but here their skills were personalized. This individual emphasis did not, extend to all of the features that I mentioned earlier. Private patients did not enquire into staff's careers, their mandate or their area of expertise, nor did staff themselves typically reveal this information. Similarly, the competence of other medical practitioners was not a subject for staff's investigation or criticism. To this extent staff's competence rested on collegial not individual authority. But various other matters were given a more personal treatment.

The individualization of medical competence within the private format had a variety of aspects. Take first the issue of the doctor's name. In contrast with the bureaucratic format, doctors routinely introduced themselves to private patients. That this was a matter of some importance can be seen in the following quotation. Here a child's grandmother, absent for long stretches in the British colonies, or their remains, and used to a private not a bureaucratic format, sought similar treatment in a Scottish hospital clinic. Several battles were fought over this during the consultation. In this instance the grandmother wanted an introduction, but the doctor at first refused to give one:

Dr I:	(to child) Can I just see you walk?
Grandmother:	Am I in the way, Doctor? ('Doctor' was drawn out and said with a markedly rising tone.)
Dr I:	No, no.
Grandmother:	Doctor? ... (pause) ... Doctor? ... (pause) ... What is your name?
Dr I:	Dr Innes.
Grandmother:	Dr Innes.

Moreover, although a doctor's career and qualifications might not be discussed in the private format, they might well be on display. Doctors in the Scottish hospitals and clinics worked in completely impersonal rooms bare of any individual reference; and the same rooms were used by many different doctors for their clinics. This was also true of the main ambulatory clinics in the American hospital, and of the various city and state clinics. But doctors who saw private patients in their own room in the American hospital did so surrounded by certificates. They did not point out the parchments, nor were they a topic for discussion, but they formed a significant backdrop for the consultation, in much the same way as the hospital itself was duly warranted by a framed certificate.

This personalization of medical work extended not merely to the doctors themselves but also to their colleagues and contacts. When Scottish doctors cited medical opinion they talked of 'we', not of particular doctors; and similarly, when they referred a child to another hospital for more specialist advice, they named the institution and not the consultant and talked simply of 'Great Ormond Street' or 'Newcastle'. But in the private format doctors talked, not just of hospitals or departments, but of specific experts. The medicine that parents received was directly linked to the 'best' available opinion. On this model the medical profession was not simply a collection of unknown experts but was staffed by named individuals bound by personal links. Here for instance an American doctor discusses a child's small size with his father, a man of considerable wealth:

Father: So it's a little too early to do this now?

Dr O: Right. We talk about this problem all the time at the moment, and I've had discussions at X and Y hospital with the experts in the field. I've spoken to A, B and C about it. We're all very interested in it but it's early days yet.... Remember, it's not just me who's telling you this, I've talked to lots of people who know more about this than I do. (He names them again, plus some others.) And they all agree that it's too risky at the moment.

Not only did doctors refer to others in these individual terms but so too did parents. In the bureaucratic format parents did not normally imply that they knew their GP personally. Indeed the naming of GPs was typically irrelevant, other than as a means to address letters correctly. In the private format, however, naming was a matter of some, importance to parents; and with it went a strong hint of both personal knowledge and an ability to assess the competence of the doctor so named. Here for example is a quotation from the grandmother in the Scottish clinic:

Usually we see Dr Charles about him. He's been the family doctor for years ever since dear old Dr York died. I don't know why Dr Charles sent me here. I've got no idea at all. I really wanted a surgical boot for him. I just wanted to go to one of the respectable surgical boot-makers but somehow Dr Charles sent me along here. I don't quite know why. It may just be wasting your time.

Staff themselves did not actually criticize other doctors, but the fact that they passed favourable judgments on some indicated that there were others who were less deserving of praise, a point which parents readily echoed. Although none challenged the competence of the doctor to whom they were then talking, most made disparaging remarks about others:

Mother: The only trouble is that the treatment will cost so much. The most competent physicians aren't found in institutions (i.e. hospitals).

Dr T: Well, I don't know about that.

Mother: Well, we've had different ones every time we've been here and they've never been any good. They've never helped.

What was most striking about such remarks in comparison with parents' behaviour in the bureaucratic format was the typically bland manner in which they were made. To question others' competence was not a threat to the proper conduct of the consultation; indeed, it was even urged by one doctor:

> Mother: We liked him (Dr Levy) particularly because he was critical of schools and said, 'Don't believe what they say.' That's what got us here.
>
> Dr Q: True. It's very important work the Learning Disability Group does in building up consumer appreciation. There's gotta be a dialogue, it's the only way.

That such criticisms were made and even openly appreciated is not surprising given the explicitly comparative stance on which these consultations were based. As good consumers and in their child's best interest, parents were openly shopping around; and such a position was honourable not shameful, something to be revealed rather than concealed:

> Intern: How did you get here?
>
> Mother: Well, he's been seeing a psychiatrist and he diagnosed minimal brain dysfunction and prescribed X. But we also want to get Dr Stein's opinion as we felt we ought not just to have a psychiatric opinion.

Just as doctors personalized their own knowledge, so they warranted their decisions far more systematically than was typical in the bureaucratic format. Parts of the following conversation are like a private tutorial for a favoured, if somewhat dim, pupil.

> Dr Q: If he's nearly three years behind then he should be in a full-time class with special education, but perhaps we can explain why he was doing OK in the nursery. (Turns to researcher.) Do you know the work of Piaget?
>
> Researcher: Yes.
>
> Dr Q: (to parents) Piaget is a Swiss psychologist. He's a far brighter man than me! What Piaget really argued was about how children started off with very concrete thoughts and then over time they progressed to abstract thought. What we want to know is, why hasn't he? As I said, if he really is three years

	behind then he should be in a full-time class of special education, but he isn't. Why isn't he? I want to know why he's not if he really is this.
Parents:	Right ... (pause ...).
Dr Q:	(leaning forward to mother and speaking in a slow, intimate voice) Now, you know what a learning disability teacher does, don't you?
Mother:	(very hesitantly) He teaches children at a level they can understand.
Dr Q:	(emphatically) That's right!

In summary, whereas doctors in the private format were obliged to tolerate or even welcome criticism of their colleagues and had to sell the special quality of their services with some vigour, their expertise was simply assumed within the bureaucratic format and was in need of no such display. In the latter mode, each and every staff member was almost automatically granted an anonymous but collective wisdom.

Medical Expertise - Parental Ignorance

Having considered the way in which the bureaucratic format granted doctors a generalized wisdom in comparison with the more individualized expertise that was sold to private patients, we may now turn to examine parents' medical knowledge and the manner in which this was handled. As can be seen; in the private format parents assumed and were granted some measure of competence to judge the service which they received, even if they were not granted any equivalent expertise. In the bureaucratic format, by contrast, parents had a far lower status. The assumption of a collective medical wisdom and the more thorough-going exclusion of critical remarks about other services were paralleled by a systematic idealization of parental ignorance.

This distinction must not be pushed too far, for in neither format were parents themselves admitted to the medical college, and in both modes the relationship was one in which there were clear superordinate and subordinate statuses. Moreover, these statuses were constantly dramatized for, whereas staff's technical competence could be idealized through the avoidance of certain topics, the establishment of their technical authority required more positive action. Colleges may be invisible and even anonymous but they are far from being entirely abstract conceptions. In professional interaction, membership or non-membership of the relevant college is invoked at every turn. The member is required to display his authority, while the client must pay due homage to the professional's expertise and indicate his own inferior status. As Werthman (1969) has argued, every action in an authority relationship has import for the maintenance, or otherwise, of that relationship.[2]

The clearest way to demonstrate this dramatization of authority is to contrast it with the very different way in which staff's expertise was treated when they talked with colleagues. The mode which such conversations took may be termed the 'clinical format', and is well illustrated in the following excerpt, which is from a case conference in the American children's hospital and concerned an adolescent girl who had suffered severe brain damage in a fall:

Dr P: There are so many unanswered questions here. She's acting so much like children we see in here who are severely retarded; grabbing, screeching, bizarre behaviour, but psychotic too.

Therapist: I'm gonna make a very profound statement (she laughs). You've got to remember that we had a normal feeling adult and then severe damage. How much of what we see is due to her losing her spatial orientation? (She elaborates on this.)

Psychologist 1: (agrees and stresses that the child is having to adjust to a whole new mode of orientation.)

Dr P: Possibly this explains the clinging.

Psychologist 1: (describes the Helen Keller case as an example of this.)

Therapist: Remember that this child was normal before. Now she will often cling as it is the only contact that she can get.

Nurse: You say she's got no sight, but I think she can see. She must have some sight. If you put a ball in front of her I've seen her pick it up. It may just be tunnel vision or light and dark.

Therapist: We've got to find this out.

Psychologist 2: Let me disagree with Jane (therapist) and Roger (Psychologist 1). I think the sensory deprivation is minor compared to the brain damage. The reason is that the whole scheme of it that has been built up in her head over years has been rearranged. What she really needs is small,

	little steps.
Therapist:	Yes.
Resident:	Can I ask a question? Can I ask if there has been a change in the nursing staff and in the routines that they perform with her, because I think it is significant that at first she cooperated, but now she doesn't. Have we over-stimulated her?
Nurse:	Yes, this could be true, especially as she's such a problem. Everybody is trying to help so we could have over-stimulated her.
Dr P:	Could we look at this? The question is what is a nurse going to do when a child refuses food?

The clinical format was used in a variety of contexts; and case conferences displayed the features which I wish to analyse rather more openly than some. While the above exchange should not be taken as typical of all interaction within the format, it serves to highlight some important differences between this and the bureaucratic mode. Several points may be made. First, note the constant orientation of the participants to a wider collectivity. Some speakers make a direct appeal to what 'we' think, see or need to do and all are oriented to this 'we'. Moreover, 'we' are the people here in this room, colleagues, people of some equivalency, with an important degree of shared knowledge and responsibility. Although a variety of technical terms are used no one bothers to explain what they mean; it is assumed that everyone knows, just as they know the sort of 'children we seen in here'. The style is essentially that of a seminar. Parents too might strive to prove their arguments in one way or another, but the bureaucratic format was not one in which there were agreed standards of proof. Staff and parents, when talking to each other, displayed no such we-orientation. They were not colleagues but individuals, with quite separate interests, responsibilities, competence and knowledge, and were referred to as such.

At the same time, although a far greater appeal was made within the clinical format to some shared orientation, the speakers also differentiated themselves from each other in a far blunter manner than was normal in the bureaucratic or even the private format. All speakers stressed their independent competence and did so as much when they concurred as when they did not. Very few parents stated that they 'agreed' with a doctor's findings, for to do so implied an independent ability to evaluate clinical data; but colleagues commonly did so. When staff disagreed among each other they did so in a relatively open fashion, each again asserting his or her independent authority. The above passage, and indeed the entire case conference, was full of remarks such as, 'You say ... but I think', 'Remember', 'Let me disagree', and admonitions about what 'we' should 'really' do. In consequence the discussion was highly competitive: a frequent feature of talk between staff. Precisely because they had some share in a common body of knowledge and a common task, each staff member's competence was on display; and a successful analysis of a particular case could lead to greater general influence within their organization and profession. Parents might seek to influence particular decisions, but they had no such organizational interests and they were not the doctor's competitors.

Finally, the free-wheeling nature of the discussion needs some comment. Dr P was in control of this meeting and he chaired it quite firmly, but nevertheless the discussion zig-zagged from one topic to another as different speakers brought different points to the fore. Some parents had problems or questions that they raised with the doctor, but in the bureaucratic format such points were presented to him for his solution, they were not topics for general discussion and collegial action or comment. It was the doctor who set the agenda and controlled it with a degree of rigour that would be unacceptable in most kinds of collegial discussion. As such, parents' questions and answers were to the point, not speculative matters intended to raise new issues, and the conversation between doctor and parent typically had a systematic feel, an air of logical progression, which was absent from most conversations in the clinical format.

This comparison of the way in which technical competence was treated in the clinical and bureaucratic formats has highlighted the basic procedures by which collegial authority was displayed and affirmed in the latter mode. Additional methods were sometimes necessary to ensure the maintenance of that authority, for the dramatization of medical expertise and parental ignorance was to be found even in those situations where, at first glance, one night expect them to be absent. For example, these twin idealizations were still present when doctors spelled out the technical grounds for their decisions; indeed, even when they denied any expertise they were still the expert. Similarly, even when medicine had failed, or parents thought it had, they typically made no direct challenge to the doctor's competence, and it was often up to doctors rather than parents to uncover such disputes as did exist. A few parents did indeed make outright attacks upon the doctor; but such occasions were extremely rare and the very way in which they made their criticisms still acknowledged some kind of medical authority. Even when parents did in fact possess some kind of medical competence, they too were normally treated as ignorant and granted a parental rather than a collegial status. The idealization of staff's medical competence and their technical authority over the child's representative was thus almost universal, though to demonstrate this and the additional procedures that it involved requires a more detailed consideration of the above instances; and it is to this that the rest of the chapter is devoted.

Warranting Medical Decisions

The first possible challenge to the rule of collegial authority came from the manner in which doctors warranted the decisions they had made; for some, but not all, staff mentioned the evidence they had considered, its various possible interpretations, and the criteria by which they had finally settled on one particular judgment or course of action. Whereas most aspects of a doctor's competence were anonymous, here there could be a considerable display of expertise. In particular, the senior American hospital doctors were most ready to impart such information, unlike some of their Scottish colleagues who produced reasons for their decisions only when asked. These variations in style are best shown by examining the different ways in which roughly similar cases were treated by different doctors.

To take one example: in chapter 3 I compared the different approaches by Scottish and American paediatricians to psychological conditions. The quotations cited also reveal a contrasting attitude to the use and relevance of medical information. The Scottish doctor was silent on other matters besides the psychological, whereas the American doctor ranged much more broadly. Here is another set of comparisons, this time both from the same Scottish clinic and both concerning possible migraine. In the first case, the doctor made only one reference to his diagnosis and this an extremely cautious one:

Dr G: Have you heard of the word migraine?
Father: Aye, it's like what my wife has ... (pause) It must be very mild if it is.
Dr G: Yes (non-committally). It's like it, is it?
Father: Aye.

The doctor then turns to another topic.

By contrast, in the other case the doctor produced a constant stream of medical information and comment, for example:

Dr H: So there has been a family history of this (migraine)?
Mother: I used to take the bile at school.
Dr H: And you used to take turns of bile as well. Well, these are always sort of inter-connected, I think.
Mother: Is it appendicitis? I had a cousin who had that.
Dr H: An appendix doesn't behave this way. You don't get a sore tummy either with appendicitis or a grumbling appendix.
Mother: It doesn't bother you chronic?
Dr H: It was a fashionable diagnosis at one time for sore tummies, but there is no real reason to think it does cause such things.

As one can see, doctors who warranted their decisions by displays of technical knowledge not only departed somewhat from the standard rule of medical anonymity but gave a personal flavour to their expertise that is reminiscent of the private format, if in a more moderate form. Such individual displays of competence, even in the extreme forms found in the private format, did not in themselves threaten the doctor's status as the authority within the consultation. When parents asked for reasons or doctors provided them, this made no direct challenge to the doctor's superior status; for the talk between doctors and parents on these matters was not an overt check on staff's competence, nor an occasion for proof, but merely a revelation of the 'obviously' competent manner in which doctors had proceeded. That such talk might covertly provide material for checking was, for the purposes of the ceremonial order, irrelevant. In the quotation cited above the body of knowledge to which Dr H refers is clearly not one to which the mother presumes she has access, nor is she granted any such status. The mother merely asks about the state of the art, but only the doctor reveals it, and does so in an authoritative fashion quite separate from the tentative manner with which staff introduced many of their remarks in the case conference. Indeed, in both the bureaucratic and the private formats doctors did the telling, parents were merely told.

Failure and the Maintenance of Medical Authority

There were, however, occasions in which parents, whatever their lack of technical competence, might well feel they had a right to do the telling. Two situations in particular posed a real threat to staff's authority. On the one hand a failure to diagnose or to cure threatened the purpose of a child's continuing attendance at a clinic. Conversely there were some occasions where doctors felt they could help, but where their actions were seen by parents as potentially or actually dangerous. Of these possible sins of omission and commission handicapping conditions were the major instance of the former and drug therapy and immunization were the most problematic examples of the latter.

Both kinds of threat were relatively frequent in the hospital clinics, particularly within the Scottish neurological clinic. However, one of the most striking features of these settings was how rarely parents voiced any direct criticisms of the doctors' actions, despite the large number of occasions on which they might have done so. To take the example of handicap: accepting that their child was handicapped was never an easy task for parents, and was often made more difficult by the relative lack of medical knowledge and capacity. A precise aetiology, diagnosis and prognosis took many years to achieve in some cases, and often cure was impossible and no satisfactory statement of cause forthcoming. In consequence many parents disagreed strongly with the doctors' verdict at one time or another. Nevertheless all but a handful made no direct challenge to their authority. Most maintained an outward pose of agreement with what they were told, even though they might say rather different things to ancillary staff such as therapists or social workers. Others did indicate their discontent but typically only by non-verbal means. Such parents kept their heads down, avoided the doctors' gaze and said little. These indirect methods presented no great challenge to a doctor's authority, for total assent is not always demanded of subordinates by their superiors. The slight distancing of the lowlier members from the due ceremony of an encounter does not threaten their master's authority, save in cases of explicit moral denunciation where, as we have seen, the defendant's demeanour is all-important. In the bureaucratic format parents could be somewhat sullen and yet still indicate their subordination to staff.

Medical incapacity did not therefore present a major challenge to medical authority. Indeed, in such circumstances the greatest criticism of medical competence came not from parents but from staff themselves. Take as examples the following two instances from the Scottish neurological clinic:

Dr I: We do like to see you just once in a while. I think I'm a charlatan really because there's nothing much we can do, but we just like to keep an eye on things to see if there is anything we can do.

Mother: Well, what's he going to be like then?
Dr I: Well, I don't think I can look that far into the future with any
           confidence. It's very difficult to say. And I might be wrong
           because so often doctors can be wrong and therefore I think the
           best thing is to keep an open mind at the moment and wait and
           see how he progresses.

To say such things was to spell out the limits of what medicine could do;
but it was not to discount medical expertise, merely to describe its potential
from an expert point of view. It was staff and not parents who typically set
bounds to medical competence for, as they were held to be the experts, only
they could know when medical knowledge was insufficient. Such comments
did not therefore diminish their general authority. Indeed, if one compares
them with those cited in the discussion of how staff warranted their decisions,
they have a very similar form. The parents are told but they do not themselves
tell, while there is constant reference by the doctor to the college to which he,
but not the mother, belongs. 'We' might be wrong but only 'we' can
accurately judge this, or point it out.

To say this is not to claim that parents never made any direct attacks upon
a doctor's competence, but such occasions were not only extremely rare but
characterized by major attempts on the part of both sides to limit and defuse
the challenge. As an initial example, here is a quotation from the case of a
child with sub-clinical epilepsy. This had seriously affected his ability to
concentrate but, after a three-month course of drug therapy, he had shown
considerable improvement and the mother now wished treatment to be
discontinued - against the doctor's advice:

Mother: Well, I must admit I don't like the idea of him taking these.
Dr I: I realize that ... but ground that is lost now (at school) may be
           permanently lost.
Mother: Well, yes, I suppose so, but I do worry about it. I worry about it,
           if it's so necessary. I worry ... I mean, that he has to have it. I
           suppose he must have it, but I sometimes think that it is not
           really all that necessary, not really.
Dr I: Oh, yes, I appreciate what you're saying but it is a severe
           problem when his class teacher finds that he can't cope, that he's
           not learning and that he's falling behind. The Educational Psy-

chologist has checked that he has a normal IQ so that's not the reason he's falling behind. They were so worried that they asked a Child Psychiatrist to look into it. There's enough to be gained here to make it worthwhile.

Mother: It's just a drug of course to *you*. I mean, you're prescribing them every day.

Dr I: (very firmly) No.

Mother: It's like all drugs, it's not dangerous....

Dr I: Yes.

Mother: If it's used properly, but we lay people do worry about it.

Dr I: Yes, I know that. I'm aware of that. But it's not a drug of addiction. Look on it more as a medicine. Unfortunately we use the same word for both.

The first point to notice about this quotation is the heightened emotional tension which accompanied the mother's challenge. If one reconsiders the mood of the case conference from which I quoted earlier, not only were challenges a standard feature of the discussion but they were done in a relatively easy way. By contrast, for a parent to question a doctor's competence in the bureaucratic format was to threaten the entire social occasion. Minor parental sniping could be done with little or no visible emotion, but fundamental questioning of medical wisdom, and thus medical authority, was usually accompanied by raised voices and flushed faces. It is thus not surprising that in the above example the mother's personal attack upon the doctor was immediately followed by a significant withdrawal. As soon as the doctor too raised his voice the mother retreated.

The precise way in which the retreat was managed is also of some interest. I have noted that authority relationships required constant dramatization for their successful enactment. But the style in which they were played was usually implicit. Doctors did not normally state that they were the expert, nor did parents usually formulate themselves as ignorant. Where there was a real threat to the ceremonial order, then such a spelling-out might well be done, though typically it fell to parents rather than to staff to do this. Just as it was normally up to doctors, not parents, to describe the limits of their own expertise, so it was parents' task, where appropriate, to depict their own ignorance and staff's competence. Each party then was expected to draw attention to its own defects. In the incident above, the mother followed her direct attack upon the doctor by a description of herself as a member of the laity. This reference drew the sting from her challenge and enabled the doctor to take on a calm and teacherly style in his reply: 'Look on it more as a medicine. Unfortunately we use the same word for both.'

This successful minimization of the offence caused by direct parental criticism of a doctor's competence was standard in cases of far more gravity than this, even though this incident was itself exceptional. Even where serious parental challenges were not overtly resolved (and there were only four such cases in the entire study) in three out of these four cases doctors and parents agreed to differ.[3] The incident was treated as no more than that: as something set apart from the rest of the consultation and in no way threatening it. Arriving at this point could, however, take time. Here, for instance, is a mother's denunciation of a doctor for having, as she saw it, misinformed her of the possible side-effects of a drug:

Mother: She took a headache on the Friday and then she was sick *all day* on the Saturday and *all day* on the Sunday and she had to stay off school....

Dr I: Well, we don't think that's the fault of the drug.

Mother: Well, Dr Hastings (GP) thought it was.

Dr I: Well, I don't really.

Mother: It all seemed part and parcel of it.

Dr I: Well

Mother: (very angrily) Look. Let *me* tell you about it. If I'd realized it was a stimulant ...

Dr I: Well ...

Mother: ... you were giving her, I'd have looked out for it

Dr I: Well

Mother: ... but you told me it was a sedative.

Dr I: Well

Mother: Well, I read the note in the chemist. And it said it *was* a stimulant.

Dr I: (with raised voice) I know, and you read that it was given as a stimulant to adults.

Mother: It said it was a stimulant when I read it in the chemist's.

Dr I: It didn't say that at all.

Mother: Well, I called in Dr Hastings and he was very upset.... There just couldn't have been any other reason for it.... There's no doubt about it at all.... And I'm not going through all *that* again.... Dr Hastings couldn't find any other reason for it.

Despite the vehemence of this attack, signified not only by the mother's anger but by her open formulation of herself as the one who was going to do the telling, the doctor eventually reasserted his normal technical authority. In the passage that followed directly from the above quotation, the doctor made an ironical but heavy appeal to his authority and the mother immediately began to treat him, conversationally at least, as a proper expert:

Dr I: My own feeling, Mrs Logie, for what it's worth, is that this illness is not related to the X. X doesn't produce these effects in children.

Mother: Do they not have fevers or sore throats, then?

Dr I: No.

The mother's protests continued for some time but in a much diminished form, and eventually the doctor drew a line under the topic and started on a fresh one; one in which his expertise was granted its normal status: ' Well, anyhow, the present position is she's off all medicine except Y.' From then on the interaction was of a completely normal form. The mother's doubts may still have been there but they were carefully segregated. Other topics were discussed in a cheery fashion, the mother even sharing in or making a joke with the doctor on two occasions. Only at the very end of the consultation, fifteen minutes later, was the topic referred to again, and then in a way which indicated an understanding, or at least a truce: (The child's condition had in fact improved considerably since the incident and the doctor had gone on to discuss cutting down drug Y.)

Mother: You're not thinking of trying anything else for her during the day.

Dr I: I don't think so. Especially after this rather unfortunate incident.

Mother: (meaningfully) Yes.

Dr I: Also, there are one or two other things that are going to happen in the future. There's going to be her glasses.

Mother: Yes, I think the glasses will be a big help.

Dr I: And, you see, if she's put on the drugs today, she might start on them at the same time as she starts wearing the glasses and we couldn't really separate out the effects.

Mother: (laughing) No.

A similar minimization, but of a slightly different kind, was practised in the only two cases where parents were openly taking their children to treatment not recommended by the doctor. These parents took pains to emphasize that it was merely a trial, that they were not ungrateful for what had been done, and that they would return if their plan did not work. Such limitation was accompanied by a similar segregation of the offending topic so that in one case the mother, after criticizing staff, gave instant indication of her continuing reliance on them. This mother was trying the Doman-Delcato or Philadelphia method of treating brain-damaged children, a non-Health Service facility:

> Mother: (aggressively) You see, nobody before Mrs Robins (Philadelphia staff) ever gave us something to work on with Ian. We came over here and you said, 'Is he getting on OK?' and that was it. My husband said when I got home, 'What did they say?' And I'd say, 'Nothing, just the same.' No one ever said, do this or do that ... (pause) ... Well, Mrs Jones (hospital physiotherapist) she's been a great help, but Mrs Robins said, 'Do X,' and 'Do Y.' The only snag now is getting a therapy table .... (abrupt change in tone) What do you do with all your old ones?

My final method for showing the near-universality of the principle of medical authority, whatever the degree of medical failure or imagined failure, is that it was staff who very often revealed parental discontent and not the parents themselves. Just as it was doctors who normally set the limits to medical competence, so it was they who quite often brought disagreements out into the open, or tried to do so, for this presented no direct challenge to their own authority. The following quotation concerns a mother who had recently seen a television programme on autism and had asked the doctor if her own, severely retarded child was autistic. The doctor spent some time explaining why he felt this was not the case, but the mother made no overt signs of accepting his arguments. Like many parents she did not express her discontent in any direct fashion, relying solely on non-verbal means to indicate her feelings. She kept her head down during the doctor's discussion of autism and thus avoided his gaze. Similarly when he had finished speaking she made no reply at all but looked most solemn. Eventually the doctor decided to bring the mother's discontent into the open:

> Dr I: I realize that you feel this very strongly and that you are not convinced.

Mother: (sharply) No.

Dr I: ... by what I say, but I am quite sure she's not. What are you thinking could happen if she was autistic?

Mother: Well, I just don't know.

Dr I: Were you thinking that if Stephanie was autistic that there would be a lot of things that one could do for her?

Mother: Well, I know that you don't know much about autistic children.

Dr I: No, we don't. In point of fact if Stephanie was autistic I think you'd have more worries than if she was just backward. I was just wondering if you were thinking that, if she was autistic, she was missing out on a lot of things that we could be doing?

Mother: Well, I wondered if there was some special kind of training to get her speaking?

This instance is particularly striking because outside the clinic this mother expressed the strongest criticism that any parent made during the study. A few days after attending this consultation she wrote an angry letter to the doctor, denouncing the competence of the medical staff in the hospital and withdrawing her child entirely from treatment. Some other parents stopped attending clinics but none formally withdrew in this fashion. Yet within the consultation it was the doctor who formulated her discontent and not herself; and he had to use repeated questions to reveal her challenge, stating what he thought she might think and asking her if this was indeed so.

Apart from giving a good illustration of the way in which parents concealed their strongest criticisms, this quotation also tells us something of the risks that doctors ran if they attempted to uncover what parents tried to keep hidden.[4] Although it was often doctors rather than parents who revealed major parental doubts, it should not be imagined that this was a routine procedure. Such revelation was certainly part of staff's agenda with the more problematic cases such as handicapping conditions, but it was normally practised only when the occasion seemed most auspicious - and even then the parents might not be drawn. Just as staff relied on the passing of time to let mothers raise doubts about their maternal competence, so they usually waited until the time seemed right to raise the issue of their own competence. To discuss such matters was no easy task, even if they themselves were first to name the topic. In the example quoted above the doctor's first remark was immediately followed by a display of anger from the mother; the first that she had shown in the clinic. Moreover, although she controlled her emotions after this, one of her following remarks was a more direct claim to medical knowledge than any she had made previously. Whereas before she had merely reported what had been said others on the television programme, she now assumed a personal authority and an inside knowledge - 'I know that you don't know' - and for parents to talk in collegial terms was to threaten medical authority seriously. Although these particular challenges were successfully resolved, at least within the consultation itself, the very dangers that the formulation of discontent might produce meant that staff normally avoided it, just as they avoided detailed formulation of their own competence except where strictly necessary.

The Challenge from Parental Competence

The final threat to staff's authority within the consultation resulted not from medical failure but from parental competence. This was only rarely an issue. Although mothers were granted a certain competence, this normally related just to their care of the child. Within the clinic, proper mothers were expected to be subordinate to staff and few claimed any medical competence. Those handful of mothers who did make a direct attack upon the doctors nevertheless phrased much of their criticism in lay terms. The mother of the child with sub-clinical epilepsy appealed not to her own expertise but mostly to her worries as a mother; and such worries were of course virtues, things that any proper mother should have. In the two other cases that I have cited the mothers certainly referred to an authority, but not their own; in one case it was a television programme and in another it was their general practitioner. Such references might bolster mothers' claims, but they themselves did not speak as members of the college whereas hospital specialists could and did.

Not all staff could make unchallengeable claims to superiority; and, while ordinary parental competence posed no threat to doctors, it might be more of a problem to staff of lower technical and social status. Doctors never complained of being socially upstaged by parents but, when asked what kinds of parents they disliked if any, the Scottish physiotherapists immediately mentioned 'people who put on airs' and 'who think they're too good for you' and, although no examples of direct parental criticism of their competence were observed, one such case was reported during fieldwork:

> Therapist B said that when John's mother came in she claimed that she could walk him better than Therapist A. So Therapist A told her to demonstrate how she did it and there wasn't any difference, except that

John lurched more when walked by his mother. Ordinarily, she said, she would have been very angry at this. After all, what was she here for? But if it kept the mother happy, well, just let her go on thinking it. She added rather sourly that the mother kept on giving her advice on how to treat John and get a good performance out of him.

With doctors, in contrast, parental competence was a threat to their status only when it was of a kind akin to their own; and this was, of necessity, rare. Nevertheless, 20 cases were seen when the parents present either had, or had access to, some kind of competent medical knowledge.[5] In two cases the mother was a doctor and in a further six the mother either was or had been a nurse. Three other parents worked in medically-related occupations and were a dentist, a radiologist and a drug company representative respectively, while another three parents worked in related academic disciplines. Apart from such occupationally given knowledge, there were some mothers who were closely related to medical experts. Four were married to doctors and a fifth was the daughter of a doctor. In four out of these last five cases, the relative was a hospital doctor and known to staff by reputation, if not always personally. There was also one mother who ran a local parents' group for handicapped children and attended regional and national conferences on the matter. Although not professionally trained, she had a wide knowledge of many aspects of the condition besides those which related to her own child.

Given the rather different claims to knowledge or influence which these parents could potentially make, it is not surprising that there were major variations in the manner in which consultations involving them proceeded. However, in the majority of cases there was in fact no challenge of any kind to staff's technical authority, and the idealization of medical expertise and parental ignorance occurred in much the sane fashion as in any other consultation. Doctors and parents stayed clearly within the guidelines of the bureaucratic format, and the competitive, collegial atmosphere of the clinical format was avoided.

This is not to say that these occasions were completely identical with those where parents had no claim to inside knowledge, but the differences were trivial. When talking to a doctor's wife one doctor put his feet up on the table - something that he did not normally do. In another instance a mother who was also a doctor displayed her child's slight cranial abnormality to the researcher with considerable clinical enthusiasm. But in other respects these consultations were little different from any other. Generally doctors spoke to such parents in a slightly more technical fashion than was usual and sometimes gave them more time than other parents received, but their consultations normally bore no resemblance to the nature of the clinical format. Indeed in two cases, both involving ex-nurses who had previously worked in the Scottish children's hospital, the mothers paid a far greater respect to the norms of the bureaucratic format than was found in most other consultations. What was normally tacit was here spelt out and both behaved as if it was wrong to ask anything of a doctor, for fear of challenging his authority:

> Dr I: Make an appointment for me then, and I'll just check her over again.
>
> Mother: Well, if you don't mind me asking, will this take a long time?
>
> Dr I: Oh, well, we might have to do it until we are absolutely sure.
>
> Mother: Well, I know I shouldn't have asked this question.
>
> Dr I: Well, it's a fair enough question. It's just that we're unable to answer it. I think (pause) ... it might be ... (pause) ... it might be a month or two.

This behaviour suggests that medical competence on the part of parents, far from automatically modifying the nature of the bureaucratic format, may in some cases merely reinforce it, at least overtly. Precisely because they were insiders and could be expected to know the rules and their value, such parents were obliged to follow or even exaggerate them. This argument is strengthened if one turns to consider those parents who did actually claim an authority in some way equivalent to that of the doctor. There were in all six cases in which parents openly asserted a medical competence; but of these three had no medical training of any kind but were academics who worked in medically-related disciplines: biology, psychology and serology. In other words, half of those few parents who asserted claims to medical competence had no professional training, whereas the majority of medically-qualified parents observed the standard rules with some care.[6]

Staff's reaction to such assertion differed. In four cases it was firmly squashed, thus upholding the rule of their supreme technical authority, but in the other two instances these contributions were actually welcomed. The four parents who failed all sought to establish themselves as independent professionals without prior invitation from the doctor. They used a variety of means to this end: a highly technical vocabulary; the indication of expert action that they had themselves initiated; sceptical comments about other issues; and offers of their own authoritative version of events:

Mother: I've been reading the journals and they were suggesting X as a cause of the damage.... I was wondering if it was something to do with the culture her father's been taking.... I mean, it's well known that such cultures can cause genetic change; for example, they cause genetic changes in snapdragons.

Dr I: Oh, I didn't know this.

Despite such displays of learning none of these parents were treated as colleagues whose professional opinion was necessary to the consultation. Thus staff did not respond, or did so only minimally, to offers of collegial discussion. Here for example is another excerpt from the above case:

Dr T: And what about your schooling?

Mother: Well, I was at the University of X and got a scholarship to Y College for my Masters. Then I had my children and I thought, I'll do a PhD, but, you know how these things work out. So now I'm working at the State laboratory. It's really quite interesting work. We publish a lot of material. Do you know Doctors A and B?

Dr T: No, I only know them by name. Well, well, I don't see any report here about urine screening.

Apart from ignoring such offers, staff also made direct moves to define these parents as subordinates and their knowledge as at best partial or even irrelevant to the task at hand. One such father, as I noted earlier, was told quite firmly that he need not worry if he was unable to answer all the questions about the child's current behaviour. For all his expertise, he was relegated to the standard category of 'ignorant father'. Similarly, the ex-nurse was told that her knowledge was only partial - 'What you're calling "petit mal" attacks' - and her professional preparations were mocked: when the notes she had made on her child's problems fell to the floor, the doctor commented, 'You've dropped your script'. Doctors might use a slightly more technical vocabulary in such cases but they took pains to indicate that their own vocabulary was still superior. They were still speaking down, even if they did not have quite so far to go as with other parents.

I now turn to those two cases in which parents not only asserted their expertise but their professional opinion was actually sought by the doctor. Instead of having to fight to win some recognition this was immediately granted them, and the consultation proceeded on a basis of some equivalence. Take, for instance, the following quotation:

Dr F: Do you think it's necessary for me to test her hearing?
Mother: Well, I think she can hear.
Dr F: Well, I suppose I'd better just ... (does so) Well, do you think
         that there is anything else I ought to check?
Mother: No, I don't think there is anything really.
Dr F: There weren't any problems on discharge then?
Mother: No ... (pause) ... I was a bit worried about her hips so I got them
         X-rayed, but they're OK.
Dr F: OK. So there's no need for me to do it really then, is there?
Mother: When is she going to catch up fully?
Dr F: Oh, I think she's doing all right now. Let's just put her on the
         couch. Sorry! It's just that these occasions do tend to turn, into
         social chat. I don't think doctors' children *ever* get fully
         examined (he grins - they both laugh).

The doctor examines the child quickly.

Dr F: She's doing fine. What's her weight?
Mother: X lbs. Why? Do you think we should be worrying about it?
Dr F: Oh, no. It's in the normal range.

This particular mother was a doctor who was known personally if not well
by the doctor, but similarly deferential treatment was given to the mother who
was actively involved in a parents' organization. Indeed, one doctor
commented of this latter mother: 'I'm rather scared of her, she knows a lot
more than I do in some ways.'

Despite this clear recognition of both these mothers' expertise, the form of
their consultations still owed most to the bureaucratic format and was only a
partial exception to the rule of idealized expertise and ignorance. To take the
case that I have just quoted, it was the doctor who by and large set the agenda,
not the mother. Although she provided expert opinion on various matters, she
did so only at his request. Moreover, despite his apologies the doctor did after
all examine the child. He may have laughed when he referred to the
difficulties of such occasions but in appealing to their notorious quality he
implicitly underlined his authority within the clinic. His earlier remarks paid
due deference to the mother's own expertise, but having done this he asserted
his superior status. She was an expert but he was, here at least, 'the' expert.
Finally, the overall pattern of the consultation was strikingly similar to the
general run of cases seen in that particular setting, the special nursery follow-
up clinic. The doctor's main task in this clinic was to detect those few babies

who still had problems and to provide the mothers of the rest with reassurance. In pursuit of the latter aim he probed repeatedly for parental worries, although it often took time before mothers revealed their deepest fears. In having such fears and having to be coaxed to reveal them this mother proved no different from the rest.

Similarly, the two doctors who saw the mother who ran a parents' organization treated her with an equivalent mixture of deference and superordination; but again they set this inside an overall framework which they, not the mother, controlled. The extent to which these two mothers were treated as colleagues depended on the topic under discussion and, where this was the doctor's speciality, he set both the agenda and the tone of the discussion. The consultations in both these cases therefore contained a mixture of formats. Parts of them resembled a predominantly clinical format, other parts a bureaucratic mode.

Thus doctors solved the problem of handling parents who might know as much as they did by recognizing their attributes as both parent and expert not jointly but separately, now treating them as parent and now as expert. In essence, this strategy resembled the segregation of topics that was used to minimize the effects of direct parental attacks upon staff's competence. The difference was that the kind of segregation practised with the competent parent was not necessarily a matter of carefully compartmentalized blocks of interaction. The switch from one format to another could be extremely rapid, with the parents' status changing from topic to topic. Such sudden transitions demand some skill and a willingness to cooperate but, in these two instances at least, these conditions were clearly met. Moreover, even though these parents were admitted to the college, they entered only on the doctor's terms. Not all of those with likely qualifications got inside, and the two who did still paid a large measure of obedience to the doctor's authority.

5 A Joint Venture

So far I have concentrated on describing particular identities within the bureaucratic format, noting how parents received an ideal character and staff were granted an ideal technical competence. What has been omitted is any real sense of their joint identity, of the way in which they were portrayed, not just as doctor and parent, but as a team. For the patient in these consultations was not the parents but the child, a child for whose sake both parties were nominally present and in whose cause they were temporarily united.

This overt alliance between doctor and parent was a central part of the ceremonial order and needs consideration in its own right, though, as we shall see, it drew much of its shape from the matters that have already been considered; the form that an alliance takes necessarily depends upon the properties of the participants.

The alliance considered here had three principal features. First, responsibility for a child was treated, not as the sole right or duty of the parents, but as in part shared with staff. This joint obligation was the foundation of the team approach. Second, just as other aspects of the participants' character were idealized, so too was their commitment to the individual child and thus to the alliance. The overt aim of their actions was to help the child, and all other considerations were secondary to this. Third, as allies who had come together in a common cause, decisions were not imposed but discussed. The allies might have different interests, powers, rights, skills and duties, but progress was by agreement and not by force. Such at least were the overt rules.

There is little to be said about the first of these principles, the assumption of a shared responsibility for the child patient. The mere fact of parents' presence in the consultation constituted evidence of such sharing. By asking staff's advice and by answering their questions, parents indicated that their child was not theirs alone, at least in this respect. This assumption was so plain that it needed no mention. Nor did it require a separate enactment for, in demonstrating their subordination to staff's technical authority, parents simultaneously granted doctors a share in the child's management.

If the way in which responsibility was shared needs only a brief mention, far more attention must be paid to the idealization of the allies' motives. For although I have devoted considerable space to parental good character and the means by which it was produced, my account of staff's character has been partial. Whereas I have examined both the moral and technical qualities of natural parenthood, I have up till now considered only staff's medical authority and ignored the moral qualities with which they were also endowed. But for a proper alliance within the bureaucratic format both parties had to be properly moral as well as competent.

Medical Motives

The demonstration of proper motivation was as complex a business with staff as it was on some occasions with parents. Indeed, in some ways staff were potentially more suspect. Parents at least had 'natural' reasons for wanting to help their child, even if these were shaky at times, but the motives of staff were merely professional; put another way, it was simply a job. They could not be assumed to have a deeply personal interest in all the children whom they saw, for the children were not their children but their work; and the attitudes we feel towards our work rarely mesh in any precise way with the ideals proclaimed in public ceremonies. Concealment was therefore necessary if staff were ever to have the qualities required of a proper ally.[1]

Let us begin by reconsidering the American case conference that was cited earlier. It will be remembered that, although there was some delicacy in what was said, the feelings to which staff were oriented were mainly professional ones. The speakers assumed a common technical interest in the case, no matter how tragic the condition and its consequences. Some were tentative in what they said, but principally so as to avoid looking foolish in front of their colleagues, or not to offend others' sense of professional pride. As the occasion was a meeting among colleagues who knew each other well, joking was in order, and was indeed a key means by which tempers were cooled and professional jealousies abated. And, since it was the child's condition that was the topic of conversation, it was this and matters relating to it that were joked about. The therapist guyed her initial remarks by saying, 'I'm going to make a very profound statement', and laughing after she said this. Later on, when it was suggested that they get just one experienced nurse to look after the child and that this might solve the behaviour and feeding problems, another member of staff, an Italian American, commented, 'What this girl needs is a good Italian Momma - and plenty of good Italian sausage.'

Thus although the discussion was a serious occasion at which serious matters were discussed, staff were at a considerable emotional distance from the personal tragedy that the case involved. The problem of how to cope with the mother and her reactions was a technical problem.

Staff's technical interest in children may be analysed under a number of different headings. There was, for a variety of reasons, a major emphasis on the unusual, and words such as 'odd', 'dramatic' or 'abnormal' were key terms in the clinical format. Moreover, children who could be described in these terms were 'interesting' and might even become 'famous':

Dr H: ... James was very well known in the newborn period. He really had a lot of problems. There was asphyxia, heart failure, hypoglycaemia, and he had an enlarged liver and spleen.

The initial reason for this interest is obvious enough. Children who were normal were of no medical concern. Not all children who were ill were particularly 'interesting', for some had normal forms of normal illnesses. This is not to say that a child's condition might not be serious, or that treatment might not be difficult, but that what was at issue was not in doubt; though here too staff were continually on watch for the unusual or the unexpected, even where it had, apparently, nothing to do with a child's condition. In the following instance the doctors had just finished discussing a routine case in the intensive care unit and were passing on to the next baby, when a doctor commented on a note in the records:

Dr H: That's a very funny selection of drugs for osteomyelitis. (The mother is being treated for this.)
Dr J: (agrees and makes specific criticisms of them).
Registrar: She's had these drugs since childhood.
Dr J: No! That's very odd.

Staff were therefore strongly biased in their attention towards the medically problematic and those that required emergency treatment. The ward-round at the special nursery devoted almost all of its attention to these cases, while most of the other babies received barely a glance.

There were in addition several other criteria which made a child of especial interest. First, the Scottish children's hospital was also a teaching hospital, and staff were always in need of good teaching material:

Dr J: It's a beautiful example of these spots.
Dr H: They're really beautifully placed. They're marvellously discrete spots. We must photograph it.

All staff had a professional interest in the unusual cases, since their study was a central means of developing both their own knowledge and that of the discipline. Just as I myself have concentrated heavily on the unusual in my analysis of medical interaction, so staff's theoretical orientation to medical conditions produced a similar focus on the abnormal. Unusual cases might provide material for research, a key orientation of many of the Scottish hospital doctors; and they were of central interest to junior staff whose qualification as competent professionals depended on their gathering as wide a range of clinical experience as possible. From this perspective, 'problems' became 'finds' as well. In consequence, when a rare condition was discovered in an inpatient, staff might be brought from all over the hospital to view the child, and such matters formed an important topic for discussion over lunch or coffee. By contrast, children who had entirely normal illnesses might be of no technical interest whatsoever, particularly to junior doctors, as is revealed in the following quotation in which two Scottish registrars examine the files before the arrival of the consultant:

Dr 1: All three of these new cases are for bleeding, not very interesting.
Dr 2: None of this lot are very interesting. One lot of fits and the rest all aches and pains.

They start to play with the toys in the room, then abandon this and look through the records again.

Dr 2: Excitement! Excitement!
Dr 1: Yes, gripping, isn't it? (One of them selects the epilepsy case.)
Nurse: Oh, you've got an exciting one there.
Dr 2: (sarcastically) Great stuff (Later on, however, it all turns out all right, for he returns to tell the consultant) This boy's been having some very interesting fits.

Apart from these personal and professional interests, particular cases might also offer lessons in management and provide the occasion for a review of current policy and practice. In the ward-round at the special nursery, staff constantly addressed a great number of general points: when should tests be done? when should blood be exchanged in transfusion cases? when was it worth referring a skin condition? when should feeds be changed? Here, for instance, the round reaches Baby Callaghan.

Dr J: Baby Callaghan seems fine. His weight is up. He's got a rash at the moment.

Sister: I don't know how bad it is.

Dr J: There's an awful lot of thrush at the moment in the Unit.

Dr H: (peers at the baby, then says) Have you been in the habit elsewhere of isolating thrush? I think I've asked you this before.

Dr J: Yes, you have. Yes, we did used to isolate it when I was in London.

Dr L: We used to where I was in the States.

Dr H: Well, the problem is of course that isolating is still a very controversial matter and in any case it's very difficult here with this acute shortage of accommodation we've got. It's been especially difficult here, with the principle we've had that anyone who was isolated had to stay isolated, which meant that you used up the isolation rooms very quickly. This needs looking at.

The enthusiasm with which doctors approached any individual case and thus the kinds of comment they made to others about it, depended not just on the degree of professional interest it held for them, but on several other matters also: the amount of work it would involve, its degree of difficulty, and how this fitted into their personal schedule. Since all patients represented work to doctors, almost every member of staff was heard to use a vocabulary which expressed this. Staff might speak of 'opening up the shop' or of 'getting this show on the road' when a clinic began. If things were slack a doctor might ask if there were any more 'customers' waiting, or comment on how little 'trade' there was today. Where tasks were difficult, clinics over-ran, emergencies occurred or staff were late for other appointments, considerable irritation might be displayed, irritation which was sometimes expressed with great force. Here, for example, is a doctor's anguished comment in the special nursery after it had been decided to carry out exchange transfusion: 'Oh, God!

Why is it always now that it happens! It'll mean work over the weekend!'

However, despite the heavily professional orientation of the clinical format it would be mistaken to assume that no reference was made within it to the more conventional evaluations of illnesses, or that patients were invariably treated as mere 'clinical material'. On some occasions in the special nursery, Sister held up a favourite baby for others to admire, and on others staff reflected on the personal tragedy involved. Indeed, the very privacy of a setting like this meant that staff expressed some feelings far more strongly than they ever did to parents. Here it was safe to criticize other services. Similarly, doctors sighed after some parents had left, and nurses commented on the pity of it all. Death, in particular, seemed to provoke such language. Whereas most conditions were simply conditions, a brain tumour was not; and the possibility of leukaemia could become 'this terrible doubt in the back of our minds'. Thus it cannot be said that lay versions of illness had no place in the clinical format. Staff took such feelings for granted in each other; what was normally at issue were other, more professionally relevant matters. This explains why the most dramatic language ever used to discuss a child's condition referred to a relatively minor injury:

Dr H: What a dreadful result!
Dr J: You should have seen what it was like before.
Dr H: What a mess. It's horrid, horrid!

Dr J: We'll need to repeat the X-rays. That's a nasty thing!
Dr H: Very nasty.

Other babies lying in cots nearby were severely ill or not expected to survive, whereas the baby discussed in these two excerpts recovered rapidly. What made staff's language so extreme in this case was that, for once, the condition had a major personal relevance, being a medical and not a natural product.

For the Sake of the Child

To say all this is not to accuse staff of callousness, merely to note that for them medicine was a job and thus their interest in it was necessarily different from that of parents. Although staff felt an obligation towards individual patients there were many other motives which also influenced their work: their career, academic interest, personal schedules, professional advancement, scientific development, departmental rivalry and general policy matters. All of these perspectives could be brought to bear on any one patient and each case was of more or less collegial interest as it combined these various qualities.

Such interests were, however, not relevant within the bureaucratic format and many would have destroyed the world which it contained. Just as staff never questioned the good character of parents, so too their own motivation went unremarked. Parents were never told that their child's complaint was boring or routine, and on only a handful of occasions was any comment made on its fascination. Words like 'odd' or 'unusual' were only very rarely used, while the work which any case involved or the degree of disruption it caused were largely hidden. The existence of other patients or of other demands upon their time were not topics of conversation with parents. In all this, each case was overtly treated as a world in itself. The present consultation stood alone, detached from other medical pursuits. Staff's interest in the general was subordinated to the particular, to this child, to whom they, like the parents, were now apparently devoting all their skill and attention.

This general strategy of avoidance fitted well enough with the medical anonymity required to sustain collegial authority. However, just as there were certain occasions when it was difficult to idealize parents' character, staff's character could also be threatened. Here too, not everything could be readily ignored, and special procedures were necessary to smooth over and nullify the more intrusive aspects of medicine.

For example, in most of the settings parents did not see staff in private. There was normally a medical audience present, usually a nurse, very often some students, occasionally other doctors; and the simple presence of colleagues or apprentices created the continual possibility of collegial discussion between them. Indeed this was often essential, particularly since teaching was a central activity in both of the hospitals. As it was teaching that created the greatest threat to the idealized moral commitment of staff to the individual child patient, I shall treat this in detail, and this case must serve as an example of the challenge that any kind of collegial discussion presented.

Teaching was especially revealing of much that was not normally mentioned. First, from the perspective of medical training, patients and those who accompanied them were best viewed as 'living textbooks', as empirical instances of types of phenomenon (Atkinson, 1976). Medical problems were of interest, not because this or that patient suffered from them and wished to be cured of them, but because this was the kind of problem students were obliged to learn about. Second, medical teaching in such contexts involved the doctor's own actions quite as much as any patient's condition. It was a highly reflexive act. Not only did doctors describe the medical phenomena under investigation, they also spelt out their own involvement in the proceedings: how they had done this and why they would now do that.

Teaching could therefore be a most elaborate affair. Doctors might sketch in the general background to a clinic and discuss their general mandate, the types of patient seen there, hospital policy for these, and referral patterns to and from the setting. More specifically, doctors could detail the nature of particular problems, their various causes, incidence and prognoses, and then describe how to recognize them, the various tests to use, their reliability and the reasoning that lay behind them. Instruction might also be given on how to read a file or a referral letter, how to get a history, and how much trust to place in it. In other words, good teaching necessarily involved making explicit many of those things that were typically concealed from parents. The difficulties that the revelation of these matters might cause were presented in a particularly acute fashion in the settings observed in this study. Teaching on these cases involved hot medicine, rather than the action-replay or cold medicine found in some forms of bedside teaching (Atkinson, 1976). Here new diagnoses were actually made, fresh problems discovered and binding decisions taken.

The principal method used to overcome the dangers of collegial discussion was the careful segregation of such talk. This was done in a number of different ways. In all but the American amphitheatre clinics, one staff member was clearly in control of the interaction. In the Scottish settings, the audience never spoke to or examined the patient without the doctor's permission, and such permission was a rarity in all but the maternity hospital ward-round. Scottish students, with this one exception, had no right to speak to the doctor in front of parents, save when spoken to; and the remarks made to them were normally statements, not items of conversation which required a reply. Medical discourse as opposed to medical pronouncement was therefore a great rarity. The same rule applied in most of the American settings. Interns or residents might talk directly with parents in the presence of their 'chief', since they had conducted the work-up, but detailed medical discussion about the case was usually avoided.

Such avoidance was possible because in most settings parents and staff were readily segregated. Detailed teaching in the Scottish clinics could be done in the gaps between patients, while in the American ambulatory clinics staff left the cubicles each time they wanted a private discussion: 'We'll be back in a minute' was the refrain which punctuated the parents' sojourn. Parents had the right to object to teaching. One mother, who complained afterwards to a nurse, was seen in private from then on, the researchers too being barred. Similarly, when an adolescent boy complained about being taught on in the American hospital the doctor and students withdrew.

These procedures minimized the amount of collegial discussion that took place in front of parents, while some doctors rarely ever taught openly on children. The staff in the Scottish neurological clinic thought their cases were too serious for overt teaching, and one of them eventually banned students altogether. In four settings, however - the special nursery follow-up clinic, the amphitheatre clinics, the maternity hospital ward-round and one of the Scottish general medical clinics - large amounts of such discussion were held in front of parents. Despite this, staff in all these settings indicated that their clinical discussion was subordinate to their interaction with parents. The clinical format co-existed with the bureaucratic format but it was a side-event. Thus, where doctors talked with students or with other staff they typically did so quietly and at the margin. In the amphitheatre clinic, staff discussion was usually confined to those on the stage and was conducted in whispers. In the general medical clinic, junior doctors who wished to discuss their cases with the consultant waited quietly at the side until he had noticed them; they did not themselves interrupt his conversation with patients.

Overt teaching was similarly given a secondary place. Some teaching comments were made in ways that fitted in naturally with the conversation with parents; the doctors' statements serving as remarks to both the mother and the students. Here are examples of how this could be done, one from history-taking and the other from an examination.

Dr F: Is she walking yet?
Mother: She's walking round the furniture.
Dr F: Children usually walk round the furniture before they walk properly.

Dr F: (lifts the baby) That's a nice straight back. Right! (He puts the baby back down.) Well, he can sit but he's a little off balance. He's got good head control. He doesn't wobble at all. Hello!

Hello! (The baby smiles.) You get nice easy social smiles.

Such smooth welding of the two activities caused no offence, but where staff engaged in any detailed teaching with students something more was needed. Here they commonly indicated that a break in the action was occurring and asked for parents' forgiveness: 'Excuse me a minute.' Such apologies were particularly elaborate in the Scottish maternity hospital ward-round where, given the Nightingale ward system, there was no private place in which teaching could be done in between seeing patients. Here, for example, are a doctor's comments from the beginning, middle and end of a case in which the doctor demonstrated how to conduct the examination of a newborn baby:

> Dr K: Hello, Mrs Angus. You don't mind all this congregation, do you?
> Mother: No.

> Dr K: (inspects the notes and makes comments to students, then says in aside) I'm sorry this is going to take a wee while.

> Dr K: OK. Thanks very much. I hope we haven't mesmerized you.

Apart from its subordinate place being indicated, many aspects of the clinical format were transformed when it was used in parents' presence. As may be seen from the examples of history taking and examination that were cited a moment ago, staff's comments related almost entirely to the good things that might be said about a child. Indeed, on some occasions the very fact that teaching was done on a child was used to indicate that there was nothing serious at issue:

> Dr K: Don't worry. Your baby is perfectly normal. I wouldn't be going into all this if it wasn't.
> Mother: (laughing) I know you wouldn't.

Even here the version of medicine that was displayed was heavily bowdlerized. Personal challenge and enthusiasm, rivalry and career aspirations were all carefully removed, and the resulting discussion had the gravity and moral purpose of some lay versions of 'Science'. Such discussion was therefore highly reassuring. At first sight, it might seem to threaten the overt order of the occasion by revealing what went on behind the scenes. But the 'private' action that was thereby disclosed was of the highest moral seriousness. Teaching might take up a large proportion of the time spent with some mothers in the maternity hospital ward-round but, since it necessarily involved the spelling-out of medical practice and manners, it could be used to display the highest motives and principles. Thus teaching could 'reveal' that the mothers, not the students, were the main focus of the doctor's attention: 'It's important to get you (baby) right up here by your mother as she's the most important person here.' Similarly, although the baby under discussion might be used as an instance of a type, the activity displayed was concerned with the well-being of all. The generalizing interest of the clinical format could therefore be shown to be relevant to a mother's own child.

Dr K: He's still looking a bit yellow, isn't he?
Mother: Yes.
Dr K: (to students) You know, don't you, that in newborn babies jaundice, what we call physiological jaundice, reaches a peak at the fifth or sixth day and then goes down. Everyone says that the peak is at five days but we've studied our own figures and found that many peak on the sixth day. So give it the fifth or sixth day. When you've had sufficient experience at handling these babies and you know that it's the third day, if it's a mild case, you can say leave it till tomorrow and test it then, but if you do have any doubts, it's important to test it right away.
Dr K: (to nurse) It is jaundiced a bit. It's very mild at the moment, but if it gets any yellower, tell Dr James here. Otherwise we'll look at it tomorrow. Bye, Mrs Morrison.

In this, Dr K not only instructed the students to be cautious, watchful and take nothing on trust, but demonstrated to the mother that this was staff's own attitude. They had not just gone along with what 'everyone says' but had conducted their own studies and produced a revised analysis. Their constant thought about such babies had resulted in better care for all. Thus, when the doctor gave the nurse instructions at the end of her lesson, her words bore a special meaning. They were not just an order but the embodiment of caring, concerned and technically sophisticated medicine. In this manner, teaching, for all its emphasis on the general, might nevertheless serve to display the personal concern for advanced knowledge that was more typical of the private format.

Although I have emphasized that teaching could be used to dramatize the serious moral purpose of medicine, it should not be supposed that all such discussions were conducted in a grave manner. Most of these clinical conversations were formal in nature, but their style could be varied to suit the occasion. Given the ineptitude of the young students who attended the maternity hospital ward-round and the normality of most babies, the doctor could turn aspects of the round into a comic turn. On such occasions, teaching was not merely subordinated to the doctor's consultations with mothers but became an amusement for mothers' benefit:

> Dr K: (to student) Now all you've got to do is to lift it up over here (i.e. to the measuring cot). Have you got the confidence to do that? Think how Mrs Laing would feel if you dropped him.
> Student: Oh, I wouldn't want her to be worried.
>   (General laughter.)
> Dr K: (sighs exaggeratedly) OK. I'll do it then. (Mother laughs loudly.)
>
> Dr K: (at end) After all that the baby's fine, Mrs Laing.
> Student: (to baby) Goodbye (very formally. Baby cries.) He's got no appreciation of my skill. (Mother laughs loudly again.)

The Rule of Reason

The tacit agreement to share responsibility for a child and the joint idealization of each other's motives and skill created characters with all the qualities of allies. Appropriate identities are, however, not sufficient in themselves to produce an alliance. To be an ally is also to do certain things, agreement has to be reached on specific issues, and there are various ways in which this might be done, ways which define what sort of an alliance this is. I have already examined one method for the production of agreement, the 'rule' of collegial authority which clearly subordinated parents to staff's technical expertise. This principle was undoubtedly a central feature of the bureaucratic format, but it was not the only relevant rule; and to understand the distinctive nature of the format one must pay closer attention to the way in which collegial authority was wielded.

At the beginning of the previous chapter, I argued that not only might a variety of social identities be invoked for any one participant in an encounter but that these might involve somewhat discrepant characteristics. Thus, all mothers within the bureaucratic format were 'naturally' incompetent as regards medical matters. Now, although particular identities may have a certain independence, when two or more are played together by the same actor, each necessarily modifies the other. Thus the idealization of any mother as naturally caring and competent had important consequences for the manner in which medical authority was wielded.

This may be clearly seen by making a comparison with the charity format. This also emphasized agreement between staff and parents but the manner in which it was arrived at was very different. Agreement here was simply a matter of parental submission to a higher authority. The oracle spoke and parents obeyed. Only the mother who took on a 'medical student' role was allowed the privilege of questioning and discussion. By contrast, parents in the bureaucratic format were treated as persons who could be persuaded, once they knew the facts. To treat parents as obviously moral, rational and intelligent was to grant them some independence from medical authority. Agreement here rested on a delicate mixture of faith and reasoning. On the one hand, parents were required to believe in staff's ultimate authority; but on the other hand, as sensible people who could read the evidence for themselves, once they knew what it was, they were permitted to argue with particular decisions; so long of course as this was done in a reasonable fashion.

The difference between the two formats may be summed up in the terms of my earlier analysis of moral work. In discussing the charity format, I distinguished between face- and character-work, and noted that the latter came in both a weak and a strong form. We also saw how the rights to character-work varied. What was legitimate, even a duty, for the doctor within the charity format was completely avoided by staff within the bureaucratic format. Now the right to criticize and to demand exposition is often given to only one of the participants in a relationship. One needs a social position from which to do character-work, and in many positions 'it's not your place to criticize'. In the charity format only the doctor had that place. But the bureaucratic format, by treating parents as independent, sensible and moral, defined them as clients and medicine as a service; and in service relationships the client typically has the sole rights to criticism.

In this instance these rights were not extensive. Thus, whereas the charity doctor used both ameliorative and reconstitutive character-work, the latter, if undertaken by parents within the bureaucratic format, would have undermined the principle of collegial authority. Indirect parental challenges to medical decisions were both normal and legitimate; but any suggestion of re-constitutive character-work was, as we have seen, quickly challenged by doctors and was in any case rare. Moreover, ameliorative work, though quite frequently done by parents, was carried out in a far more restrained fashion than was the case with the doctor who used the charity format. Criticism was allowed but reason ruled; and since staff were treated as entirely competent, the kinds of criticism that could be made were limited in their force.

Nevertheless, 'reasonable' parental criticism was tolerated and even welcomed, for without it how could rational agreement be reached? Indeed, parents who never had any questions and who accepted everything that staff said might be regarded as old-fashioned. Thus doctors at the Scottish hospital distinguished sharply between their urban parents and those from the remoter rural areas. Here, for instance, is a short passage from a consultation for epilepsy, followed by the conversation between doctor and students afterwards:

Dr I: Well, I think we'll keep him on the X (drug) as he has had another attack.
Mother: Oh, aye, oh aye. That's right, doctor. I think that's for the best. Oh, aye, he should be on it for a long time.

Dr I: Well, that was a classic patient, what traditionally most patients were supposed to be like, although few are these days. That's the sort of patient Dr Finlay had.[2] We don't see very many nowadays.
Student: (imitating mother) I know the sort - 'Oh, aye, doctor, aye, you're right, doctor, you're so right, aye, you're right.'

For some doctors this attitude was a distinct fault in their patients. Some criticized working-class parents as far too accepting of what was said to them, even if they did not display their agreement in such elaborate terms as rural parents. Here, for instance, another doctor contrasts the kind of parents found at different local authority clinics:

Dr D: The more intelligent people tend to ask far more questions and they're less likely to accept one's answers without querying if there could be an alternative answer. And in this respect, I do think that the population who attend the Green Lane Clinic and some of the other ones, I think they have far too much confidence in us as doctors, they don't realize that we are human and we can fail in things.

Not all doctors shared this attitude. Some saw parental questioning of their decision as a waste of time, since the parents were incapable of judging the wisdom of any one line of action. Others expressed both points of view, pleased that parents took a keen interest in their child's welfare but irritated by those who tried to 'score points off them'. Nevertheless, even the doctors who were most dismissive of parental questioning did not challenge parents' right to question them, merely the efficacy of their so doing.

Such toleration was normally matched by the careful way in which parents phrased their questions, if they had them. As I have shown in the previous chapter, parental questions were commonly information questions, ones which asked for the doctor's viewpoint but treated that viewpoint as authoritative. Even the criticisms were normally indirect and carefully based on appeals to lay, not professional, knowledge.

Such procedures offered at least a chance of rational agreement being produced. Staff were sometimes obliged to uncover criticism and certainly required to listen to it, even if they did not accept it, just as they were obliged to answer questions, even if the detail in which they did so varied considerably. Likewise, although parents had rights to question and criticize, they were obliged to use these in a moderate form which did not challenge the entire basis of the interaction.

This rule of reason meant that staff tolerated almost all criticism, so long as their personal authority was not questioned; and even then they made exceptions and tried to preserve some notion of an alliance. Take first the following instance, which involved a child referred to the neurological clinic for general delay, but who was still being seen at an orthopaedic clinic. The child was three years old and not walking, a state of affairs which the doctor blamed principally upon the parents, who carried the child everywhere; blame however was apportioned only by the parents not by the doctor:

Father: What about this leg? We come to the hospital but no one says nothing about it?

Dr J: Well, he's flat-footed but he's capable of walking, the muscle tone is all right. (Examines child's leg for second time.) He will walk. It's just that he's flat-footed. I think what we'll do is refer him to physiotherapy, umm, to see if we can get him walking.

Father: Well, I'm not complaining but I want an answer. We've been coming up here for some time now.

Dr J: Yes, he's past his third birthday, isn't he? Yes, I think he needs some physiotherapy.

This example is of additional interest in that although both parents were present it was the father who did the criticism. Such a division of labour was typical of many couples. Although mothers attended far more often by themselves, there were many cases in which it was commonplace for criticism or detailed questioning of staff to be done only on those infrequent occasions when fathers also attended. If it was the father who complained about other services, or demanded to know if a child would ever walk, or what the problem really was, then such questioning, however direct, posed only a marginal threat to the central relationship, that of doctor and mother. Their alliance was still secure, for the criticism was done by an outsider, someone with no great knowledge of either the child or the clinic.

Third parties were not the only means of rendering parental criticism more acceptable. Special circumstances could also minimize the gravity of any offence. Particular latitude was given to the parents of severely handicapped children. Indeed, as we have seen, doctors actively searched for any difficulties that they were experiencing. In the following instance the doctor listened calmly and seriously to the mother's criticisms. He did not join in with all the mother had to say, neither did he dissociate himself entirely from it. He nodded at various points and generally gave the impression that her problems or criticisms were either reasonable or intelligible, that he quite understood why she felt like this:

Dr G: We did talk at one time about the special school at Atholltown, but nothing came of it, did it?

Mother: It all fell through. Nothing happened.

Dr G: No.

Mother: They didn't want her.

Dr G: It may have been the distance.

Mother: It was a fantastic distance.

Dr G: Yes.

Mother: If only there was a school near the city, I'd like that.

Dr G: All right, then. We'll just have to see. Is there anything else that you'd like to bring up?

Mother: No. Miss Sutherland (area social worker) said that she didn't know what to do with her. Well, she's a dead loss. She comes every month but, I mean, she doesn't know what to do with her.

Dr G: Uh-huh.

The strong concern to demonstrate agreement meant that even major parental revolt could be rewritten after the event. I have already noted the way in which direct parental challenges to the doctor's authority were segregated and their overall effect minimized. What was even more striking about some revolts was the great efforts made by both parties to translate them into an agreed plan of action. Thus parents who sought alternative treatment to that which they were offered were typically incorporated within a shared agenda. Take the following instance, the only example in the study where a mother asked for another medical opinion. Despite its rarity, and despite the fact that the mother twice asked for a second opinion, first from the senior neurologist in the adult hospital and then from a London specialist, the request was still managed with great delicacy by all parties. The mother presented her demands as coming, not from herself, but from her family, and observed the greatest courtesy towards the doctor; thanking him profusely once he had agreed to a referral, apologizing for her actions, and even offering to pay: 'Money is no object.' This enabled the doctor to be polite in his turn and to present the referral as a jointly agreed decision.

Dr J: You mentioned last time that your husband was a bit unhappy, that he wants a second opinion. I've discussed this with Dr McAllister and he and I are quite happy for you to have a second opinion.... Would you like me to write to the London hospital?

Mother: Yes, that would be very nice if you could.

Dr J: If we feel it is going to be a help we don't hesitate to ask the advice of other centres. We can't guarantee that this would help but it will certainly help in the sense that it should satisfy you and your family.

A little later in the consultation the decision has become a joint action, not an individual one, and one in which, as usual in the format, the doctor has the major say:

> Dr J: Well, as I said, I think we are clutching at straws a bit but I think we just have to try.
>
> Mother: I'm sorry to be such a pest.
>
> Dr J: No, that's all right. You're asking just the questions that you should be asking, that any mother should ask.... I do think that if we get nothing from the London hospital we shouldn't bother with anywhere else.
>
> Mother: No.
>
> Dr J: There's nowhere else to go really.
>
> Mother: It's very hard to take in.
>
> Dr J: I know, it's very difficult.

A similar incorporation of revolt occurred in the majority of these Scottish cases where the parents sought treatment outside the National Health Service. During the study, an American film which made large claims about the Doman-Delcato method of treating brain-damaged children was shown on British television, and this resulted in a large amount of publicity in newspapers, magazines and other televised programmes. As a result, several parents of handicapped children became interested in the method, even though the treatment was available only in the private sector and was viewed sceptically by hospital staff. This major challenge to medical authority was resolved in all but one case, with both parties contributing equally to this. Far from being a threat to the alliance, it was transformed into something which the allies considered together. One couple did in fact withdraw their child from the clinic without mentioning their disagreement in the consultation, but in five other cases parents raised the topic themselves and asked the doctor's advice. In doing so, they still treated the doctor as the authority and allowed him in turn to treat their ideas as reasonable. Thus in the one case where the parents openly tried the Doman-Delcato treatment it became an experiment, something which they did with his blessing and on whose progress they reported at regular intervals.

Reaching Agreement

So far, in considering the way in which alliances were actually made and agreements reached, I have emphasized the special stress that the bureaucratic format placed on the rule of reason. Clinics offered a service and clients had rights to rational criticism and discussion. Staff did not simply impose their views upon parents. But reaching agreement was a rather more subtle process than I have made out. Alliances cannot be made solely out of debates, however reasonable their form and tone. What is never mentioned is often as important as what is said, and just when things are spoken is equally crucial. Such considerations apply with all the more force to matters as delicate as the health and future of children. Although overt agreement was essential if the alliance was to be maintained, it would be wrong to imagine that this was actively sought on each and every occasion. Moreover, although parental questioning of staff was from one perspective a search for agreement, the seeking, finding and display of consensus was primarily a task for staff. It was largely staff's decisions that were at issue, and it was they who controlled the agenda and set the tone of the occasion. In consequence when agreements were sought, it was staff who did most of the searching, whereas so far I have emphasized actions that were principally initiated by parents.

Before going on to consider the different ways in which staff sought agreement, I must note two points. First, the debate in clinics did not concern some abstract proposition but a particular child in whom most parents had made a heavy emotional investment. Second, the children were conversationally endowed with a variety of special properties which distinguished them from adults. Ignorant and messy, but intelligent, amusing, joyful and wonderful; these were the essential properties of children in the everyday usage of the clinic. As such, these were the terms in which any discussion of a child's medical normality had necessarily to be argued:

> Essential normality cannot be demonstrated by a doctor merely ticking off a child's accomplishments on some standardized check-list, although such work is a routine part of assessment, but must be directly addressed and established by the entire manner in which the child is treated. The doctor has to demonstrate a correspondence between the clinical version of normal childhood and the everyday version. To treat the occasion solely in a clinical fashion would not be to establish the child's normality in the everyday world (Davis and Strong, 1976b, pp.158-9).

This passage describes the task facing a doctor engaged in developmental assessment, but the same principle applied whatever the medical work or the condition of the child. The entire manner in which the doctor discussed a child with its parents reflected on its medical status and was therefore a central method through which debate proceeded. Since its formulation of the child was necessarily indirect, it served as a delicate means for setting the boundaries for more overt discussion. Where a child's condition was held to be serious, then a relative absence of wonderment and laughter by staff could indicate that this was a child for whom marvelling and fun were not wholly appropriate. Conversely, where staff held parents to be worrying without real need, great jollity helped to banish those doubts.

In some consultations such indirect methods were the only ones used to reach and demonstrate agreement. In the developmental screening carried out by the local authority and city clinics, children were not there for the solution of particular problems. Most mothers assumed that their children were normal and doctors likewise held that most were right in this belief. Given this shared assumption, there was no need to spell out their agreement in the matter. Indeed, to search for agreement would have been to imply that there might well be cause for disagreement. Staff and parents simply treated the children as 'lovable rascals', and the jolly discussion of their rascality served to indicate their medical normality.

Where a child came to a clinic with a specific problem, that problem had to be directly as well as indirectly addressed, and use was made of more formal procedures for seeking agreement on staff's decisions. Take first the occasions when parents were assumed to be deeply worried about a child, but staff had few such doubts. Apart from adopting the jolly air that suited a normal child, staff searched actively for parental fears and knocked them promptly on the head when they surfaced. Given their assumption that the deepest worries were often the hardest to reveal, staff often asked the same question several times in order that every fear might be dispelled and complete agreement reached on the child's normality. In the following quotation from a follow-up clinic, the doctor asks the mother four times if she has any problems or worries - and only at the fourth time of asking are the mother's fears revealed. Her baby had been kept in the special nursery at birth and was thus initially certified as medically problematic. The doctor's task was therefore not just to convince himself of the child's normality but to convince the mother as well:

Dr F: How old is your son now? Nearly one, isn't he?
Mother: One more month.
Dr F: Good. Have you got any worries about him?
Mother: No.
Dr F: So there are no problems?

Mother: No.

Dr F: He's eating the same food as everyone else?

Mother: Yes.

Dr F: Does he have any extra vitamins?

Mother: No.

Dr F: Has he got any other problems? I know you had him in here for quite a long time with rhesus problems.

Mother: No, he's all right now. He's been OK for a long time. He does have some problems with his teeth - but he seems OK. He dribbles a lot.

Dr F: Uh-huh. That'll be due to his teeth.

The doctor then asks a series of developmental questions and the mother says the child is doing fine.

Dr F: So there are really no problems?

Mother: No ... (pause) ... Well ... he is small, well, I think he is but no one believes me.

Dr F: Well, he's smallish ... (pause) ... What's his weight? (Mother gives it.) Well, he's *well* within the normal range....

This 'search and destroy' method for reaching agreement rested on the standard assumption of medical expertise and parental ignorance. Parents produced the worries, though often with guidance, and the doctor dispelled them. A second method was that of conferring a joint expertise upon parents. In this, mothers and fathers became colleagues who clearly agreed with doctors and validated their opinion. Such granting of medical authority did not threaten the doctor's own status, since he alone had the power to confer it, and it was merely a temporary phenomenon. Where a child was considered to be healthy, this procedure could be used with considerable rapidity and ease. Here a doctor makes 'guesses' and then 'checks' them with the mother:

Dr F: And is he standing and walking?

Mother: Yes, though not so much as she does.

Dr F: So, despite the fact that she's smaller she's ahead by about ... well, I would guess three or four weeks?

Mother: Yes.

Similarly, Dr F, in such cases, could overtly discharge a child as much on the parents' authority as on his own:

Dr F: Well, if you've no worries about him?
Mother: No.
Dr F: Then I've no worries about him. What about his teething?
Mother: Yes, he is.
Dr F: Yes, I can see he's a handful. Well, I don't think there's any
            need to see him again if you don't think so.

In this case and the preceding instances, the doctor's aim was to normalize the children, to indicate that they were fine and healthy. But the procedures that were used to reach agreement here, the search for doubts and the appeal to joint authority, were equally suited to occasions when a child was in fact ill. In these circumstances any parental worries that were uncovered could now serve as grounds for the doctor's own doubts. Both staff and parents could be shown to agree that there was something wrong. Where the diagnosis was relatively trivial and easily treated, this appeal to a joint authority was easy enough. Where neither of these conditions was satisfied, reaching agreement became far trickier. Doctors used the same methods but they did so in much more cautious ways.

For example, in cases of delay where parents had already mentioned their own grave doubts about a child, doctors often referred to these when giving their own version: 'Well, I don't know if I've got anything to tell you that you don't know already.' Conversely, if parents had given no indication of any such worries then doctors would normally ask for these. Before he gave his own version of the child one doctor routinely said to such parents, 'How do you yourself feel about John?' speaking the words slowly and seriously and looking them full in the face. Coming after the history and the examination, such a manner indicated that the occasion was a serious one and that now was the time to reveal any deep anxieties about a child. Other doctors asked parents for such comments after they had given their own diagnosis:

Dr G: I am, I must admit, concerned that she's not walking. She's
            beyond the age where she should be walking, and she's not
            talking as well as she should. I'm inclined to think there's a
            general delay here. How do you think she compares with other
            children?

Mother: I still feel she's more easily tired than other children are. But she seems quite good with her hands.

The mother talks about other things and the doctor asks the child to look at a book which they all watch. Eventually he comments.

Dr G: You see, I'm not ... well, certainly I'm not saying she's seriously backward.
Mother: No.
Dr G: She seems interested and alert but she is a little behind. At her age one can't say what will happen. (The doctor elaborates.)
Mother: But she is bright at play. She has a ball she likes, she plays with that very well.
Father: And, when you take off her clothes, she recognizes all of them and the order that they should come off in. She knows that.
Mother: Yes. What about her feet?
Dr G: You know, I don't think there's much wrong there. I'm sure it's not her feet. (He gets parents to walk child.) Yes, she's using her legs a bit but she hasn't got her balance.
Father: No. She's not got her balance.
Dr G: No.
Mother: She has come on slower than average.
Dr G: Yes. She's coming on but just at the rate of slower than average. I don't know whether she'll speed up or not.

Although this too represents a search for agreement, this quotation has several important differences from those cited in the cases where a doctor was normalizing a child. There is no assumption of an immediate and easy concord but instead a careful discussion of the evidence, conducted in a relatively unhurried fashion, whereas the search and destroy method was used with speed and vigour. When parental doubts were to be amplified rather than dismissed doctors proceeded more slowly and indirectly. Dr G did not repeatedly probe the parents about their doubts or worries, he merely asked them a question which might lead to such talk, as might his own statements and the various demonstrations he provided, such as the book and the walking. Doubts and their discussion were allowed to develop gently over, time. Thus, although agreement was certainly a high priority for staff, search is perhaps too active a word to describe their method in such cases.

Agreement here was stalked rather than sought after; doctors lay in wait and watched, and the end was no sudden spring but a gradual luring towards acceptance.

For what was at issue was the parents' whole conception of the child: its present, its future and their own future as well. And, whereas normalizing a child might be done in a session, as might the revelation of minor illness, stigmatizing a child could take many months or even years. Although it is conventional to refer to the telling of bad news as something that occurs at one point in time - 'When they told me' - such a description does not capture the complex nature of the process by which such news was broken here. To some extent this depended on clinical uncertainty. As doctors saw a child over time, so they gained a more accurate version of the child's condition and capacities. Just as crucially, however, the stages depended on the doctors' belief that bad news should be broken slowly, that parents had to prepare themselves for the worst, that they could not take everything in at once, and that the news staff had to tell should match parents' expectations:

Dr J: She's a very nice mother. I think what we're trying to do is to introduce her very gradually to the fact that the child is very small, though we know she will look like a circus dwarf. You know the sort of child I mean? Well, we haven't really told the mother that. We've just said that she's going to be very small. Anyway, she seems to be a candidate for delayed development and there's also this increased intra-cranial pressure, that's going to be a problem. Now at six months I saw her, that was at the special nursery follow-up clinic and she had a head-lag there, but of course then it wasn't necessarily developmental delay. So we saw her again at eight months, and by then she had got some head control but she hadn't her sitting balance. She had some hand movements and was vocalizing all right. So that seemed to be on the credit side. But at ten months we found that she wasn't sitting. The mother feels that otherwise she's doing all right there. She's not a very bright thing but I think in this case she's a pretty good judge of what the situation is. Then she was referred here. There has been this query about brain damage but we've not mentioned any of this to the mother. In fact the child had this very bashed-about head, she looked really awful when she was born.

The breaking of bad news was therefore an extremely delicate operation, in which staff probed to see how much parents suspected; produced some information and saw how they reacted; elaborated if they were challenged; withdrew slightly if the parents looked angry, and so on. Staff played a waiting game, not enforcing their own definition of a child but always leaving a part to be negotiated in each consultation, trying to build on last time's definition, but first waiting to see how parents commented on what had happened in the intervening weeks or months. As far as the two can be separated, the movement was from diagnosis to prognosis, first indicating what the child was and then saying what it would be. The movement from one to the other varied with the parents' receptiveness. No parent was told everything immediately, but some achieved detailed and dispassionate discussion far more quickly than others. The following example indicates both the difficulties that might be faced and the way these were surmounted by making little agreements at each stage. The excerpts are from three consecutive consultations.

This was the child's first visit to the neurological clinic. He was four months old at this point and had already been seen three times at the special nursery follow-up clinic. The mother had several other children, was highly competent and had made detailed comments on some of her child's problems. She had not however noticed the more serious ones, the child's spasticity and microcephaly. In his summary, the doctor started out by appealing to the shared agreement on the child's delay and then moved on to his own diagnosis. But this was phrased tentatively and the entire discussion of the child was in the present not the future tense:

Dr I: He is very behind in what he's doing *of course* (my emphasis) and although you yourself are not very impressed with it, I think that his muscles are rather stiff. He does have some spasticity, this is what it's called.

Four months later, at the next visit, the mother indicated at the very beginning of the consultation that she was sceptical if her boy had made any progress and the doctor's own history-taking revealed very few signs of this. This time he looked towards the future in his summary:

Dr I: Well, I don't find anything new. From what you say he has made a very, very slight progress, not very much, not very much, but a little.... I hope that there will be further progress, and don't be too upset if it is slow. It looks as if Alan is going to be handicapped to some extent.

On the third visit, eleven months later, the mother talked freely of the child's severe handicap: 'He's absolutely ruined.' The doctor's summary was in turn far more specific about the future than on the previous visit.

Dr J: He's a long way off walking now. I don't know if he ever will. He's got to get sitting balance first, if ... (pause) ... When he gets near weight-bearing age we might ask the orthopaedic surgeons if there is anything that can be done to improve the mechanical performance of his feet. He seems well, he's avoiding any deformities, but he's certainly got quite a way to go before he's got complete head control. His head is lagging back a bit. The next stage after that is sitting balance, he's nearly got head balance. (The child is in sitting position.) How long can he stay like this? Just for a few seconds?

Mother: Yes, for a few seconds and then he keels over.

Dr J: So we want to work on sitting balance and then the next stage is weight-bearing, but he's a long way off that at the moment. OK, that's fine. At present you are quite happy coping with him at home?

Mother: Oh, yes (cheerfully).

Even at this stage some matters went undiscussed. The doctor did not press the mother on her ability to cope, though privately he felt her to be unrealistic. Further, the full extent of the child's handicap had not yet been revealed. The microcephaly had not been mentioned nor, as can be seen, was any detailed statement made about the child's mental abilities. Although the mother defined the child as 'ruined' at one stage in the conversation, she was eager to try and bring him on. Such eagerness was treated as laudable but unrealistic, and an indicator that she had still not grasped the true nature of her son's injuries. More detailed discussion was thus postponed until the mother herself clearly accepted such facts; that is, until a 'reasonable' discussion of the child was possible and reasoned agreement could be reached. Parents and staff preserved their alliance and its rational form by seeking agreement only when this could readily be made.

Moral Character and the Alliance - an Exception

One partial exception should be made to two of the rules that I have described in the last three chapters. I started out by emphasizing that, no matter what a mother's actual qualities, staff treated her as ideal. This principle led to the further rule that whereas staff could not criticize parents, parents could criticize staff, for they were clients who had rights to question the service they received. It should, however, be noted that two mothers, whom staff privately felt to be a danger to their child, did in fact lose some of their rights as clients. Their moral character was not directly impugned, but they were not allowed to criticize or object in quite the same fashion as other mothers. In the following instance, the mother, who had been brought to the clinic by a health visitor and adopted a sullen attitude throughout, started to criticize the hospital:

Mother: He got that (scabies) when he was in hospital.
Dr I: (rather sharply) I don't want to allocate blame.

Here the doctor felt strongly that the mother was responsible for the scabies but refrained from saying so. She was also suspected of severe neglect, even perhaps assault. As his remark indicated, she retained her good character only so long as she did not impugn that of others. Similarly, such mothers could lose their normal rights to question or object to what was done with their child. Here is a quotation from the second case, which involved a mother who readily admitted that she could not cope with her child. The child was already partly in care, but the mother objected most strongly to the new arrangements that were suggested. Beyond a certain point the doctor ceased to reason with her; she was treated as lacking the ordinary rights to object and was spoken to in a far more authoritarian fashion than other mothers:

Dr J: I've just been on the phone to the social work department. What's been the problem?
Mother: Well, she attacked her sister and grandfather and she was throwing things - like kitchen things and ornaments. She's knocked the windows out and she's had two fits since I last saw you.
Dr J: Well, why did she do it? She knows she mustn't.
Mother: Well, I smacked her then she went quiet, then suddenly it all

came out. I had to kick her to get her off her sister when she was mad.

Dr J: Well, there doesn't seem to be any medical problem apart from these turns that she's been having. Now there's been a case conference and they decided that really what she needed was day care. They discussed where she might get it but there was no firm conclusion. Craiglee was felt to be inappropriate (the child attends this during the week at present), except that the housemother has a very good relationship with her.

Mother: Yes, she has.

Dr J: But sometimes they're not going to be able to accommodate her and then day-fostering....

Mother: (very sharply) No, I *won't* accept that.

Dr J: Well, you'll have to accept one or some other. (The doctor mentions a nursery as another possibility. The mother raises transport difficulties. From now on the doctor was distinctly curt in tone with the mother, for example:) But are you interested?

Mother: Well.

Dr J: Well, *are you interested?*

Kicking the child was not treated as an overt issue, but such behaviour provided a covert warrant for the removal of the mother's normal rights to question staff's decisions. The mother was still offered a choice but her rights to refuse it were shown to be limited, by turn of phrase and by tone of voice, if not directly. Such parents were expected to come quietly. The rule of reason still applied, in that they were reasoned with and not shouted at, but they themselves were not allowed to shout. Thus, although parents were allies, certain rules had a higher priority than others. All mothers were naturally good, not all had quite the same rights to criticism.

6 Medical Control

One further element in the theatre of the clinic must be considered before we go backstage and examine those more covert activities and sentiments which the bureaucratic format concealed. So far I have depicted the masks of the players and sketched in the broad themes of their relationship. Yet one quite central feature of the drama has gone largely unremarked. I have noted how parents, though allies, were nevertheless excluded from the medical college and cast as subordinates. What I have not shown is the extent to which that subordination was manifested within the various activities which made up a consultation. Put another way, we must distinguish between those matters which pertain to actors' overall status within a relationship and those rules which govern their actual participation within the action. The two are clearly related but the one does not follow directly from the other. In some encounters the lowly may be granted considerable speaking parts, while in others their baseness may be reflected both in their exclusion from large areas of the action, and in a heavy control upon those parts which they do get to play.

Here parents were both excluded and controlled. They might be partners but they were not equals, and the imbalance of power within the bureaucratic format was one of its most striking features. Although parents had some rights to question and to criticize they could use these only within an overall context of medical dominance. The technical authority given to doctors was matched by an equivalent authority to control almost every aspect of the consultations' shape, sequence and timing.

My emphasis on medical control should not be taken to mean that parents had no power to negotiate with staff. As other work has clearly shown, there are various ways in which patients may influence the course of action within consultations (Roth, 1963; Stimson and Webb, 1975). However, although we still need to know more about such influence, its effect should not be exaggerated.[1] Within the bureaucratic format, and indeed within all of the formats discussed here, medical control of the consultation was systematic, all-pervasive and almost unquestioned. Although various writers have commented on this control (Johnson, 1972; Byrne and Long, 1976), not all of its features have been explored; and it is such exploration that is the aim of this chapter.

129

Objects of Involvement

The medium through which control of the nuts and bolts of interaction is exerted is the same as that used to create the rest of a format. Selective attention is the basis on which the whole of these little worlds rest, and participation within them is a matter of what may be defined as relevant for whom. Thus one of the central matters governed by the ceremonial order is the allocation of 'objects of involvement'. To put this less formally, encounters may involve a variety of activities apart from talk, but rights to involvement in these may not be distributed equally. We have already seen how children were typically excluded from many areas of the medical consultation. A similar, if less extreme, exclusion applied to their parents. Whereas doctors had rights to engage in a wide variety of actions, parents' rights were singularly limited.

In clinics, doctors might do many things. They could break off conversation with a mother to read or write a note, or to look at the child, or to ask the nurse a question, or to teach a student. They were also allowed to be 'away' for long periods. Some doctors spent considerable time lost in thought, their eyes unfocussed or their fingers drumming. They therefore had a wide variety of sources of involvement within the consultation, and parents typically recognized the legitimacy of such engagement by not 'interrupting' doctors when they were so involved. By contrast, parents had no such rights to other activities but maintained themselves in a state of permanent alertness during gaps in the conversation. While the doctor read or wrote mothers waited, ready to spring into conversation when requested to do so. They did not read, smoke or suck sweets; and talk with their children or their husband was strictly subordinate or, in Goffman' s terms (1972), a 'side-involvement'. Many mothers abstained from discussion altogether, particularly with older children. Only if a doctor left the room might a conversation of any normal volume or gesture begin.

Given this suppression of other involvements, it could not be said that staff interrupted parents when they took up their conversation once more, for there was nothing of any substance to be interrupted. Parents were at the doctors' disposal, and talk could begin or end at any time of the doctors' choosing and typically without any need for permission or apology.

The way in which parents were allocated and accepted a dependent role within the consultation can also be illustrated by the highly restricted set of bodily actions in which they engaged. Staff could move freely around the room: now standing up; now sitting down; now looking at this; now doing that; but parents sat in the chairs provided for them and did not move from these except to facilitate medical examination. The one mother who, of her own accord, left her chair and walked round to the doctor's side of the desk was greeted with immense surprise. Some parents even seemed unsure as to how far they could make themselves comfortable. Parents who arrived in overcoats often sweltered in the heated rooms rather than remove them, and one mother who arrived in a thunderstorm sat there and dripped until the doctor asked if she wanted to remove her coat.

Three alternative objects of medical involvement need a further consideration. The first of these, the discussion of medical matters with an audience of colleagues and students, has already been noted in the previous chapter. There I emphasized the way in which such discussion was overtly subordinated to the consultation between doctor and parents. Nevertheless, staff's ability to talk with an audience was an important assertion of their power, for such rights were not symmetrical. Some parents talked at nurses and other staff as well as to the doctor, but no one except the doctor normally responded and such communication disappeared into a void. By contrast, staff's right to engage in discussion with others could be used to influence directly their relationship with the parents. In the following instance, the doctor used the researcher to help to pacify a recalcitrant mother who had made a series of complaints in a rather aggressive tone:

Dr F: Apart from her food, are there any problems?
Mother: Well, there's her sleeping.
Dr F: Well, what, doesn't she sleep?
Mother: (firmly) Well, she does now because she gets something to make her sleep.
Dr F grins at the baby and dangles his stethoscope in front of it. He then says to the researcher:
Dr F: Isn't it marvellous having a baby like this? (Researcher smiles. Mother smiles back at researcher.) But it's not always marvellous. What's this about her not sleeping?

This use of an audience was exceptional. Nevertheless, it illustrates a potential resource that was always legitimately available to the doctor but was rather more dubious if parents attempted it. Including the audience in their remarks was one thing, manipulating them another.

Besides, such manipulation was normally a most difficult task, for the audience was on the doctors' side and could not be used against them - or so parents seemed to assume, for in none of the consultations which used the bureaucratic format did parents make any direct appeal to others to intervene on their behalf. By contrast, this happened in three out of the fifteen cases in the charity format, and in two of these a nurse actually stepped in to aid the mother: in the case of nappy rash cited earlier, the nurse joined in to say that she too was guilty, that she had always washed her babies' nappies in Ivory Snow and had not known of its inadequacy.

The doctors' power in the bureaucratic format was therefore reinforced by their access to an audience which acquiesced in their handling of the occasion and could be manipulated to further their own ends, a resource which was not available in quite the same manner to the parents.[2]

Two further asymmetries also had important consequences for medical control. The first of these involved children. I have already noted that children were treated as mere side-involvements for parents. Staff's authority extended, temporarily at least, to the relationship between parent and child and not just to that between parent and doctor. Indeed, the maintenance of their authority depended on a rigid segregation of parent and child. Staff might interact with the children whenever they chose but parents could not do so. Staff might switch openly between the two; parents must attend to whatever they were bid. Staff might address parents through the child, but they themselves were only to be spoken to directly. Where parents' presence was deemed to affect the relationship between staff and child too greatly, parents were removed from the setting. After the initial visit, both occupational and physiotherapy staff in the Scottish hospital did not permit parents to be present during treatment. Staff were also in charge of the allocation of praise and blame for the child's performance. Further, even though parents might normally be considered to have the most extensive knowledge of their child and to be the best interpreter of their words, actions and feelings, such knowledge was treated as partial and as able to be overridden where staff saw fit.

When doctors did interact with children, it was parents' duty to assist staff in their management. In this they were principally required to ensure that children recognized staff's paramount authority; or, put another way, they were obliged to underwrite the temporary loss of their own control. Alongside this they were expected to bring the child in a suitable condition for examination or therapy and to aid during these as appropriate; to hold children when they struggled; to encourage them when they failed to respond; and to soothe them when they cried.

Such an alliance might seem to have imposed heavy burdens upon parents, for they were deprived of most of their normal rights over their child. Yet almost all were loyal subordinates, even though cooperation was not always easy, for their duties were ambiguous. On the one hand their children were removed from their control, but on the other hand they were still expected to help in controlling them. Some did nothing at all but hovered uncertainly near the child, some intervened occasionally and hurriedly withdrew; others, as in the following instance from the orthoptic clinic, saw it as their duty to reinforce everything that staff said:

Therapist G:	Take your time.
Mother:	Take your time.
Therapist G:	This is the last one.
Mother:	This is the last one.
Therapist G:	Look at it.
Mother:	Look at it.
Therapist G:	Look properly now.
Mother:	Look properly.

Despite this partial removal of the child from their keeping, parents had some rights here. They might still interact with their sons and daughters even though such action was clearly subordinate to, and in the end controlled by, medical staff.

The medical records were a very different matter. For all practical purposes these belonged to the doctor and not to the parents. In the American clinics parents had a legal right to inspect their children's records, but none was observed to ask the doctor if they too might consult the file during the interaction. In all settings the notes stayed with the doctors and in no sense were they common property. Moreover, in many ways the presence of the medical record was as essential to medical interaction as the presence of parents or children.[3] Just as Dr J found it hard to continue where only the child's brother accompanied him, so a consultation without a record was a difficult task. Where the file for a particular case was not present, as when a child was attending another clinic at a similar time, doctors deferred the case until the file had arrived. If they were forced to carry on without it, as where records had to be acquired from another hospital, they made continual mistakes. Such constant correction challenged their normal professional ease. Proper medicine could only begin when the file as well as the patient was present, for it constituted an alternative biography to that available from the parents, and one that had been medically warranted.

Writing that biography was a medical and not a parental task, and was one of the main tasks in the consultation. Everything that parents said in clinics was for the record. For them to speak was to permit their words to be written down at the doctor's discretion. In all the cases doctors made notes: some wrote as they went along, pausing to do so after each question or test; others waited until their investigation was complete; but all devoted part of their time to writing. Indeed, where official forms were used, writing could be as central an activity as conversation with the parents. In particular, discharges from the maternity hospital, adoption cases in the general medical clinics, and developmental assessment in the local authority and neurological clinics all centred around the filling out of a form. Doctors and nurses worked with the form openly displayed and ticked off items one by one as they were covered. The presence of the form and of an official pen hovering over it defined the nature of the parental task: the production of brief answers that could be filled in as quickly and efficiently as possible.[4]

The record was not as obtrusive on those other occasions when there was no official form to be completed; but it nevertheless played a major part in the action for here too it constrained the speed, length and shape of parents' answers. When asking questions of parents, doctors would often not address them directly but simply speak as they consulted the file or added fresh contents. Only when presenting their conclusions did they routinely look parents continuously in the face as they spoke. For attention was not guaranteed to parents. Although they had the right to ask questions or introduce topics of conversation, they had no definite rights to an answer. Doctors could demand this of parents but parents could not do likewise, for doctors, as we have seen, had other legitimate objects of attention through which they could ignore their remarks. In the following instance, both the child and the notes were preferred to the mother's comments. (The child was suffering from minor mental retardation.)

Dr G: (gives the child a ball) What's this? (The child plays with it.)
Mother: She's rather smart now she's older. She knows her figures and she can write her own name now.
Dr G: Yes, yes. (He gives the child some cubes and writes a note, half-watching the child.)
Mother: She doesn't like sitting, she always likes something to do.
Dr G: (carries on writing a note, then watches the child intensively, then says) All right now I'll have a word with Mr James to see what's happening. There's no need to make an appointment for

	this clinic in the meantime.
Mother:	No.
Dr G:	All right, then, bye-bye (to child).
Mother:	Bye-bye.
Child:	Bye-bye.

Not only did doctors control the medical records and use them to enforce their general control of the encounter, but parents rarely made or at least used any records of their own. There were only seven cases in which parents brought along their own notes, and in three of these it was the doctors who had asked the parents to do this. More importantly perhaps, no parent was ever observed to make notes during a clinic.[5] Doctors wrote down what they said but parents did not reciprocate. Minutes of a kind were kept, but only staff made these, stored them and had ready access to them.

Not only did staff have special rights to involve themselves in a wide variety of activities, but they also largely controlled the overall timing of the consultation and the scheduling of individual pieces of the action. Thus it was staff who decided when a consultation both began and ended: in only one case in the entire study did a mother rather than a doctor end a consultation. Time was the doctors' and not the parents'. Not only did parents have to arrange to see the doctor and not the other way around, they might also have to wait even where they had been given a set time. Doctors usually apologized for major delays, but parents had no right to interrupt and be seen at the time that had been formally set aside for them. Similarly, once in the consultation it was typically the doctors who scheduled events and not the parents. As such it was doctors who normally made comments like 'Right', 'Fine' and 'OK', which signalled changes in the topic or the action.

Controlling Talk

Just as doctors had special rights to engage in a variety of activities besides talk with parents, and could also largely determine the sequence and timing of those activities, so too they exerted a major control over talk itself. In considering that control three points need particular emphasis. The first of these is the general absence of small talk from consultations. When staff talked to children all kinds of personal matters might be discussed: their school, Christmas presents, holidays or favourite television programmes. By contrast, conversation with parents was all of a piece. Normally the participants talked of nothing besides medical matters either before, during or after the consultation; with doctors there was no pre- or post-activity talk.[6] Parents were ready to start as soon as they entered; and as soon as they entered doctors started. Doctors opened the talk and almost always did so with a remark that initiated medical action. With new patients they asked them what the problem was; with old patients they commonly inquired, 'How are things?' or 'How have you been?' Remarks such as these might in other contexts be taken as a general inquiry or as an occasion for talk about the weather, their jobs, or whatever parents wished. Here, however, 'things' meant the child's problem, and was invariably taken to be so. Such questions constituted an opening which initiated the activity, they were not a prelude to it. Similarly the ending of medical activity was also the ending of talk. Once doctors had either discharged the patient or fixed a new appointment, patients left the room.

Not only was talk confined almost exclusively to medical matters, it was also largely question-and-answer talk, and rights within this were unequally distributed. Doctors by and large asked the questions; parents did the answering. On some occasions, after breaking bad news, doctors did ask parents to bring a list of questions next time. But to do so was to recognize that typically it was they who asked the questions and not the other way round. Parents did get some chance to ask questions but it was at the end of the consultations, after doctors had asked theirs.

The questions that doctors asked were also of a distinct type. In his analysis of conversation in psychotherapy, Blum (1970) distinguishes two kinds of question and answer talk. In the kind that is special to such occasions, the therapists' questions are to be heard simply as occasions for general talk. Simple 'answers' are not wanted, for the therapist is concerned with making inferences about the patient's 'mind' and this requires some display of that entity. By contrast, the questions which were asked in the children's clinic were typically requests for specific information and not a warrant for general discussion. The majority of parents' answers were therefore brief and to the point. Here, for example, is a quotation from a developmental assessment case in a Scottish local authority clinic:

Dr A: Is he eating and sleeping all right?
Mother: Yes.
Dr A: Now, when I saw him last his eyes were a bit watery, weren't they?
Mother: Oh, they're fine now.

Dr A: Right. Now, was the pregnancy all right?
Mother: Yes.
Dr A: There were no troubles during it? No kidney troubles or anything?
Mother: No.
Dr A: It was a normal delivery, no forceps?
Mother: No.

The third major feature of clinic talk, apart from its specificity and its concentration on medical matters, was the 'hidden agenda' (Scheff, 1968) to which that talk was directed. Doctors asked for information but they did not normally explain why they needed it, nor did they reveal the criteria by which they judged its relevance. Some doctors might give a brief resumé of their thinking when they produced their conclusions, but no one gave this at the beginning of the consultation or during the actual questioning. Doctors had parents' answers at their own disposal and could do with them as they wished. They could accept them and pass on to something else, as in the above quotation, or they might make demands for greater precision and even on occasion check this out with the child:

Dr G: And there's no question of his inhaling or swallowing anything that afternoon?
Mother: No, he didn't have anything in his mouth.
Dr G: (to child) You're quite sure, Arthur, that you didn't have anything in your mouth and you hadn't swallowed anything?
Child: No.

Similarly, where a doctor was not happy with an answer he might continue to ask the same question until he was satisfied. In the next example the doctor asked the mother to describe a typical attack, but she talked instead of a particular one. Only when he had repeated his request three times did she rearrange the way she told her story and start to use the general present rather than the past particular tense:

Dr H: Now, tell me about a typical attack of sore tummy? What does he do?
Mother: Well, eh ... In October he had an attack he was off school for a week with the sickness and then he was sick again.
Dr H: Is this the typical time off for an attack? Is it a normal one? Is he

off for a week usually?

Mother: Well, um, not usually, but that was in October.

Dr H: Will you tell me what a normal one consists of?

Mother: Well, in the winter he had two attacks, there was three months between them.

Dr H: Uh-huh, ummm. What's the first thing that goes wrong?

Mother: He complained of being sick that time, it was just starting up.

Dr H: Yes. Is there any pain in his tummy? Does this occur?

Mother: Aye, there's this pain in his tummy.

Dr H: And does this pain happen before he vomits?

Mother: I think so, and then he just, there's the pain and then he's sick, or sometimes it's just the pain.

Just as doctors repeated their questions until they got what they wanted, they also ignored things that they took to be irrelevant and might even interrupt a reply to ask about the matters that really concerned them:

Dr F: Can he drink from a cup?

Mother: Yes. He's still got a bottle but....

Dr F: Can he hold a cup?

Mother: Yes, he can manage to hold one.

Not only could doctors make whatever they liked of answers to their questions since their agenda was largely concealed, but they also used that agenda in an extremely rapid and routinized fashion. Such routinization was most obvious when doctors worked from an official form, but it was equally true of other cases. Each doctor had set methods for handling the kinds of case which he saw and used the same questions and the same formulations, in much the same order, in case after case of any particular type.[7] Thus, although parents were given opportunities to talk they could do so only within a systematic framework laid down by the doctor, a grid that was in daily professional use but in which they themselves had little practice.

Controlling Topics

As we have seen, doctors controlled the action in clinics by limiting the amount and kind of attention they were prepared to give to parents. Not only could they direct the conversation but they alone had the right to engage fully and openly in other activities outside that conversation. The right to control the consultation in this fashion was also used to restrict the topics of consultation even more narrowly than has hitherto been mentioned. Clinic action was not only exclusively medical, but also the medical remit was overtly defined in a most limited fashion. Staff focussed on the individual case and, within this, on the current physical problems which that case involved. Only in exceptional instances was this focus broadened.

Take first the individualizing tendency of medical work. I noted earlier how in any one consultation staff concentrated on that particular child as if it constituted a world in itself and was not just another example of X or Y. In doing so they avoided the twin dangers of treating the child as either mere work or just clinical material. At the same time this focus also prevented parents from gaining general knowledge about medicine and its ways, and those few parents who dared to seek this were actively discouraged. Take for instance this example from the maternity hospital ward-round:

Mother: Why do they measure the baby's length?
Dr K: Well, we measure all children as it is related to their adult height. You probably wouldn't be interested.
Mother: (eagerly) Oh, yes, I'm fascinated by all the things you do, but I just wondered why you were doing it. I must have been about four inches long at birth. I'm so small.
Dr K: How tall is your husband?
Mother: 5 feet 10 inches.
Dr K: (tells the mother the average length of children at birth and adds) There's not much variation in this. (The mother smiles eagerly again and looks as if she wants to continue the conversation, but the doctor turns to talk to a registrar.)

Besides the omission of general discussion about medical matters, the range of topics covered was highly restricted. Fundamentally, doctors were only interested in problems. Let us reconsider the quotation from Dr A's clinic which is cited earlier in this chapter, a quotation which is typical of interaction in almost any clinic. The key words and phrases that recur in each interchange are 'all right', 'fine', 'no troubles' and 'normal'. As soon as normality was established the doctor passed on to the next topic. If there was no problem there was nothing to talk about. Indeed, where the doctor was rushed this might constitute the end of the interaction. Here, for example, are two fairly typical consultations with old patients on the maternity hospital ward-round:

> Dr K: Hello, Mrs Jones.
> Mother: Hello.
> Dr K: Is baby feeding OK?
> Mother: Yes.
> Dr K: Fine.... No problems?
> Mother: No.
> Dr K: Super.

We move on to the next bed.

> Dr K: Hello. You're an experienced mother, aren't you? No problems
>   here?
> Mother: No.
> Dr K: Fine.

We pass on to the next bed.

Not only were doctors interested solely in problems, but their definition of the problematic was severely limited. This had several aspects. Let us start with child development. This was a matter of major concern in all the clinics, and all the doctors and therapists had some training in the matter. However, staff only took notice of those who were retarded. Although local authority clinic doctors graded the children that they assessed, parents were not normally informed of the grade. Indeed, the fact that the child was being assessed was not normally mentioned. Only where a child was delayed were mothers told the result of the assessment.

Similarly, in all clinics mothers of delayed or handicapped children were routinely given advice on how to aid their child, but no such advice was given where babies were judged to be normal. Children, it seemed, needed to be 'brought on' only if they were 'behind'. This is not to say that doctors assumed that normal babies could not be aided in this fashion. Mothers whose babies were exceptionally competent sometimes received lavish praise by local authority doctors after they had left, but such praise was not given during the clinic, nor was criticism or advice offered where a baby was merely average. Mothers of normal children who tried to discuss the child's development in detail, and who asked about the stages at which children did this or that, were treated as 'worriers'.

Similarly, doctors normally showed little interest in the everyday difficulties posed by children. As children grew they created all kinds of new problems for their care and management. Outside clinics, among mothers waiting in the corridor, such problems were a standard topic. 'Mother-craft' was however normally excluded from clinic conversation, even where the doctor felt the mother to be relatively incompetent. This was simply not the doctor's business, it did not fall within their remit and therefore it was not dealt with. Only where it was sufficient to cause a 'medical' problem, for example severe nappy rash, was it raised, and even here its handling was often delegated to others such as health visitors or nurses.

Psychiatric matters were another topic that was normally excluded from paediatric consultations within the bureaucratic format. The avoidance of this area has already been considered in my discussion of parental character. It is worth noting here that almost all emotional issues were side-stepped and not just those which involved possible psychiatric disturbance. Clinics were not bereft of every emotion, some indeed were marked by jollity, but the emotional range was a foreshortened one. It ran simply from joy to neutrality. Where the occasion was a happy one both parties might express happiness; where it was not then by and large they expressed nothing. Here as elsewhere doctors set the tone. As we have seen, parents who tried to import a language and emotional tone appropriate to other and more cheerful occasions by laughing or displaying great affection for their child often failed. Staff reciprocated in this manner only when they felt it appropriate. Developmental testing on a normal child was accompanied by all kinds of congratulatory remarks from staff. Bad performance received no comment. Apparent exceptions to this rule of a limited emotional range in fact exemplify it. Staff used dramatic language about conditions only when these were easily remedied. Here, for example, are two doctors' remarks to mothers on the maternity hospital ward-round:

Dr K: Oh, what a nasty septic spot! I think that had better be punctured. We'll take it through to the nursery and do it there.

Dr L: (to a nurse) Could you get this (sticky eyes) seen to right away as it is rather nasty.

Serious conditions were examined without any such comment to the parents and, just as doctors refrained from using dramatic language, so too did almost all parents. Clinics, it seemed, were not places for emotional display. Bad news was broken in a matter-of-fact way and received in much the same fashion. Doctors indicated the tragic nature of events only by indirect means. Some, for instance, used a quieter and more intimate tone of voice. Some parents likewise lowered their eyes, looked embarrassed and said little or nothing, but almost none displayed any open signs of grief. Only three parents in all were observed to cry and then only briefly. This does not mean that others felt no such emotions, but that clinics were inappropriate places to express these:

> Dr J: I think they often express some of their emotions as soon as they get outside the room. If I go out to get something or to test the urine of the next patient I find them in tears in the corridor, when they would seem nowhere near tears in the room.... They demonstrate relatively little in clinic. I'm sure the picture they present at home or on the bus on the way back is quite different.

The absence of open grief in clinics seems linked to the absence of any occasion formally provided for its expression. In Sudnow's (1967) study of dying in hospitals, he noted how, when doctors broke news of a patient's death to their relatives, they paused briefly to allow an expression of grief. Not all relatives in fact displayed such emotions, but all were allowed an opportunity to do so. However, when bad news was broken in the paediatric consultations no such opportunity was provided for parents nor did they seem to expect this.[8] Having revealed the existence of a serious condition, doctors simply moved on to a discussion of further visits and possible treatment.

Such absence of occasions for grief did not mean that staff were annoyed when it was displayed, for they saw tears as 'natural' and as 'one end of the continuum'. However, they acted as if those who were on the brink of tears would rather not cry if this could be avoided. They therefore carried on with their normal routine, or else, when this became impossible, paused to allow parents a chance to master their emotions. Here is the end of a case in which the doctor had broken the news that a child was very severely handicapped. Up to this point the mother had been fully in control of herself; indeed she had taken a lead in identifying problematic features about her baby:

> Mother: Of course, if there is anything that could be done you would let me know?
> Dr I: Yes, of course. I don't think I'm telling you anything that you don't know already.
> Mother: Yes, and you would let me know if there was anything that could

be done? You would let me know? (As she says this the mother becomes very red in the face, her eyes begin to glisten and she has difficulty in getting her words out. The doctor pauses and says nothing. Eventually the mother masters herself and asks a further question.) And when do I come back?

Dr I: In six months' time, and you'll be seen once a week in physiotherapy, and otherwise I'll see you in six months' time.

Grief then was treated as a private matter by both sides and not something that was appropriately expressed in clinics. Even when mothers did cry their tears were their own affair. The action might pause to allow them to recover, but sorrow was not itself a topic. Doctors did not put their arms round parents in such circumstances, nor did they encourage them to express their feelings further. The most that any doctor did was to murmur softly, 'I know, I know'. These matters were not entirely neglected, for staff did act where they were particularly worried about parents' reactions; but these were dealt with, not in the clinic, but delegated to other specialists such as social workers.

Not only did staff focus solely on the strictly medical problems of a particular child, but those problems had to be current ones, problems that were of immediate import. Consider this apology made by the mother of a severely handicapped child as she entered the neurological clinic:

Mother: I feel I'm here under false pretences. I called in at the desk to see if I could have a word with you and they said, 'Come in', and they gave me an appointment. There's nothing wrong.

To arrive at a clinic without a current problem, unless one's child was there for screening, was to lack any proper reason for being there.

Changing the Rules

There is one final aspect of the medical control of these consultations that requires mention, although it need only be brief since I have touched upon it several times in the preceding chapters.

Far from being immutable, the bureaucratic format could itself be modified when the occasion arose, and the right to control such alteration formed a crucial part of the doctors' armoury. There were basically two kinds of changes that might be made in the rules. The first and most fundamental of these was to shift the entire format and substitute another, or at least blend in elements of two formats into the same encounter. As we shall see later, doctors were not entirely free agents in this respect; nevertheless it was they who chose when to admit parents to a collegial discussion and not the parents themselves; and it was largely up to doctors to decide how far a clinical discussion with other staff or students might be permitted. The occasional parent might try to enforce the conventions of the private format but, unless they were also paying for the service, such attempts did not succeed.

The fact that the format was in some sense at the doctor's disposal was one of the principal constraints upon parental criticism or complaint. To step too far out of line might produce a change to another and far less pleasant ceremonial order. No such complete switch was actually observed, although doctors hinted at its possibility in censuring mothers of revealed bad character. Nevertheless it remained a permanent possibility and one that is certainly exercised in other kinds of medical setting, as will be seen later.

The second right which doctors had in this respect was to modify one or two of the rules while still retaining the overall form of the bureaucratic mode. Two good examples of this procedure have already been given. Parents were normally cast as technically incompetent but, where it suited doctors' purposes, as when they wished to normalize or to stigmatize a child, they might be granted a temporary equality - so long at least as they supported the doctor's own judgment. This right to confer identities upon the other participants, or the privilege of 'alter-casting' in Weinstein's (1966) phrase, was also seen in the removal from two mothers of the normal parental rights to criticism.

But other sorts of rule might be modified as well. Indeed in some therapy sessions the heavy control of conversation was so relaxed that the ceremonial order no longer resembled the bureaucratic format. What happened on such occasions is nevertheless worth a brief inspection since the contrast may still tell us something about the normal mode. We must also examine the somewhat lesser relaxation of control that could occur with the parents of severely handicapped children, for such instances formed the major, though only partial, exception to the rule of doctor domination of the proceedings.

Special Cases - Therapy

In two of the settings where therapy was done - the occupational and physiotherapy departments of the Scottish hospital - parents were excluded from the treatment sessions and were seen, usually briefly, before and after each session. Compared with medical consultations in clinics, such meetings were casual and relatively easy affairs. This was partly due to the therapists' status. They too were women, while they had no formal responsibility for assessing a child's condition, or for informing mothers about it. They were also much lower in the hospital hierarchy than doctors, and for some of them, their social origins were rather nearer those of the majority of patients. Moreover, although they routinely discussed the child's performance in therapy, such discussion typically lacked a heavily controlled agenda. Indeed, other identities besides those of therapist and parent were used to generate topics of conversation. A discussion of the child's performance could on occasion be followed by all manner of general topics which had little to do with therapy. Since they saw parents so often, usually either weekly or fortnightly, and over such a long period - often several years - therapists could become part of the routine life of parent and child. As such they might acquire details of the parents' interests, mood, holidays, home and work. While doctors had no time in which to get to know a child, therapists' whole management technique was based upon such knowledge. For some children, therapists - like teachers - became central figures in their lives, and their mothers commented on how they looked forward to therapy and on what they had said about it last time. Finally, whereas clinic visits were infrequent, the weekly visits to therapy corresponded to the parents' own time-scale and to their everyday perception of change in the child.

All this meant that each side could take so much more for granted, both about each other and about the child, than was possible in clinic consultations. Whereas for doctors most children were part of an undifferentiated mass, to and about whom they could say little more than repeat the standard adult formulae used to inquire of the young, therapists could display a rich store of personal information about each patient. As such, mothers could simply assume that their child was well known to the therapist, they did not have to explain, merely allude. Since meetings were frequent both sides could raise matters as they arose and when they felt the time was right. Topics could flow 'naturally' out of the conversation and did not have to be openly enforced. This greater ease was heightened by the absence of any overt records or record-taking in normal conversations with parents. Doctors pooled their records in a central system and for them continuity resided primarily with the files and not with their personal knowledge of the patients; but therapists knew them from acquaintance as much as from their notes.

Despite these differences one must not overemphasize the contrast between doctors and therapists. The latter did not devote much of their time to parents, for mothers often brought and fetched their children with barely more than a minute or two's conversation. Some mothers were reticent and staff never got to know them, while, whatever their relationship, therapists owed their primary allegiance to the hospital and not to the mothers. Although there was often no overt agenda in their chats with parents, in practice they were searching for information about mothers' attitudes or family conditions and, where relevant, this was passed to other staff. Therapists asked mothers about their lives, mothers did not normally respond in kind.

Special Cases - Serious Conditions [9]

The second exception to the principle of rigorous medical control concerns cases that are far more central to my analysis. Where a child was seriously and chronically ill then medical control might be relaxed to suit the special medical tasks which such conditions created. As we have seen, severely handicapped children placed a major strain upon their parents. The assessment of their ability to cope with this burden could not be done solely by the interrogatory style typical of more normal consultations. For this purpose, staff used the psychotherapists' style in addition to their usual manner and sought to produce displays of talk as evidence of parents' frame of mind. Such general conversation served a further goal. We have noted how slowly doctors broke the worst news, how they waited for signs that the mothers themselves had come to realize the facts of their child's condition. Again, the accurate judgment of parents' version of their children required a more relaxed, more equal conversation than that which was typical of less serious conditions. In consequence, staff allowed parents rather more opportunity to set the agenda. Mothers' interest and wonder at the minutiae of their child's development, something which was normally excluded from clinic interaction, might here be a most relevant topic. In this quotation a mother talks about her very severely handicapped son. The mother, after discussing blood tests, an EEG and the child's hearing - all topics initiated by the doctor - introduces a topic of her own:

> Mother: We've seen Mrs Sheila (physiotherapist) today and she's very pleased with him and said he was coming on well. She said he may be ready for his shoes soon. He seems to be making another spurt. He's altogether stronger and asserting his rights. For

Dr I: example, you can't shove food at him either. If he doesn't want to, then he won't.
Dr I: He's becoming more of an individual?
Mother: Yes, it's lovely to get this feeling that I just can't manipulate him as I want, that he's got his own will. I've got some exercises now for him from Mrs Sheila. He's splaying his legs out now so he can sit quite nicely. He's actually managing to sit on the floor by himself. Another problem that we had was him rubbing his head on the back of the settee. Mrs Sheila said we should stop him doing this as it would put him back into wrong positions, so that's sorted too.
Dr I: I get the feeling that you're reasonably pleased with the way things are going at the moment.
Mother: Yes. Another thing is that he would never put his arm around you when you carried him and if he fell over he would never put his arm out to support himself, he just squealed. But in the last few weeks he's started to grab hold of you and if I carry him upstairs he'll put his arm round me. These are very small things, I realize, but they're things he's developing now.
Dr I: They're signs of progress, however small.
Mother: Yes, like the first time he broke a cup for me. I was thrilled that he'd got to the stage where he realized that if you threw something over the side of the cot it made a nice noise. And now he's started to have odd nocturnal dreams, I think.

As can be seen, the doctor allowed the mother to talk freely, not imposing his own agenda but simply repeating what she had said in a polite fashion and allowing her to raise fresh topics. The medical agenda might be broadened in other ways as well. In the more serious cases where children attended repeatedly, it was common for parents to raise all kinds of minor medical problems which had little or nothing to do with the main condition, or with the doctors' specialist skill. These were dealt with cheerily along with all the rest. Attendance at the clinic might also be continued long after it had any real medical relevance. Thus whereas normally the agenda was highly restricted, in some cases hospital staff took on the role of the general practitioner:

Dr I: There's no real point in some ways in still seeing Angela but I like to, as you can't really rely on GPs. I'm hopeless at working out which GPs are the really good ones. The only contact I have with them is through their letters. I hardly ever meet any GPs in the city. Some doctors can work it out but I can't. It takes years to do anyway. Doctors who have been here a very long time, like Dr Fitzsimmons and Dr Simpson, have got to know which GPs are reliable and obviously it helps if you've been trained here. Dr McAllister trained here and knows quite a few of them personally. Really, it should be the GP's job to check up on children like this, but as so many don't you can't rely on it. So in the end the paediatrician has to take on the responsibility of keeping an eye on them.

As was noted earlier, not only did paediatricians discuss a much wider range of personal problems with the parents of such children, but they also assumed a managerial responsibility as regards other hospital and local authority services and checked on parents' attendance at these and their feelings about them. This broadening of the agenda meant that parents had rather more control over the discussion in such cases. Once again, this point must not be over-stressed. As we have seen, doctors were cautious about the information they produced and shied away from any criticism of other services. Moreover, although they allowed parents to talk more freely about their children such conversation was still linked to the doctors' agenda and took place under their control.

7 Ease and Tension in the Alliance

Having examined the various components which together made up the bureaucratic format, we can now step back a little and consider the overall fit between this surface ceremony and the more covert sentiments and actions of the participants. The outer form in which it cast the relationship of doctors and parents was flattering, if rather tightly controlled. In a strictly technical sense the format proved most successful for, despite the extremely varied circumstances in which it was applied, it was only on quite exceptional occasions that any major modification was necessary. Another good indicator of this achievement is the way in which almost all the participants managed to contain whatever personal feelings they may have had, either about each other or about the events under consideration. Consultations were both formal and polite, and strong emotions were suppressed. No doctor who used the bureaucratic format was ever seen to get angry with a parent, while only a handful of parents came anywhere near anger and overtly such emotions were quickly dissipated. Similarly, despite the great tragedy that was sometimes involved, almost no one cried.

It must not be supposed that this technical success meant that all consultations were managed with equal ease. As I have emphasized, a role format is primarily a matter of surface ceremony. It is an entity to which participants pay formal respect but it does not necessarily reflect how they actually feel about events, nor is it an accurate guide to all the action within any particular encounter. Many things may be done so long as they are decently clothed. Sometimes, of course, there is a ready fit between the ceremonial order of an encounter and the wider worlds of those who act within it. On these 'easeful' (Goffman, 1961) occasions the participants may feel no sense of strain and become completely engrossed within the action. But if there is any serious discrepancy between surface and substance, between the overt order and the covert reality as perceived by one or all of the participants, then such occasions are marked by a continuous tension, a tension which is reflected in continual efforts to bridge or conceal the crevasse. Since my data is largely observational my account will focus primarily on these visible signs of strain rather than on the subjective accounts found in some other work (e.g., Stimson and Webb, 1975; Strong, 1977a).

I have, of course, already considered a wide variety of sources of tension. However, my account has been partial for, in seeking to show the universality of the format's rules, I have concentrated on the especially adverse situations and neglected those features which posed systematic difficulties in every consultation. Up till now it may have seemed that, where parents were relatively competent and the child's condition amenable to medical treatment, then the alliance could be made with great ease. The one possibly harsh note has been the ubiquity of medical dominance. There were, however, a number of other, general features which were equally potent sources of strain. Great ease was in fact a relatively rare occurrence; and the alliance, although constructed for mothers, was, as will be seen, more suited to foster-mothers - fellow-professionals whose knowledge and involvement more closely matched that of medical staff.

Medical Time

One major source of strain lay in the marked discrepancy between the overt medical emphasis on service to the individual client and the actual setting and timing of that service. Certain potentially offensive matters might be carefully excluded; but the bureaucratic setting, and the medical control of action within that setting, these could not be wished away. Doctors did not see patients in their own homes and at their own times. Instead patients waited on doctors. To attend an outpatient clinic was to enter an elaborate and formalized bureaucracy whose rituals had an iconographic as well as a functional significance, revealing both the precise nature of the doctor's time, and that each client was simply one amongst many. Simply to get the attention of a doctor, parents had to make a formal appointment, for which they received a card. On arrival at a hospital they were confronted by a large building whose interior, though full of bustle and activity, was also permeated by a sense of seriousness and enforced quiet. Entrance to this, or to a city clinic, required investigation by a receptionist and after that there were still further intermediaries, nurses or health visitors in uniform, who controlled immediate access to each doctor. Time did not belong to parents but to doctors, and mothers could only be seen when staff were ready for them. Thus, even before the consultation began certain crucial features of its form were already present in embryo. Waiting for an appointment or waiting outside the clinic told parents what their status would be once they were inside.

Within this framework, the amount of time allocated to parents was both brief and bureaucratically regulated, even though doctors had some flexibility in the amount they gave to individual cases - a few patients might receive two or even three times their official allowance. But such time was bought at a cost; other patients had to receive less than their due or else doctors had to skimp other work. Further, such variation took place within very narrow limits compared to the complexity and importance of some of the issues that were addressed. Here are a doctor's comments on reading through the file of a child who had been referred to him from another clinic with suspected developmental delay. The clinic is running half an hour late.

Dr J: I don't understand this. James was seen last week but none of the relevant tests have been done. What on earth can I do? I suppose all I can do is the milestones.... Oh, heavens. (reads out notes) 'The mother fears that there is a diagnosis of leukaemia which is being hidden from her!... The child lives with granny and is best seen with the grandmother.'

Nurse: Well, it's the mother and father that are here with her today.

Dr J: Oh, no! I wonder if the mother is being upset by all these referrals? And it says here that I'm to decrease the mother's fears. In *fifteen minutes* (the time formally allotted for the case)!

Given such narrow limits the only feasible solution for staff was to control the nature, sequence and timing of the action as tightly as was described in the previous chapter. Exceptions were possible only for the exceptional patient. To circumscribe the consultation in this fashion had effects well beyond the rather dramatic problems of the case cited above. Things happened at the doctor's pace and not at that of the parents. They had little time to pause for thought or to modify a previous answer. Since time was the doctor's they could not ask him to slow down or request an extra ten minutes at the end. Once topics had been dealt with they were normally gone for ever, for it was hard to return with second and fresher thoughts. Since time was limited and questions were pointed, answers had to be brief. The vague and circuitous nature of everyday talk about illness had no place here, nor could there normally be any mention of the ways in which that particular illness had a meaning in parents' lives. As we have seen, how they felt about their child, the practical problems of its condition, their ups and downs: all of these were normally excluded. The transaction was rapid, focussed and, above all, impersonal.

This impersonality was always a threat to the ideology of the 'alliance', but posed a special threat to the more long-term and serious cases. Not only was the agenda sometimes broader here, but the regularity of parental visits could lead to the expectation of a more personal friendship. However, not only was there a considerable staff turnover but also, even where the same doctor continued to treat the same patient over the years, his recollection of the case rested as much in the records as in his own memory. On occasion, almost everything, even the parents' name, might be forgotten:

Dr I:	Hello. Do come in.
Grandmother:	Hello.
Dr I:	Mrs Hutchison, isn't it?
Grandmother:	Mrs Innes!
Dr I:	Mrs Innes.... Sorry! I thought I remembered it. She's been in for ... (pause)
Grandmother:	For therapy.
Dr I:	In the inpatients for therapy!
Grandmother:	Yes, as an inpatient.
Dr I:	She's not in Marchbanks yet?
Grandmother:	No, no. She's not in there yet. I've been up to see it as you suggested but she's got to wait for a bed. They've put her on the waiting list.

Medicine and Morality

A similar discrepancy between ceremony and substance may be found in the treatment of parents' character. The ideal nature ascribed to parents within the bureaucratic format was one of its most striking features. Yet to understand fully the working of encounters within that format one must at the same time grasp a quite opposite proposition. Despite the surface neutrality of the ceremonial order, medical work in all these consultations necessarily involved routine and systematic moral investigation. On the one hand doctors treated parents with the greatest delicacy, on the other hand they covertly scrutinized their competence and character in a myriad different ways.

The assessment of the patients' or their representatives' moral character is a central feature of medical encounters in any kind of format. To see why this is so, some brief remarks are necessary on the nature of medical phenomena. In analysing any kind of event one makes use of what Goffman (1975a, p.22) has termed 'two broad classes of primary framework, "natural" and "social"'. In natural frameworks, events are seen as unguided and un-willed. Since they are purely physical and quite separate from human action, there can be no standards of success or failure here. By contrast, social phenomena are viewed as aimed and controlled and are thus subject to assessment as regards their efficiency and morality. Despite this apparently clear dichotomy, the actual application of these frameworks is often a difficult matter, for the natural and the social are interwoven in complex ways.

Medical matters are a good example of such complexity. On the one hand many medical phenomena have clearly physical causes and are treated by largely physical means. As such, sickness often serves as a legitimate excuse. On the other hand, illness is embodied and is thus also part of the social world: many conditions are caused by or partly correlated with social events, while their recognition and treatment are in many ways social phenomena, as are many of their consequences. The investigation of illness in any one patient is therefore as much an inquiry into the social as into the natural sphere, and is necessarily a moral as well as a physical inquiry.

The extent to which staff, on the basis of such assessment, actually condemned parents when in private, varied considerably. Some, as in this instance, were forthright:

TD: When she (social worker) first made contact there she really wanted to change the family, but she soon learnt that you couldn't. You can't change things with the Millers and people like them. It just goes on.... I've given her lots of clothes and things, I've really tried to help that family but she's just pawned them straightaway.... Her husband is a pig, he's a big man with pop-eyes, a very nasty piece of work.

Others avoided such judgments. Here another therapist argues that one should never condemn parents:

TE: I don't think we're here to judge the parents. I think that the parents, they've got that child twenty-four hours a day ... trying to put oneself into the position of having a child twenty-four hours a day ... I think that's what we've constantly tried to do.

But even though staff differed in the extent to which they moralized about their clientele, all routinely engaged in social and thus ultimately moral assessment. Some might not in fact condemn parents, but their inquiries provided the material from which indictments could always be made.

This moral assessment had several important dimensions. First let us consider the cause of the child's condition. I have already touched on the possible psychiatric links with many childhood complaints, but even in more clearly physical ailments, parents might still be held partly responsible. The conditions in which the family lived, their knowledge of health and diet, and the care which mothers had taken, all played a part in the incidence of disease. One crucial indicator of these matters, or so staff felt, was social class; and data were gathered on all aspects of this. Staff noted parents' accent, asked about their occupation and examined their address with some care:

> Dr G: They're from Danzig Terrace. That's a notorious place in the city for problem families.

The doctor next looks at the child's height and weight which have been given him by a nurse.

> Dr G: Well, they're in the normal range. ... (pause) ... I suppose they are about average for Danzig Terrace.

Apart from noting such background features, staff routinely assessed, in so far as they were able, the care that parents gave their children. Besides considering the extent to which parents had complied with medical advice, routine questioning and physical examination gave them the opportunity to note the child's general state and to check its nourishment and cleanliness. Indeed, this was a mandatory part of staff's work. Although children still belong legally to their parents, in both Britain and the United States the State has increasingly intervened within the family and medical staff are crucial agents in such intervention. This showed itself in a number of different ways. In the developmental assessment carried out in the Scottish local authority clinics, doctors were required to grade parental care on an official form, and strong attempts were made to assess every young child in the City. Under State law the American doctors faced legal action if they failed to report any case where they suspected the possibility of child abuse. Although it was extremely rare for children to be removed from their parents on medical grounds, in all settings the doctors had access to paramedical workers with both the training and the mandate to intervene within the family. The Scottish local authority had large numbers of health visitors who regularly visited all newborn babies, while both hospitals had their own social workers who could investigate any family matters about which doctors were worried.

Although the threat of potential investigation hung over every clinic, relatively few parents were in fact investigated since most attained what doctors took to be a reasonable, if not perfect, standard of care. But at the same time, however well they cared for their children, all mothers were likely to fail on at least one central aspect of a parent's duty. I have noted how fathers were openly distrusted as reliable witnesses but, although mothers were overtly treated as fully competent in this respect, in private doctors were sceptical:

Dr G: The mother I think had observed them (small fits) in the child but just hadn't noticed them. We're used to this sort of thing, but this is her first baby. It shows you, you just can't rely on mothers knowing what to expect and what to understand from the baby's behaviour. When we asked her about them she said nothing about it.

Such scepticism about parents' ability to notice the problematic informed whole areas of medical practice. Developmental screening, for instance, was premised on the assumption that parents were unable to detect many forms of delay, at least in their early stages. Not only did parents not notice things that doctors defined as important, but staff also suspected the accuracy of what they did report. Here are Dr G's comments to the students as he reads from a referral letter:

Dr G: 'The mother says the child has right occipital headaches.' Now is it likely that a five-year-old could say to his mother that he has a headache? It's very rare. It's even rarer to locate it. So I immediately say that this is the mother's interpretation.... Is it likely that a five-year-old would come up to his mother and say, 'I've got a right occipital headache' (laughter). So immediately one has to think about how reliable the mother is.

These matters were often summed up in a word. The most common medical classification of parents was whether they were 'bright' or 'dim'; 'intelligent' or 'unintelligent':

Registrar: The mother *claims* it's a thirty-two week pregnancy. She also says X.
Dr J: She doesn't sound very bright.
Registrar: She's not.

Dr Y: It sounds as if the father hasn't got two neurons to rub together.

Dr G: That mother's not very bright either. She says that she thinks that the child is going to become smart in time, yet there's no doubt that she'll be a very backward child.

The other key quality for which doctors searched was how far parents were 'sensible'.[1] Being 'sensible' meant putting things in their proper context; not worrying without any cause; not letting ones's emotions influence what one reported to doctors; accepting one's fate; and making hard decisions when these had to be made. In other words it meant an active and competent compliance with medical staff. While some mothers, 'worriers', saw problems where there were none, and others tried to overcome the impossible, the ideal parent had a nice balance of involvement and detachment, subordination and concern. Here, for example, a therapist discusses the mother of a severely handicapped child:

TE: She's marvellous. The best of them all. She's ever so detached and yet ever so loving and she genuinely wants to know what's best for her child.

Whatever parents' actual qualities, however much they loved their children and cared for them in sensible and intelligent ways, the routine background questioning which was a central part of taking a history might well uncover other shameful matters that were never normally revealed. Some children were illegitimate and so, on occasion, were parents. Spouses might be separated or divorced, alcoholic or mad. Such matters were only rarely mentioned, but where they existed there was always the possibility of their discovery. Indeed, medical questioning might even reveal discrediting identities of which a parent was previously unaware. The following quotation is from the case of a boy with suspected epilepsy:

Dr I: And your husband? How old is he?
Mother: 25.
Dr I: And he's in good health?
Mother: Hmm.
Dr I: Now *he's* had some attacks, hasn't he?
Mother: Well, I don't really know. Not since we were married.
Dr I: Oh, Dr Martin (GP) mentions that he was in Benlogie Hospital (principally an institutional hospital for the retarded).
Mother: He was in for three years.
Dr I: You don't know what he was in there for, do you?
Mother: I don't know. He got himself into trouble. Stealing, I think it was.
Dr I: How old was he then, do you know?
Mother: About 16. He cane out when he was 19.
Dr I: When he was 19, yes. But you....
Mother: I thought he was in for trouble.
Dr I: Uh-huh. You didn't know then that he'd had some attacks?
Mother: No.
Dr I: He's had some blackouts. I think your husband will have told Dr Martin about them. (Mother looks blank.) What's your husband's work?
Mother: He's in the cleansing.
Dr I: He's in the Street Cleansing Department, is he? Uh-huh. Did you go to an ordinary school?
Mother: Yes, an ordinary school.

Thus no matter how technical the manner in which staff asked their questions and however much they abstained from comment, medical inquiry could always be read by parents as a check on their competence and good character. Even if staff denied that assessment was being done, this offered no real guarantee:

Dr I: Are you still pumping her valve?
Mother: Yes.

Dr I: How many times a day?
Mother: *You* told me ten times.
Dr I: I'm not trying to catch you out. (Mother laughs disbelievingly.)

Parents' awareness of the underlying nature of consultations was shown most clearly in their appearance. Children were scrubbed, shined and dressed in their smartest clothes,[2] as indeed were their representatives, who often wore their best suit for the occasion.

Of course, the display of moral worth extended beyond the matter of appropriate costume. Take the matter of compliance with medical advice. Some parents were quick to reveal their effort and motivation:

TG: Hello, and how's Peter?
Mother: Fine. Show Miss Carson your white patch. It proves you've been
          wearing it (she laughs).

A rather more subtle strategy can be found in another mother's comments when she arrived to collect her child from therapy. The mother was suspected by the therapist of cosseting the child and carrying her rather than making her walk:

Mother: Do you want a walk?
Child: Yes.
Mother: Thank Goodness!

Such displays of righteousness could be elicited by almost any question; for not only were staff engaged in covert moral judgment but the criteria which they used were necessarily unclear to parents. This was not simply a matter of this judgment being hidden, for the interweaving of the natural and the social was ambiguous in itself. Moreover, in a society with major ethnic, class, occupational and religious divisions, there are a variety of standards by which action may be judged, and the opinions of any one person cannot be known in advance. In the essentially middle-class setting of the hospital clinic, working-class parents were at a particular disadvantage. They were often unsure of the proper behaviour expected of a young child and controlled their offspring with considerable severity. Middle-class parents looked on in amused tolerance as their two-year-olds played on the floor or interrupted the doctor, but many working-class parents went red with embarrassment at such behaviour and were plainly worried how far it reflected on themselves. In addition to these other uncertainties, one must also note that parents have a great variety of responsibilities, many of which contradict each other. As regards their child they have to care for it but yet not spoil it and, apart from their child, they have many other duties. They have responsibilities towards their spouses, their own parents, their other children and towards themselves. Each of these may conflict in some way and it is always a matter of practical judgment as to which rule should prevail in any one instance.

As a result of all these ambiguities, parents could never know for certain just when they were being judged and whether or not they had passed. On one occasion or another any medical remark might bring forth a parental justification or display of moral concern:

Dr I: He still uses both hands?
Mother: He's left-handed. But I don't try to stop him being left-handed.
          I've left all my children to use whichever hand they want.

Dr F: And is she feeding herself with a spoon yet?
Mother: Well, I haven't had time for that yet.
Dr F: (to students) Well, they don't usually feed themselves at this
          stage.

Dr J: Well, she's been a model patient.
Mother: She hasn't been like this the last two or three times she's come.
          I was so ashamed of her.

Besides the considerable difficulties of managing young children, parents faced many other problems in fulfilling their duties towards staff. I have already discussed the conflict between, on the one hand, the twin rules of collegial authority and medical control and, on the other hand, parents' own right to reasonable criticism. Several other such conflicts must also be noted. Parents had a right, even a duty, to raise their worries about their child. But to do so was fraught with danger. Since most parents were ignorant they could not always know what would count as a proper medical problem worthy of staff's consideration. Moreover, since fears are an emotional as well as a rational matter and are known to be so, even medical training gave parents no guarantee that they were right. If there was in fact no problem, then the parents not only wasted the doctor's time but discredited themselves. They might, perhaps, be judged as silly, needless worriers. Even if they were correct they might still have done something wrong. The child might have a different problem from the one they thought it had, or else should have spotted it earlier, or handled it in a different way. In consequence, some parents prefaced their worries with apologies or made disclaimers afterwards:

> Dr B: And what can we do for you, Mrs Mitchell?
> Mother: Well, I may be daft but I think he's teething.
>
> Dr C decides that there is no problem.
> Mother: It's just these spots.... Other people notice it and.... (her voice trails off)
>
> Father: There is one thing. I don't know whether it's relevant or not, but Michael never moved as much before he was born as our earlier baby.
> Dr I: Well, some children just do move and others don't.
> Father: Well, it's probably stupid of me to bring this up but I just wondered.
> Dr I: Not at all.

More seriously, the possible embarrassment which such statements portray may have deterred many parents from raising those matters which troubled them most deeply. I have already noted the elaborate search procedures which were required to uncover certain parental doubts. Yet typically these were used only when staff were certain both that the parents were worried and also that there were no real grounds for such worry. In other words, for worries to be dealt with parents had normally to raise them themselves and, as we have just seen, there were several powerful deterrents to this.

I shall give just one example of the difficulties that this may have caused, that of chronic handicap. In many cases the precise cause of the condition was unknown. Quite why a child was spastic or retarded was usually uncertain, something which led to a good deal of parental speculation. In discussion with students and with the researchers doctors often mentioned this and the mistaken theories parents often produced. They had, it would seem, all kinds of worrying beliefs about causation, many of which centred round personal responsibility. One mother ascribed her child's condition to bumping into a lamp-post when pregnant, another to hanging curtains too near term. Yet these theories were only discussed if the parents themselves raised them, and this applied to a strictly limited number of cases. Most parents showed a marked reluctance to reveal such fears and, correspondingly, doctors seemed unwilling to explore them in any detail. No doctor made routine inquiries into these matters and even when the topic was raised, it was usually dealt with in a brisk, no-nonsense fashion that seemed unsuited to the possible agony and embarrassment that the issue might cause for parents.

The following instance brings out several of these features. Quite often the matter seemed so difficult to raise that it was fathers and not mothers who asked about it. Here, the question is asked even more indirectly:

Dr J: Well, all seems to be going fine. I'll see her again in a year's time.

Mother: She's very bright, it's as if she's tired, her hand ... (the child is spastic).

Dr J: Yes, more than her leg.

Mother: Yes, I think she will be all right ... (pause) Shona Brown is in Jane's nursery too and *her* mother blames herself for it.

Dr J: Does she come here?

Mother: Yes, she can't work out why this happened to her. They said something about her heartbeat being down in labour.

Dr J: Well, it's very often that we can't find a reason for these things.

Mother: It may have been that I knocked myself when I was seven months pregnant.

Dr J: I shouldn't think it would have been that.

Mother: Well, the cord was trapped.

Dr J: Yes, that's more likely. Hey, she's away with my bricks

Mother: Yes! (grabs child) And so we make an appointment for a year.

Dr J: Yes, for a year. That's fine. Bye.

Mother: Bye.

This mutual difficulty derived from a combination of factors. I have just noted the problem that these issues created for parents, while medical avoidance of the topic also seems based on matters treated earlier. The pressure of time meant that staff had every incentive to ignore anything that was not placed firmly on the agenda, while the exploration of these matters could seriously threaten the doctor's status. Where staff could say nothing with any certainty, their technical authority might well be placed in doubt. As one doctor admitted, 'You might as well ask a man in a fairground as me, we just don't know.'

Another source of embarrassment and potential judgment for parents lay in the distinctly positivist conception of a parent's duties that was embodied in medical interrogation. As can be seen from staff's treatment of parents with medical pretensions, the ideal parent did not theorize about what they had observed but merely reported 'the facts' and left the doctor to consider what these might mean. Parents who offered their own diagnoses created yet more work for doctors. Yet this ideal was quite unworkable in practice. As Bloor and Horobin (1975) have noted, many types of medical practice are based on the assumption that patients or their representatives possess the ability to diagnose that they have a medical problem. Yet, having used their skills and made the decision to seek advice, they are supposed to remain passive during the consultation, a situation that may often lead to conflict. Besides this, the positivist model is internally incoherent. To cite a previous quotation: 'The mother I think had observed them (fits) in the child but just hadn't noticed them.' In other words, since the mother lacked any proper criteria for investing medical significance in her child's behaviour, she was unable to report on it in any fashion relevant to the doctor's purposes. In other words, competent observation depended upon having an appropriate theory and this was something that most parents lacked. Even when parents attempted to stick to 'the facts', it quickly became evident that some facts, such as teething, on which they placed great significance were of no interest to staff, while other matters into which they had made no inquiry themselves were probed in great detail. Parents' inability to provide consistently accurate or relevant information was also indicated by doctors' recourse to competing sources of data such as the medical record or physical examination.

Telling a story in such circumstances could thus become most difficult for parents. The mere fact that a doctor asked a question might be seen as containing an implicit assumption that any competent mother could answer it. Moreover, just telling their story to an expert could shake any confidence that parents might have held in it, for it was necessarily constructed according to lay criteria, criteria of which they might only become aware when in the presence of experts. Even if staff made no comment on what was said, their mere presence might produce all kinds of doubts and modifications in the stories parents told. And if they asked about things that parents had not thought of or ignored matters that they had taken to be central, then any coherence of or confidence in their story could easily disappear. In the following instance the mother was reduced to long periods of silence:

Dr I: When did he have the first one?
Mother: He was three years old, about a year ago.
Dr I: What was it like?
Mother: His eyes roll up and he stares.
Dr I: Did he have a temperature?
Mother: Yes, and a sore throat. He went a bit rigid the second time. (She
         elaborates.)
Dr I: Can we stick to the first one?

Mother stops but then continues to describe a typical attack drawing on
various attacks he has had.

Dr I: I just want to know about the first one for the moment. (Mother
         stays silent.) Did he do anything else? (Mother stays silent.) Did
         he jerk or shake at all?
Mother: Yes, a bit.

Thus the idealized competence granted to mothers, the overt assumption
of their intelligence, rationality and reliability, was potentially undercut by
the most routine of medical practices. A request for elaboration or for
rephrasing, the asking of a question, or the examination of a file, all of these
carried with them a consistent threat to that pristine parental image that was
so central a part of the ceremonial order. Nor were these the only risks that
parents ran, for threats to their character and competence came, as we have
seen, from a wide variety of sources. Medical work was necessarily social and
thus moral work.

Audience Effects

A further systematic threat to clinic ceremony came from the presence in
most settings of an audience to the interaction between parents, child and
doctor. In my earlier discussion of this audience, I emphasized the variety of
procedures that were used to minimize its effect upon the consultation.
Students or other staff were typically placed to one side of the action, and
conversation with them was carefully controlled. Not only was the use of the
clinical format restricted but the version in which it appeared was sober and
sanitized. Nevertheless, despite these various attempts to moderate its

influence, the presence of an audience routinely altered the nature of consultations and undercut the idealized version of a private, confidential and uniquely focussed relationship. The presence of an audience gave the proceedings a very public air. The settings were not made for the easy revelation of matters of great intimacy. Staff did not assume a confidential manner, for it was plain that nothing was in confidence; anything that was said was available for discussion, if not now then later on. This lack of privacy was most marked in the large wards of the maternity hospital. As has been seen, the round had some of the aspects of a show, but this was a show not just for the individual mother and her child but for all the other mothers present in the ward, who watched the round's progress with some interest. A discussion between the doctor and one mother could set this other audience talking loudly amongst themselves:

Dr K: How do you manage to look so good? You've got a marvellous hairstyle.
Mother: (blushing) Well ... fairly....
Dr K: Have you done anyone else's hair while you've been here?
Mother: Oh, just one.
2nd Mother: She makes us all look like drudges.
3rd Mother: She must get up at 4 o'clock to do it.

Audiences did not normally talk amongst themselves or comment on the action, but their mere presence transformed the occasion. Teaching in particular had a striking force, regardless of whether any individual child was actually taught on in the presence of its parents. The importance of teaching in many of these settings was enshrined in their actual construction. Outpatient clinics were designed to accommodate particular types of teaching, and as teaching styles varied so too did their ecology. The 'amphitheatre' was built to enable patients to be treated as clinical material and had a stage, floodlights and banked seats for that purpose. Even where teaching was less overtly the dominant activity, its impact could still be reflected in the bricks and mortar of the setting. The suite of three rooms in the Scottish hospital clinics and the cubicle system in the American hospital both enabled teaching and clinical discussion to form a regular part of outpatient work. Even though they might say nothing, the audience on these occasions could be very large. Six or seven students sat in on some of the Scottish hospital clinics, while the numbers in the amphitheatre clinic could reach as many as thirty. On entering these settings, parents were immediately presented with a mass of faces, all watching them with interest. Indeed, in the amphitheatre they were quite literally on stage:

(Father, mother and child enter floodlit stage.)
Mother: (nervously) Hello.
Dr W: (sitting in front row) This is your first child, isn't it?

Dr W: And there weren't any other problems?
Mother: No, she's fine otherwise. It really floored us when we walked in to see all these people here.
Dr W: Uh-huh. OK. You can put her up on the couch. (Mother does so. Three doctors get up from their seats and go up on to the stage.)

Parents had normally no real choice as to the presence of an audience. In many settings they were there for each and every case. It is true that the objections made by one mother after a consultation in the Scottish neurological clinic led to the doctor banning students from that clinic, but this was the only mother whose criticism was mentioned by staff and even she did not object during the clinic itself. Since the hospital was a teaching hospital there was no possibility of banning students from more than one or two of the more specialist clinics. Although teaching while parents were present was typically limited, doctors did not normally seek permission for this except in the most serious cases.

There was in fact one setting, the maternity hospital ward-round, where requests and apologies of a kind were routinely made; but these were not phrased in such a manner as to permit ready refusal, as witness these quotations from the beginning, middle and end of a consultation in which the doctor supervised the standard examination of a newborn baby:

Dr K: Hello, Mrs Mackie. We've come to look at your baby. (To baby) Here's a big audience to look at you. (To mother) Do sit down, Mrs Mackie and you won't tire yourself. Don't worry, we'll move baby near you for the examination.

Dr K: (to student) You just do it and we'll comment on what you've missed. You won't mind, will you, because it's the only way to learn. (To mother) And you won't mind either, will you, because we've all got to get experience.

After the student has finished the examination and Dr K has commented on this:

> Dr K: (to mother) Your baby's super, Mrs Mackie. You don't mind putting up with all this, do you? And she's a very good little patient. (Mother smiles weakly, and looks exhausted.)

When teaching was done it took up an important part of the time allocated to the patients. For example, of the four special nursery follow-up clinics that were observed, two contained students and two did not. Cases in the latter clinics lasted between eight and ten minutes, whereas those where students were present lasted no more than five minutes. Where teaching was carried out in the presence of the child even less time was allocated directly to parents. Some staff summarized the history of a case after the parents had arrived and made occasional comments to students during it. On some occasions where parents were keen to stay and full of questions, doctors still ended the case rapidly, in order to address the students' questions instead.

The domination of the action by teaching was at its most extreme in the maternity hospital ward-round. Indeed, in some of these cases it would he more accurate to talk of the mother, and not the students, as constituting the audience.

Teaching had other effects besides these. Even where doctors never openly taught in front of patients and where the segregation of teaching and treating was apparently complete, the mere presence of a student audience could transform each case into teaching material. The action that apparently centred on the child and its parents had a dual role; the doctors were not simply doing diagnosis and treatment, they were also demonstrating how to do these tasks. Such demonstration was done by first telling students what to see in the interaction they were about to witness, and then enacting it in such a way as to make the lesson visible; a feat which enabled yet further teaching to be done on the case once it had been processed. Conversations that took place solely with parents might, in consequence, be thoroughly informed by the requirements of teaching. In some cases topics were inserted which were of relevance only to the students.

For example, Dr F used the cases in the special nursery follow-up clinic as a general resource to teach students about normal babies. Each case was used to illustrate one particular aspect of a normal baby, with the aim of building up a composite picture by the end of the clinic. Since there was no guarantee that the babies who turned up would match each of the aspects to be considered, the choice of a baby to illustrate any one feature was often arbitrary. In the following instance the doctor had been teaching about smiling prior to the baby's arrival. The baby was already known to be smiling but nevertheless, although the consultation lasted only four minutes, the doctor used the opportunity (a) to show how to check 'real' smiles; (b) to reveal the normal age at which babies smile; (c) to show how to produce a social smile:

Dr F:	Now, the last time we saw him I think he was smiling. Is he smiling? Really?
Grandmother:	Yes.
Dr F:	You're sure it's not wind?
Grandmother:	No.
Dr F:	He smiled at eight weeks, didn't he?
Grandmother:	Yes.
Dr F:	(to baby) Hello, hello. (Baby smiles. To students) You get easy social smiles. (To baby) Come on, give us a smile, give us a smile, give us a smile.... (To grandmother) And he laughs and chuckles, does he?
Grandmother:	Yes.

The imposition of such a rigid teaching format was found only when the doctor faced a similar kind of task in case after case, as in those settings where developmental assessment was routinely done. In other clinics doctors taught from whatever happened to turn up, from 'inside' a case, although still relating this to what they would normally expect to see. But however it was done the impact of teaching was considerable. This was particularly true of the American hospital's ambulatory clinics. The patients waiting in their cubicles were auxiliaries to a floating classroom, for right in the centre of the clinic the doctors, interns and residents had a private room from which they worked, taught and learned. For them, this was where the day's action centred and their interaction with parents was informed by the manners peculiar to that classroom:

> Mother: This kid has had everything done to her. (She describes various
>   tests and then mentions that her teeth were slow to come
>   through.)
> Dr O: Where did they do this?
> Mother: St Cyprian's.
> Dr O: Oh. (To resident) When the teeth are slow what's the first thing
>   you think of? (He smiles and waits.) Just like that! (He snaps his
>   fingers. Resident does not answer.) Hypothyroidism!

In such instances there was an important sense in which the parents, the child and the doctor were all on display for the benefit of others, a sense which might undercut the primary assumption that consultations were for the child's benefit. More subtly perhaps, the physical presence of such an audience could make it yet more difficult still for parents to discuss their child and its problems. To do so was hard enough, given their medical ignorance and their fear of seeming foolish, but such uncertainties were only compounded by a setting in which informed medical discussion was so patently an integral part. In any consultation parents ran the risk of being covertly judged, but where students or other staff were present such judgment was clearly a central part of the medical agenda, even if it was carried out in private.

Quite apart from the more subtle intrusions of the audience, not all attempts to subordinate and segregate this other action were in fact successful. Three particular difficulties may be noted: the technical problems of managing the same interaction for different audiences; the difficulties of physical segregation, and the problem of controlling equals. Doctors in fact might have three or even four separate audiences, each of whom had to be taken into account in some way. Students required one thing and mothers another, nurses might need instructions and researchers needed information. To do all these things simultaneously and to examine and treat the patient as well was not easy. For beginners, conversing with mothers might be difficult. One registrar who examined children on the maternity hospital ward-round not only took far longer to do the actual examination but also complained afterwards, 'I just don't know how to talk to mothers yet.' Even those who were practised in such situations might still omit to take all the members of their differing audiences into account simultaneously. Here, for instance, Dr F, in trying to combine both teaching and consulting, uses a series of terms such as 'unusual', 'damage' and 'surprise' which were never normally said to parents in such circumstances:

Dr F: How old was he then?

Mother: Five months ... (pause) ... Oh, they both had chicken-pox.

Dr F: Really! That's very unusual.

Mother: My oldest son brought it home from school. I had four of them with it at the same time and associated with it they had an irritating dry cough which he's had ever since.

Dr F: Yes, chicken-pox can cause a bit of lung damage at the time. That's not a surprise. As you know, chicken-pox is normally mild.

Mother: Yes.

Apart from these technical problems, physical segregation could sometimes be problematic. Even where clinics were relatively private, as in the Scottish settings, doors were sometimes left ajar, and in the maternity hospital privacy was very hard to find. Mothers were to be found in the corridors as well as in the beds, and Dr K urged the students to caution, reminding them that 'even the walls have ears in the Matty'. The American clinics faced the greatest problems here. The cubicles in which parents sat were windowless and too small for the door to remain shut for long, while the room from which staff worked had no door at all. In consequence some consultations took place with the door open, while the supposedly private talk of staff in the corridor and operations room could sometimes be overheard in the cubicles.

Finally, it should be noted that not all doctors actually wished to subordinate all other action to that with the parents, while in some instances other staff would not let them. On several occasions when staff of some equivalence to the doctor sat in on a clinic they assumed rights to intervene and discuss that were never granted to students or nurses. More generally, in the American amphitheatre clinics and in one of the Scottish hospital clinics, patient and parents, though still perhaps *primus inter pares* constituted only a part of the agenda under consideration.[3] Other staff and nurses might discuss things among themselves, if quietly, and, in line with this greater prominence of the clinical format, the atmosphere in the clinic was both technical and informal; jokes were made, journals cited and gossip exchanged. This point should not be over-emphasized. The backstage medicine that was revealed was still a selective version of the medical world. Nevertheless, it was different from that which was normally revealed, as witness the following quotation from a Scottish clinic. In this consultation the doctor had spent ten minutes talking to parents about their child's retardation, explaining that he felt it most unlikely that their child would attend a normal school. All of a sudden he noticed a registrar hovering in the background:

> Dr H: (to registrar) Sorry, you've been waiting while I've been chattering. (Registrar hands Dr H an X-ray.) It's still a bit spotty; could they come back in six weeks' time, it could mean cystic fibrosis. Sorry, I didn't see you coming in. Have you been there long? I am sorry, help yourself to another patient because this really requires a bit of explanation.

Medical Incapacity

In considering the divorce between the rhetoric of the bureaucratic format and what was in fact on offer, some attention must be paid to medical incapacity. Unlike the tensions discussed so far, this was not a universal difficulty, for many medical problems were solved. Nevertheless, some conditions were difficult to cure or ameliorate, and in others there was no cure at all. Some of the special difficulties that this failure created have already been discussed, but a more general point remains to be considered. I have noted the way in which our culture divides the world into natural and social spheres. On this analysis medical incapacity, so long as it is not simply a matter of personal incompetence, and so long as there are no other more viable methods, cannot strictly be judged in moral terms. Medicine may have failed but it is more a case of Nature defeating Man than of personal or professional dereliction. Children are not artificial products for whom we can hold the manufacturers or the mechanics responsible when they go wrong.

Nevertheless, there are senses in which it seems legitimate to talk of moral failure, even when there is no question of a merely personal inadequacy. Take, for example, the following comment, which followed a consultation in which a mother had denounced the medical service and praised the Doman-Delcato method:

> Dr I: As she says, we stand indicted. We haven't been able to do anything

for her here. We just see her every three months and say, 'How are things?' 'Oh, much the same,' she says. And I say, 'Right, I'll see you next time.'

Similarly Dr I confessed to another mother, as he broke the news of her child's severe retardation, 'I feel such a fraud.' To feel fraudulent or stand indicted is to accept the validity of moral judgment in these cases, and such opinion seems related to a basic belief about science which permeates our culture. In this, the constraints of the natural sphere are acknowledged but it is also held that, through the application of human thought and experiment, the natural will become known and socialized. On this analysis, all phenomena both should and will become subject to human intervention and modification. Scientific medicine has been amongst the most striking examples of this plan of investigation and alteration, and its sales pitch is based upon its increasing ability to intervene within the natural on its customers' behalf. Where striking advances had been made both doctor and parent could rejoice in its success:

Dr F: (to researcher) This baby was very ill at birth. She was nine weeks early and had very severe hyaline membrane infection. We had to put her on the ventilator. She was pretty ill in every respect. Now she's fine in every respect. (Grinning at baby) You're lucky you weren't born twenty years earlier, my girl.

Mother: (laughing) Otherwise, you'd be dead.

Dr F: (as mother gets up to leave) A triumph of modern medicine.

Given these human hopes in the progress and capacity of medicine, problems for which there were no solutions could undermine its credibility. All that parents could be offered was that 'one day' medicine might have the answer, but such consolation was of little use to parents whose children had such problems now.[4] This failure to meet the implicit claims of high-technology medicine resulted in, or was compounded by, a series of other features, all of which might reinforce a sense of defeat and thus threaten the overall meaning of the consultation. If established medicine had no ready answers this left the field open to its competitors, to parental pressure groups such as that for autism or to non-establishment medicine like the Doman-Delcato method. Just as parents might feel cheated when medicine could do little, so staff could find working with such cases an equally depressing experience. It was pleasant to administer triumphs, less so to admit failure. Here in a quotation from fieldnotes a doctor is talking enthusiastically about success:

> Dr McIntosh said that he had worked 32 hours that weekend but it was worth it because he liked to see the results. He'd had two meningitis cases and had also been involved in saving a baby's life. He had worked out what was wrong when it came into casualty and had managed to get treatment underway immediately. Areas of medicine where you couldn't get good results, for example, geriatrics, handicap and psychiatry, didn't interest him very much.

Thus in chronic conditions such as handicap the criteria of success had to be totally altered from those that prevailed elsewhere. Others have noted how parents alter their time-scale and look for small rewards (Voysey, 1975). A similar process was essential for medical staff if they were to gain any satisfaction from handling such cases:

> Dr J: There's a tendency to think of chronic handicap as the least interesting aspect (of paediatrics) because the rewards are so small and because there's a general feeling that you can't do much anyway.... I like to feel that I'm achieving something and it's less easy to feel that in this sort of clinic. What I have learnt is that, if you look for small gains, and that if your expectations are realistic, small gains can be as rewarding as major cures in general paediatrics.

Such redefinition might prove difficult, as might the other strategy in which staff engaged, that of switching from a therapeutic to a managerial role. The rationale here was that, even if cures could not be provided, at least some other form of help might be given. But although paediatricians might broaden their remit, they lacked control over non-medical resources. They themselves were not responsible for assessing whether a child should go to a normal school, nor had they any real say over access to nursery places, to special schools or to special institutional care. They had no authority to provide special housing or to find money for special clothes, furniture or toys. Yet such matters might be of far more practical importance than the little that they themselves could offer. Doctors might take it upon themselves to inquire about all these wider things and to contact the relevant authorities, but they were distant from the real sources of power.

Even the limited things that medicine itself had to offer could still place extreme burdens on some parents. Certain chronic medical conditions demanded continual parental care, special therapy by parents, and regular attendance at several different outpatient clinics; very often for no great reward. As such, medical services might be both overwhelming and fundamentally disappointing, as one doctor remarked when discussing severe cerebral palsy:

> Dr I: Orthodox medicine hasn't got very much to offer apart from physiotherapy to those parents who want something to do. In fact, there's a greater variety of parents of handicapped children than there is of handicap. Large numbers of parents won't do anything, they won't even bring the child up to the hospital. Either they can't get it organized or they're just not able to do this. Very often it's a single-parent family or if it is two parents they're both at work and it's just too difficult to arrange. For them orthodox medicine provides almost too much, and yet for Mrs Miller it doesn't provide enough.... Now she's doing so much that she's almost harming herself. She's searching for more and more to do, and a lot of medicine is just palliative.

Finally, in considering the strains that medical incapacity posed for the ceremonial order of the clinic, some mention should be made of those problems to which there were certainly technical solutions but which could present major practical difficulties in their implementation. Several of these have already been discussed. There were, for example, the unwillingness to investigate parental theories of aetiology, and the discrepancy between the implicit assumption of a more personal relationship and the anonymity of medical work in large bureaucracies. And things might not even get this far. The very offer of help might well be rejected by parents, since to accept it was to define their child as handicapped.

To these difficulties one more should be added. I have already discussed the complex way in which bad news was broken. Looked at from another angle this could also be seen, not as a search for agreement as I described it earlier, but as a lack of frankness. For doctors displayed no such qualms in less serious cases. In his intensive study of 14 children with poliomyelitis, Davis (1963) argued that, in the less severe cases, medical staff revealed far more at a much earlier date. This finding was confirmed across the whole range of cases and clinics in this present study. Just as doctors used dramatic language only for trivial complaints such as septic spots, so too they were immediately frank about the less severe problems which they encountered. Here for instance a doctor discusses a urinary infection that he has just diagnosed:

> Dr G: Now these urinary infections in little girls are quite difficult to get rid of. There's nothing serious usually but it's worthwhile checking up that there's nothing wrong with her kidneys, and that means doing an X-ray and we'll also get a sample of urine sent off to see if it's infected. The best thing is to arrange for her to have an X-ray and I'll see you again in a month's time. If something is wrong then we need to do something about it. If there's not anything wrong then we'll still need her to attend to see what's going on. I might have to see her repeatedly. The treatment might take as long as six months. I'm afraid there's no easy way around this. We need to stop it now. There's no easy answer provided by clinical medicine but it's best to do it now so that it stops recurring.

Similarly, here is how a doctor broke the news in a case of relatively mild cerebral palsy. Again this was the child's first visit to the hospital and, unlike the more serious cases considered earlier, the future was spelt out very directly:

> Dr I: She does walk but her walking is never going to be, um, well, perfect. She'll always be adequate on her feet but I don't think she'll ever be able to walk long distances.
> (Mother looks upset and goes very red.)

Despite this crucial difference in the extent to which doctors revealed information, it should be noted that even in the less serious cases staff were not completely open with parents. Not only did they conceal the inner workings of medicine but, since the future was always unclear and many conditions were no more than remote statistical possibilities, they routinely suppressed any marginal doubts that they might have about a child. Indeed, this bowdlerization was practised even where staff were legally obliged to be frank. The consultants in the Scottish hospital were required to assess all children being considered for adoption and to produce a detailed medical report for the benefit of the social work department, the magistrates and the prospective parents. Yet here too they concealed certain doubts where they felt it to be necessary:

> Dr G: (speaking to the adopting mother and social worker, after filling out a form for the magistrates) ... I certainly think everything's all right.... I can't find any abnormalities so it'll be through by the end of January.

> Dr G: (afterwards) ... That was a difficult one. I'd have been happier if she'd reacted to the rattle and happier if she'd lifted her head up earlier. She did it in the end but I felt she could have done it earlier. One has also got to take into account that she is an Indian baby, they might be slower to develop. Negroes, of course, are faster. One has also got to take into account the reason why she's adopting this baby. She may be one of those people who have a thing about underprivileged children. I would like to see her again in two or three months' time perhaps but, as she seems to be so set on this thing, I won't implant the doubt in her mind. But she seemed a pretty lively thing.

This general difficulty in being frank constituted the last of those tensions which systematically informed any and every medical consultation. However trivial the condition there was always the possibility that the doctor was not being completely open in what he or she said about it, a possibility that was strengthened by the brevity with which these matters were normally considered. Such strain was kept well below the surface on most occasions, and was only visible in the more serious cases where parents too found their doubts hard to discuss and the relevant questions difficult to put. 'Will she ever grow out of it?' 'Will he catch up?' 'Will she ever walk?' - all these were usually asked in a manner quite different from other kinds of inquiry. They were said with embarrassment or with defiance, mumbled or barked and generally treated as awkward, both for themselves and for doctors.

Easy Alliances

In considering the sources of ease and tension within the bureaucratic format, I began with the latter since these were systematic features of any medical consultation. There was, in other words, the permanent possibility of a serious disjunction between the ceremony and the substance of such occasions. Staff were constrained both to investigate their clients' competence and morality and to preserve their good name. Likewise, parents were obliged both to reveal their doubts and problems and to ensure that they did not waste staff's time or challenge their authority.

In consequence, for the alliance to be of any ease, somewhat special conditions were required. The fewest difficulties occurred where there was no medical problem and no expectation of one on either side. Routine developmental screening in the local authority and city clinics was typically a pleasant, humorous affair where mothers and doctors joined in mutual admiration of the young child (Davis and Strong, 1976b). Overtly, the medical interaction served as merely an occasion for such activity. Wonderment and joy were legitimately displayed even prior to medical inspection, and tests were simply tricks which enabled a child to display its virtuosity.

In more standard forms of consultation where there was a medical problem of some kind, it obviously helped if the condition was trivial or easily cured. Moreover, the less reliance that staff needed to place upon the parents, either for information or for care, then the easier their relationship could become. There was one important exception to this rule for, in the right circumstances, medical dependence upon parents might lead to an extremely close alliance. Such conditions were found in some cases involving drug therapy and in some of the milder cases treated by the occupational and physiotherapy departments. Here parents might be given an important but relatively simple part to play, something which was their own and which depended on their motivation and skill but which stood a good chance of success. In such cases, it was common for staff not merely to treat parents as allies but to formulate them as such. Here is an example from a Scottish general medical clinic where the child is suffering from encopresis:

Dr H: So we're well on the way to winning but we've not found the
          right adjustment yet.
Mother: As I say, I've been giving him 20ml a day but that turned out to
          be too much.

Dr H: Too much?

Mother: Yes, it was like dirty water. We gave it a try but it wasn't any good....

Dr H: Well, I feel we've reached the stage where you're almost the doctor and I'm just watching what you're doing.

And here is another from physiotherapy:

Therapist   Well, I think the reason she's come on so far by herself is
    A: just due to you doing this sort of thing with her. I think
            that's what's done it. That's what's brought her on this far.

Mother: Well, I've learnt a lot already.

In replying in this modest fashion the mother paid due deference to the alliance and recognized her subordinate relationship within it. Here then was a nice allocation of praise by both parties. In more serious cases where doctors could do little, an easy alliance depended on parents' open acceptance both of the facts of the case and of medical limitations. Even the most 'sensible' parents took time to adjust. When they did so alliances of some ease could on occasion be managed; doctors might compliment a child without any danger of such praise being taken as a warrant of the child's normality, and parents might criticize the service without staff taking this as any personal challenge.[5]

It must be emphasized that many apparently easy relationships rested on a distinctly shaky base. Their surface smoothness and even celebration was premised on the avoidance of some important matters and parental ignorance as to others. Here for example is a brief description of a close alliance during one consultation with Dr I. The patient was a nine-year-old girl with epilepsy:

1   When the parents arrived in the clinic the doctor asked the mother if she would mind summarizing her daughter's medical history for the benefit of the students present, a task that doctors normally reserved for themselves.

2   Later the mother introduced the topic of a book on epilepsy that the doctor had recommended. She talked about this enthusiastically and the doctor joined her in this, adding his own comments.

3 Unlike most mothers, this one let her daughter speak at length in answer to the doctor's questions and, when she herself discussed her child with the doctor, she continually looked towards her daughter to check the accuracy of her remarks.
4 After hearing how the child had fared since her last visit, the doctor presented future management as something to be jointly decided upon - 'I'm not sure but I feel inclined to let it go for a bit' (i.e. to continue without medication) - 'How do you feel about this?'

Epilepsy was a condition in whose management parents had a major role to play. They monitored the child's progress and were responsible for seeing that drugs were taken daily. There were, however, additional unspoken grounds for the alliance to be so strongly expressed here. The girl had been very seriously ill after a previous drug treatment and the doctor had every incentive to share responsibility for managing the condition with the parents. Further, although the mother did most of the talking, her husband was also present. He only came occasionally but it was he who always asked the awkward questions, in this case 'Will she ever grow out of it?' Such a division of labour enabled the wife to play the part of loyal ally and safeguarded her future relations with the doctor. No detailed reply was actually given to the father's question. The doctors suspected that the attacks might turn out to be temporal lobe epilepsy and possibly permanent, but there was no clear way of knowing until the child reached adolescence. Thus, as Dr J commented after a visit from them nearly two years later:

> Dr J: They're not worrying nearly enough about the future ... but you can't really tell them off otherwise they won't tell you the truth and it's very, very important to get at the truth. It's very difficult to know how to play such cases.

The nurse entered the room and said she had just heard the parents telling the girl how nice the doctor was.

Professional Mothers

In summary, although there were circumstances in which alliances could be made with some ease the possibility of tension was always there. In fact the only sorts of mothers with whom staff routinely had an easy alliance, almost regardless of the circumstances of the case, were not natural mothers at all but foster-mothers. Foster-mothers were the ideal client precisely because they were not parents, but colleagues and junior colleagues at that.

In all, 17 foster-mothers were observed in a total of 26 consultations.[6] Those patients who were in the care of these foster-mothers were mostly babies, and only six children were seen, their ages ranging from between two and eight. Most fostered babies were quickly adopted and, whatever the reason for their attendance, their fitness for adoption was a central theme in most settings, even if this was not always openly discussed.

When compared with natural mothers, foster-mothers had several distinct advantages as medical allies. Whereas parents were only supposed to be competent and caring, these qualities could normally be assumed in foster-mothers. Indeed they were essential qualifications for the job and as such implicitly guaranteed by their employers. This is not to say that doctors placed immediate trust in foster-mothers, and it was common for them to begin by checking the number of children that the mother had fostered. But once a certain level of experience had been established all could proceed with relative ease, for immediate weight could be given to what they said. Here is an excerpt from the beginning of a case in the neurological clinic:

Dr J: You have children of your own?
Foster-mother: Yes, one, and I've had nine foster-children.
Dr J: Ah, well, your opinion is worth its weight in gold.

Similarly a foster-mother's visit to a clinic where students were present was often an occasion for stressing that one must pay careful attention to what they said:

Dr G: ... I thought he was a little slow. His head was falling back a little early. I asked the foster-mother - they must be very experienced women who've had a lot of babies, one gets very acute answers from them - I asked her what she thought. He was a little slower than others she'd had, which is a very significant thing. So the adoption was postponed.

Doctors relied on foster-mothers in this way, not just because they were experienced but also because they were emotionally detached. Indeed, for the job to stay a job they had to remain so. As one foster-mother said at the end of a session:

> I hope it's quick (the adoption). I told the social worker that I wanted it to be as quick as possible, as I'm getting far too attached to her. I hope it's done within a month.

Because of their normal emotional distance, foster-mothers could discuss their charges in quite distinctive ways. On the one hand their lack of long-term commitment to the children meant that they could display a very open affection towards them, or at least towards the babies, all of whom received far more overt affection than was normally given by natural mothers. With natural mothers, such display could be read as evidence of an overwhelming attachment which might render technical discussion of the child's condition problematic; but not with foster-mothers. On the contrary, doctors felt able to use a clinical format in their presence, treating them as they did their other professional colleagues. Where they had worries about a child, both doctor and foster-mother could speak about them freely and in very similar terms. Thus great affection could be readily combined with a much greater emotional distance than was usual. Medical problems were not potential tragedies for either party, merely unfortunate things about which one might be worried or even upset, but only in a professional kind of way. Doctors' incapacity in some cases was of no great personal consequence and, since the child was not the foster-mother's ultimate responsibility, a serious condition threatened no major blight upon her life. Since she was not the child's actual mother she could not normally blame herself for its condition.

In such circumstances the impersonal bureaucratic setting of the consultations was a source of far less tension. The infrequency of visits to hospital clinics, the brief time available for each to be accomplished, the gap in formal education and social class that was often present, the formal agenda and formal surroundings and the obtrusive nature of official records and recording: each of these features could increase the distance between doctor and parent. Yet with foster-mothers such bureaucratic arrangements were a part of and might even enhance their status. The foster-mother was a professional herself and her responsibility towards the child was arranged on a bureaucratic basis. To be treated in a formal manner was simply part of the job. Since doctors commonly treated them with great respect and often deferred to their experience and expertise, their visits to the clinic could be a professionally rewarding experience.[7] Bureaucratic arrangements were best suited to those who were themselves at least partly bureaucrats.

At the same time, although foster-mothers were in a sense the doctor's colleagues they did not represent the independent and competitive threat to medical authority that was typical of some discussion in the clinical format. Their knowledge, though extensive, was derived from experience rather than professional training and as such they were clearly subordinate to medical staff. On no occasion did a foster-mother challenge a doctor and, although some emphasized their individual agreement with doctors' observations, none placed any stress on the distinctive quality of their own judgment or claimed any special rights in their children.

Their behaviour therefore contrasts strongly both with that of natural mothers and with that of some other professionals who accompanied children on occasion. This latter group of social workers and house-mothers shared the foster-mothers' professional detachment but most of them lacked their detailed knowledge of the particular child, while, as was seen in the case of the social worker who accompanied the mentally retarded mother, some of them posed a distinct threat to the doctor's own authority. Social workers did not define themselves as subordinates but as equals and claimed their own special competences and rights in the child, claims that were not made by foster-mothers.[8] Given the subordinate but insider status of the latter, doctors could relax more freely with them. Indeed, whereas no doctor ever criticized another doctor to a natural mother or to a social worker, one general practitioner received heavy criticism when the child was represented by a foster-mother.

Given these features, and the additional fact that foster-mothers were a scarce and valuable resource and thus to be encouraged, such consultations were not only easy affairs but they took on a different form from those found with natural mothers. As competent but junior professionals, foster-mothers did not so much raise problems with doctors as make semi-formal reports on their observations. Consultations were typically straight to the point. Doctors asked immediately what they had observed and foster-mothers replied in a careful and detached manner. Several of these points, the status of foster-mothers' evidence, the manner in which they reported rather than simply spoke, and their considerable emotional detachment are revealed in the following two quotations from the beginning and end of a consultation. Here we may see a clinical rather than a bureaucratic format:

Dr G:	Hello.
FM/SW:	Hello.
Dr G:	Now, how long have you been fostering him for?
FM:	Yes, six weeks.
Dr G:	Since a few days after he was born, isn't it?
FM:	Yes. I noticed he was a bit slow.
Dr G:	In what way?
FM:	Well, he was a bit wobbly, a bit slow to smile and his balance is bad.
Dr G:	And is he smiling now?
FM:	Yes.
Dr G:	Of course, it is normal to be wobbly at this age.
FM:	Yes, it is.
Dr G:	Well, there are just one or two things. There's an annoying little heart murmur. There's also his posture; he was a little bit floppy when I held him up.
SW:	Yes.
Dr G:	I'd be a little uneasy about that, but then someone has to be below average, and what do you do about it?
SW:	Well, we'll let Mrs Miller (foster-mother) keep him (for the time being).
FM:	Yes, I'd like to keep him. I'm not happy about it.
Dr G:	No, I'm not either.

The relative ease with which consultations with foster-mothers were conducted emphasizes yet again the many tensions that underlay paediatric consultations with parents. Of course not every consultation was a tense occasion and some clinics were relaxed, even jolly, affairs. But, as we have seen, doctor-parent interaction was often a most complex matter. Discussion was circuitous and guarded, words had to be carefully chosen, messages must be indirect. Even the easy alliances had to be made with care and, although one might still stand on ceremony, the somewhat rickety structure beneath one's feet did shake alarmingly from time to time.

8 Conclusions and Generalizations

A fairly standard and not unreasonable response to a detailed sociological description of some small segment of the world is 'so what?' Description can become an end in itself and, in so far as there is any pleasure in the rigours of analysis and writing, most of the joy comes from making one small piece fit with another and tidying up all the loose ends. (In this respect ethnography has a good deal in common with housework.) These obsessions are rarely shared by readers, who are more concerned with the point of the whole enterprise. And here the analyst is faced with a problem, for the conclusions which may be drawn from a description such as this are at many different levels, while the evidence for much of what one wants to say is strictly limited, case studies not lending themselves too well to the sociological urge to explain the world in a swift paragraph.

This final chapter has therefore a rather jumbled and somewhat tentative character, for in it I shall essay a considerable variety of rather difficult tasks: a reconsideration of Goffman's work on frames; a suggestion as to the extent to which the bureaucratic format is in general medical use; a hypothesis as to its origins; and finally some discussion of its possible drawbacks. Here then is a wide range of topics about which I can only offer suggestions rather than draw definite conclusions. Nevertheless, to make the whole thing readable I shall often abandon caution, in so far as this is compatible with a modicum of academic respectability.

I shall begin with some comments on Goffman, though once again the non-sociologist may prefer to pass rapidly on to the next section.

Frame Analysis

In introducing the concept of role format I spent a little time in considering Goffman's own approach to the analysis of interaction. Having analysed one particular role format in some detail, as well as reflecting on some of its rivals, we may now go back to Goffman's work and see if we have learnt any general lessons about frame analysis.

183

Before we do this it may be useful to summarize Goffman's interests in this area. The first point to note is that although Goffman's approach to interaction is fundamentally structural he has in fact devoted relatively little attention to the analysis of particular frames. While Gonos (1977) is therefore right in describing frames as the basis of Goffman's vision, and indeed his analysis is a valuable corrective to many previous interpretations, his article is misleading if it is taken as a guide to what Goffman actually does.

To write such a guide is a most tricky enterprise but, in essence, Goffman's interest in frames themselves has been restricted to the following four areas: first, to the general procedures by which *any* frame is established;[1] second, to the ways in which a frame may serve as an original against which copies or transformations of various kinds can be made, such as jokes, dreams, deceptions, experiments, rehearsals, demonstrations and plays (Goffman, 1975a); third, to an emphasis that frames represent a moral as well as a cognitive order; and finally, to the delineation of certain very broad classes of frame, like those distinctions between natural and social frames, focussed and unfocussed interaction that were considered in chapter 1.

This is in itself a formidable body of work. However, it must be noted that Goffman's method for studying frames is quite different from the one that I have used here. His work is largely of the essay form, and is typically based, not on the detailed observation and recording of particular frames, but on the consideration of a huge variety of different frames studied through close attention to the materials of his daily life and through very wide reading. Conventional fieldwork has played a part in all this but only a part, for one of Goffman's basic aims has been to produce a series of very basic propositions which relate to all frames, universal generalizations which hold true regardless of time and place; and for this project what is most needed are first, a wide range of comparative materials and second, illustrations which have an unusually dramatic power - frames which have the capacity to illuminate the workings of all others.

It is this latter concern which explains why games and the theatre are the only two areas where Goffman has studied particular frames in any detail, for these serve as 'natural metaphors' (Garfinkel, 1956a) to reveal the way in which all activities are framed. Their very artificiality, the fact that they are consciously framed in a way in which other activities are not, can help us to grasp the framing of more conventional matters.

The scope of Goffman's vision and his powerful use of metaphor have added greatly to sociology. However, it must be noted that, since the only distinctions he makes between frames are at very high levels of abstraction, he has nothing to say about many of the particular frames in which sociologists and others have major substantive interests. This is not to deny the great value of Goffman's classifications, merely to observe that his concerns, as he himself notes, are somewhat special. Moreover, Goffman has another set of interests which are in many ways as important as, or more important than his concern with the frames themselves and which explain the peculiar elusiveness of his work, touching on frames at one moment only to dart away the next.

For Goffman, perhaps, the principal interest in frames lies, not in their particular contents, nor in their origins, nor indeed in their specific links with the wider world of which they are a part, but in the relationship of persons to frames. This concern is well stated in the introduction to 'Interaction Ritual' (1972), though here he picks out only one aspect of his interest in individuals and reality-construction:

> I assume that the proper study of interaction is not the individual and his psychology, but rather the syntactical relations among the acts of different persons mutually present to one another. Nonetheless since it is individual actors who contribute the ultimate material, it will always be reasonable to ask what general properties they must have if this sort of contribution is to be expected of them. What minimal model of the actor is needed if we are to wind him up, stick him in amongst his fellows and have an orderly type of traffic emerge.... Not then men and their moments. Rather moments and their men (Goffman, 1972, pp.2-3).

Two things should be noted about this statement, apart that is from its elegant phrasing. First, that what Goffman defines as the proper area of study for the student of interaction, 'the syntactical relations among the acts of different persons mutually present to one another', is not in fact a field which he himself has entered, save in passing, for to do so requires an interest in particular acts, identities and frames.

The second point is that this quotation highlights only one aspect of Goffman's interest in individuals. In the version presented here, people are mere creatures of frames, and what we normally conceive of as a person is reduced to a set of devices for the re-creation and careful maintenance of pre-existing and super-ordinate frames.[2] At the same time as offering us this insightful but highly alienated vision of ourselves, Goffman provides us with a quite separate model; one that emphasizes the margins of freedom that allow the individual some space for his or her own interests, identity and purposes.

Rather than being mere puppets, individuals, on this other version, are shown to manipulate frames to their own advantage (Goffman, 1971a), to make elaborate copies and parodies of more serious frames (1975a), and to distance themselves from frames even while acting within them.[3] Indeed there is a strong moral emphasis in much of Goffman's work and an anger at the way in which certain disadvantaged individuals are treated as if they were no more than the frame, or identity inside that frame, within which others have encapsulated them (Goffman, 1968a, 1968b).

If these are Goffman's principal interests, much of the task of frame analysis still remains to be done, though it must be emphasized that what remains is in many ways the easier and more conventional work. Despite this, something may be gained from it, and in the next few pages I shall attempt both some amendments and some additions to the general model and suggest some propositions about particular kinds of frame.

My first point concerns the extent to which individuals are trapped within particular frames. As we have seen, Goffman has gone to great lengths to establish the various subtle ways in which people detach themselves from frames and use them to their own purposes. This argument is clearly supported by the data presented here. Parents who disagreed with doctors would subtly alter their demeanour. Similarly, despite the overt ban on moral investigation, doctors could nevertheless still carry out complex re-constitutive work. At the same time we have also seen that the extent and manner in which they could do this were severely constrained. Goffman is aware that such constraints exist but his very concern to establish that there is a margin of freedom here may well mislead. There is perhaps in his work an over-emphasis on the more playful and free side of interaction. Certainly studies such as *Asylums* (1968a) and *Stigma* (1968b) cannot be viewed in this light, but these treat of special situations and identities, whereas in the more general discussions of the relationships of persons to frames there is a tendency to see distance as always available, parody and joking as a constant resource.

A good example of this tendency can be found in his study of surgical team work (Goffman, 1961).[4] Here Goffman explicitly treats the activity as a test-case, as a situation in which above all we would expect to find a total commitment to the role and thus a complete identification with and control by the frame:

Here, if anywhere in our society, we should find performances flushed with a feeling of the weight and dignity of their action. A Hollywood ideal is involved .... If the role perspective works, then, surely it works here, for in our society the surgeon, if anyone, is allowed and obliged to put himself into his work and get a self out of it (Goffman, 1961, p.116).

What in fact Goffman found there was a good deal of joking and by-play; surgery was often conducted in a far from serious manner. But to conclude from this that such major role distance is a standard feature of frames is surely mistaken, for there is no good reason to see this as a test-case; indeed one might argue, following Goffman's own work elsewhere (1971a), that it is precisely in a back-stage area such as surgery that one would expect to find large amounts of fun. The frame used in surgery is another instance of the clinical format, a format which in this study was often characterized by a high degree of joking and distance, at least where it was used away from patients. (One good example of this is the American case conference which I cited at some length earlier on.)

By contrast, the bureaucratic format was a highly serious affair. This is not to say that no joking ever occurred - certain matters were indeed routinely laughed about, for children were agreed to be an endless source of amusement. But more fundamental things were treated with considerable gravity. The doctor's competence and authority were no laughing matter, nor indeed was the child's illness. Only one mother tried to laugh off inquiries about her child's condition and make fun of the doctor's remarks, and she was quickly humiliated by the simple, serious repetition of the questions. It was certainly possible to parody the frame on occasion or to distance oneself from it, but the matters at stake were too serious to allow for much leeway. Parents might show a little non-verbal dissent but no more. The mother who refused to play the ideal character ascribed to her was investigated by social workers. Similarly, a doctor might lightly parody his trade - 'a miracle of modern medicine' - but only when an apparent miracle had in fact occurred. Outside this context such a remark might constitute a serious breach of frame, a sign that the doctor's attitude was not all it might be.

In other words, although some distance was permitted on occasion there were clear and important limits. Goffman (1976b) has emphasized the 'dance' of interaction, the movement to and from the frame; it is equally important to note that there are usually clear rules on both the amount and type of dancing and that there are many circumstances in which no more than a brief and stately minuet is permitted. Moreover, even though he takes care to emphasize the way in which role distance may in fact serve the ultimate end of the activity system (1961), Goffman still tends to write as if playing with frames or formats was somehow separate from the frames, whereas I would see such acts as governed by rules that are themselves part of the form. Each format then contains within it guides for respectable transformations and transgressions.

My second point concerns what Goffman has termed the 'syntactical relations' among the acts of individuals in encounters. As I have argued, since he has not studied the grammar of particular relationships he has left the area almost untouched. Clearly a large number of case-studies of different relationships would be required before one could map out these things with any accuracy. However, even with one study such as this, it does seem possible to make a start on compiling a list of what the basic elements in such a syntax would look like. (For a related attempt at systematization, though in a slightly different area, see Lofland, 1976.) That is, it seems likely that there are a restricted number of components out of which all role formats are constructed. I cannot make any claims to comprehensiveness, but the following six seemed crucial in the formats I have considered. Each could vary independently of the others, and their particular combinations underlay the special nature of both individual formats and particular encounters.

1 The right to criticize: this may be allocated to one, some, all or none of the participants. In the bureaucratic and private formats it was the right of the parents; in the charity format this prerogative belonged to the doctor.

2 Where criticism is allowed, is character-work permitted and if so of what type, ameliorative or reconstitutive? (Reconstitutive character-work seems to carry a much greater risk of challenges to the frame and is therefore normally restricted to particular identities and to highly formalized settings - at least as between strangers.)

3 Who, if anyone, has rights to the overall control of the interaction? (The central dimensions of power here seem, at least in this study, to be: the range of legitimate objects of involvement for each participant; who controls the setting, if anyone; who controls the timing, sequencing and agenda, if anyone; who chooses the frame, if anyone; within any one frame, who has rights to choose identities both for themselves and for others; who can authoritatively formulate what is

going on; who controls the criteria for admission to membership within the frame; who can modify which rules.)

4   How far are topics, speaking-rights, etc. pre-allocated? (For instance, it was normally doctors who asked the questions and parents who did the answering, but such rights are not an automatic indicator of control, for on some occasions doctors asked parents to come along next time with any questions they might have. In these latter instances parents were pre-allocated the right to question but overall control of the frame still lay with the doctors.)

5   Are the participants of overtly equal competence in the matter at hand or not?

6   What are the criteria which specify the qualifications necessary to be granted membership status within the frame? (For example, although some situated roles within formats are supposedly for anyone, that is anyone can be a patient or client, not everyone in fact has the particular competences or qualifications required. Examples in this study were the Puerto Ricans who could not speak English, the brother who accompanied a child and, most importantly, child patients in general; none of these quite fitted the demands of the bureaucratic format as used here, and various other kinds of accommodation had to be devised.)

My third point also relates to the syntax of particular kinds of frame, but in a somewhat different fashion. One of Goffman's major concerns has been to specify the procedures and skills by which frames are maintained. But since he has been interested only in propositions which are universally true his approach is necessarily limited. In this study the rule of irrelevance, that is the tacit agreement to avoid all those things which might subvert the reality of a particular frame, was indeed the basic procedure by which formats were kept intact. Nevertheless, there were other methods of almost equal importance which could not be understood without reference to the syntax of particular formats. As we have seen, not everything that threatens a format can be avoided; the very work of an activity system may run directly counter to its ceremonial order, while that order itself may contain contradictions: the rights, duties and character of one status may conflict with those of another. Where such contradictions occur, then means must be found for their reconciliation if the activity system is to proceed smoothly; and such means will themselves form an integral part of the frame.

Once again, although there are likely to be a very large number of different formats in any society, the contradictions which occur are likely to be relatively few in number, since the fundamental dilemmas are posed by the different combinations of the basic elements to which I referred earlier. Thus the solutions which are learnt in one format will apply, more or less, to all those others which embody a similar difficulty. Two basic contradictions have been considered in this monograph, and the nullificatory methods noted here may be summarized as follows (though, again, this is not to claim that these lists are complete).

1 How may a superior criticize and correct the actions of an ideally good and competent subordinate?
   a by emphasizing the spotless future.
   b by treating the subordinate as ignorant and therefore guiltless in the past.
   c by proffering good excuses (thereby showing that the matter is something which needs excusing).
   d where reconstitutive work is considered essential, by letting the subordinates do the work themselves, i.e. by letting sinners name their own sins. (This is an extremely delicate time-consuming method, save where confession is institutionalized as in the Catholic Church.)
   e by passing such work to a subordinate.

2 How can authority be sustained when a subordinate has the right to question that authority?
   a by limiting severe dissent to the level of demeanour, a tactic that is fine save where character-work is involved.
   b by leaving it to the superior to formulate his own incompetence and the inferior's disagreement, thus preserving the authority rule.
   c by the superior threatening to switch frame if the inferior tries to break frame.
   d by the inferior explicitly formulating challenges as non-serious (e.g. I don't know about this but ...).
   e by the inferior formulating challenges as coming from others, e.g. friends, colleagues and relatives.
   f by limiting a challenge so that it constitutes just a small section of the encounter, with an agreement to disagree and other normal business being transacted as before.

g by switching between formats (as here between bureaucratic and clinical) though only on the superior's terms.

h by the transformation of successful challenges into joint plans.

A rather different kind of nullification also needs some consideration. Goffman tends to write as if there was one and only one frame available for each activity-system. He does indeed note how in any particular 'strip' of action a person may engage in a series of different activities, each of which has its own frame (Goffman, 1975a, p.561). He also notes how customers are often portrayed in very different ways by service-providers when they are alone in back-stage areas (1971a), thus contrasting the different frames which may exist for overt and covert activities. But these are separate points. So too is the argument that within any one frame, participants may make various copies or transformations of that frame.

These things are not at issue. My concerns here lie with 'basic' frames and not with their facsimiles, and with just one activity-system, not with a sequence of different systems or a contrasting pair.

As we have seen, there were a variety of ways in which medical consultations could be framed. Moreover, in any one encounter it was possible for more than one format to be employed; a phenomenon which immediately poses the question of how the reality of each format was kept intact. Goffman treats the phenomenon of alternative versions solely in terms of gaffes, mistakes, breaches and asides - as a temporary slippage for which repair-work might be necessary. But this is a quite separate matter. The problem for staff and parents was: how could dual versions of reality be maintained; how was it possible for a clinical format to co-exist with the bureaucratic format?[5] Once again the tactics used here may well apply to other instances of twin framing and may be stated in summary thus:

1 by the segregation of topic areas, reserving different formats for different topics.

2 by the segregation of participants, so that not all take part in every format.

3 by one format being given secondary status, e.g. by apologizing for its presence.

4 by bowdlerizing the contents of one or both frames - an extension of the rule of irrelevance.

5 by revealing the worthy aspects of one or both frames, i.e. by showing how each was important and might contribute to the other.

6   by turning it into a joke, an amusement for participants in the other frame.

Finally, Goffman's analysis of the origins of a format is distinctly limited. His account of the development of situated roles sees the process as merely one of repetition (Goffman, 1961, p.96).[6] If the same activity played through often enough, then a stable ceremonial order and division of labour simply emerges. A rather more fruitful though equally brief suggestion is made in *The Presentation of Self in Everyday Life* (1971a). Here Goffman describes the ceremonial order of encounters as:

> ... a kind of interactional modus vivendi. Together the participants contribute to a single overall definition of the situation which involves not so much a real agreement as to what exists but rather a real agreement as to whose claims concerning what issues will be temporarily honoured. Real agreement will also exist concerning the desirability of avoiding an open conflict of definitions of the situation. I will refer to this level of agreement as a 'working consensus' (Goffman, 1971a, p.21).

Such images point to a process of negotiation and exchange as underlying role formats, even if this essentially political analysis is taken no further in Goffman's own work.[7] We ourselves however may build on this and, based on my reflections on the origins of various medical formats, a number of points may be made about the creation and re-creation of social forms.

Let us start then with the model of ceremonial order as essentially the product of political compromise between the participants. Any one encounter is a social world in miniature, whose outward form relies upon a miniature, tacit contract. The shape that that contract takes is largely the product of the particular interests and resources available to the participants.

At this point we must distinguish different levels of institutionalization. In one-off encounters the ceremonial order will be a fresh creation, but where the same activity-system engenders a number of routinely repeated encounters then, so long as the balance of interests and resources is perceived to be the same, the same overt form is likely to be repeated. Under these circumstances repetition may indeed result in institutionalization.

The possibility that one general solution will emerge is strengthened by two further considerations. First, a routinized solution to the problem of choosing a ceremonial order saves time, effort and worry. It diminishes uncertainty, cuts out initial skirmishing, avoids trouble and enables a rapid concentration on the task at hand. Second, as such a form enters general use, it acquires a moral as well as a political and technical force and becomes, not merely one way of solving things, but the way these things ought to be solved.

Given this institutionalization and its accompanying moral aura, role formats can become somewhat separate from the material interests that initially brought them into being. These little worlds can assume their own independent reality and status, set apart from the actions of their creators and re-creators. The original negotiation may have taken place many years, decades or even centuries ago, and current users may remain entirely unaware of the political and historical reality which they embody.[8]

This reification also enables a further kind of slippage. Since formats, once created, have an independent existence, they constitute a resource for all kinds of action. A form which has been invented to suit one set of purposes and interests may be used later on, under a different set of circumstances, to quite different ends. Something which started out as a rather deviant, daring use of a form may end up years later as the conventional means, the original usage having been forgotten.

Perhaps the most crucial aspect of this process of change is the gradual modification of one central element of the format: the rules that specify just when, where and with whom the format may be used. It is changes here that may permit the rest of a format to go relatively unchanged and yet be used in very different ways. A format that may have originated in and been intended for a highly delimited set of participants may become generalized throughout a population. Conversely, a form that was in general use may, over time, be restricted to a small minority of occasions or persons. In consequence, although the rules governing setting and membership are, at any one point, an essential part of a format, historically viewed they may be seen as slightly to one side and separate from the rules formulating identity and action.

One other major aspect of change may also be noted. Under new circumstances, bits of an old format may be combined with new elements, blending 'traditional' with 'modern' forms to create a new compromise. Indeed, all formats must have their origins in this fashion, for none can be created from totally new components. We build on a stock of pre-existing forms and their elements, taking bits from here and there and combining them as it suits us. God may have created the world from chaos, the Earth being without form and void, but the humbler products of mankind are strictly secondary creations. The totally new would lack both meaning and validity.

Indeed it is the very fact that forms are reified that lends them some authority and weight.[9]

The General Incidence of the Bureaucratic Format

Having emphasized the importance of seeing role formats as political products with a particular historical location and set of uses, I now want to examine the bureaucratic format in this light. Before I proceed to this, there is one prior task. In deciding where to look for explanations it is essential to consider not just the nature of the phenomenon but its incidence as well. If, for example, the bureaucratic format is found only in medical consultations with parents, then its origins are likely to be different from the origins of a format that is used with both parents and adult patients.

As we shall see, although my own data relate solely to children's clinics, there are quite good grounds for suggesting that the bureaucratic format, or something like it, is a far more widespread phenomenon. In fact I shall argue that this format, with one or two alterations, is likely to be the predominant type of ceremonial order in medical consultations within the National Health Service. Its incidence within American medicine is more difficult to estimate. There are no readily comparable American studies that I know of, while the greater diversity of types of medical service seems likely to produce a more varied range of formats. Nevertheless, it seems likely that it is at least a common mode of practice there, perhaps the most common.

In making these suggestions, I shall engage in two principal moves. The first is to argue that although medical work with children has some clear differences from that with adult patients, there are some important internal devices, at least in outpatient consultations with parents, through whose use the format can remain relatively unaffected by the presence of children. The second move is to compare my own findings with those of other studies conducted elsewhere within the British health service. There are clearly not enough of the latter, nor are they sufficiently detailed, for any definitive statement to be made. What evidence there is does suggest that the bureaucratic format, or something fairly like it, is in standard use.

To see how children were excluded from the consultations we must first understand why this was done. The reasons derive from the very special nature of children's abilities and the equally special attributes which they are granted by adults.[10] In brief, young children lack even the most basic health knowledge. They do not necessarily know they are ill and may therefore lack any motivation to get better. They are also incapable of reporting on their illnesses in any precise fashion or of co-operating with staff in any normal adult manner.

Rather than treating medical consultations in the highly focussed manner of adults, young children create their own meanings and activities out of the proceedings; files, telephones and medical instruments can all be turned into toys. Just as they lack an adult version of the consultation, so too they lack a corresponding version of themselves. Without an adult version of the future they lack a self appropriate for medical work, for medicine is concerned with prognosis, prevention and care.

Given this incompetence, adults treat children in a very special fashion. On the one hand, they are granted some highly attractive qualities; they are, for instance, seen as wonderful, amusing and innocent in ways that adults cannot be (Davis and Strong, 1976b; Strong and May, 1980). But on the other hand, they are given a strictly subordinate status and placed under very tight adult supervision.

It is this latter factor which explains children's continued exclusion from consultations, even when they are of an age to play some sensible part within it. At first children are excluded because they cannot cope, save by the use of an extremely inefficient, complex and time-consuming mode - the game format (a mode whose use is considered elsewhere (Davis and Strong, 1976a)). Later on, they are excluded because their parents or guardians still have the ultimate responsibility for their welfare, while their own contributions are less skilled than those of the normal adult.

This exclusion was no simple matter in the clinics studied here. Since children were actually present in the consultations, indeed their physical presence was normally essential to the activity-system, they presented a constant challenge to the smooth working of the adult formats.

This dilemma was neatly solved by a judicious adult use of whatever blend of competence and incompetence was possessed by a given child, though for descriptive purposes it will be simpler to create two straw-children, the 'young child' and the 'older child'.

With younger children or with the mentally retarded, adults turned their incapacity to focus on the consultation to their own advantage. Since children read other meanings into events they were actively encouraged to do so. Not only did many clinics provide toys, but staff often gave them items of equipment to play with. The child thus engaged, staff and parents could continue their conversation undisturbed. Where there was an audience present they were commonly expected to help out by playing with the child - nurses, students and researchers all having to muck in. Fathers, when they accompanied mothers, often had this as their major role.

Children's exclusion from the main action was reinforced by the special qualities that adults attributed to them. Just as parents spoke for children, they also spoke to and about them in ways that adults did not speak of each other, at least while in their presence. The laughter and wonderment that might greet the actions of young children were as much an indicator of their status as incompetents as the open and routine criticism which these might also earn. As incompetents they were clearly subordinated to the adults present. Parents overtly and continually instructed children on how to behave. They warned them when they were going too far, rewarded them for good behaviour, and punished them when they transgressed.

Their character as incompetents was therefore publicly established, indeed in clinics their character was public property. Adults had majority rights not only in their own characters but in those of the children present, and examination of the latter was a common feature of clinic work. Parents openly commented upon the sort of person their child was, while they were regularly asked questions about such matters, for many medical conditions commonly had behavioural problems associated with them.

Young children themselves were obliged to play a part in their exclusion from the adult conversation. Despite their permitted engrossment in other activities, they were expected to give due acknowledgment to the presence of the main action.

If an adult encounter's integrity is to be maintained in the presence of young children, a set of rules is needed to govern the relationship to it of those bit-players. Of these 'minimal encounter rules' the first that children were expected to recognize was the obligation to acknowledge the beginning and end of the action. Saying hello and goodbye was commonly expected of one-year-olds and considerable time could be spent on getting it right. Young children were also expected to recognize the primacy of the adult encounter by dropping whatever they were doing when required upon the adult stage. They were also obliged to keep their own activities unobtrusive - though considerable leeway was allowed here: by a series of brief, infrequent and usually murmured comments, many parents sustained an intermittent interaction with their child, both pacifying it and yet paying some attention to the main encounter.

The fundamental principle that underlay all these procedures was that of adult authority. 'Because I say so' was the implied rule that gave reason to events. In this, adult-child interaction was marked, not just by an assumption of childish ignorance, but by a parallel and equally basic rule of adult omniscience. Adults had authority because they knew. Among adults such omniscience was often a matter for joking. Parents and staff laughed at children's assumption that they would know the answer to every why? and what? Yet such a premise was fundamental to their interaction with children. Most children took the fact of such authority totally for granted and their revolts were transient affairs, rebellions not against the reasonableness of the authority itself but against some minor edict. As such they were treated as unimportant by adults. Young children were not expected to recognize adult authority, indeed their very incompetence might reasonably hinder them in this. Their shyness, moodiness, their sudden swings of involvement, all these might prevent obedience to doctors' or parents' wishes. Besides, medical demands were often novel and sometimes difficult or painful.

Given such incompetence, children's failure to observe the medical conventions presented no serious threat to the reality of the bureaucratic format. In other words, although the co-presence of two adult formats for the same activity could present a severe challenge to the little worlds which frames create, the presence of children was a far less fundamental danger. The level of noise or the constant interruptions might produce some technical difficulties, but the world in which young children lived was of a clearly subordinate status and there was no need to treat it with the seriousness accorded to adult frames.

Young children or the severely retarded could therefore be readily excluded from most of the action, and even such intrusion as they did make could be written off. But older children possessed a much greater capacity to participate sensibly in the consultation. What happened to them? In fact, despite their larger abilities their exclusion was often yet more pronounced. The very powers which might have given them a greater part than their younger brethren were used against them. For such children were now deemed old enough to obey adult authority fully. Allowances could be made for the very young. They might even be given special activities to keep them occupied. But older children were caught in a dilemma. As children, they were subject to the fundamental rule of childish incompetence and as such accompanied by an adult representative who spoke for them. But as older children, they were expected to stay excluded without any necessity for effort by the adults; in other words, to have learnt fully the minimal encounter rules required of subordinates.

Thus, beyond the age of five or so children were expected to pay much greater respect to the social priority of the adult conversation. Good behaviour equalled sitting quietly on a chair of their own, and pleasant distractions were not provided. Children were now required to look as if they were ready and able to participate if called upon to do so; that is, some version of adult demeanour was expected of them. But even for the oldest children the call rarely came and when it did their participation was closely supervised. Eleven- and twelve- year-olds typically waited in silence while parents and doctors discussed their case. Only exceptionally did such children initiate topics and even then their participation was still minor and treated in quite distinctive ways.

Since parents and others spoke for children they had the right not merely to define what was in the children's best interest but even to formulate their experiences, that is to define what they had perceived, what they felt, and how they would react to things. Their parents apparently knew them better than they knew themselves. Their own versions of events were routinely overridden by those who 'really' knew what the child had felt or would experience. When older children were asked questions by staff their parents often spoke for them, not waiting for the child to answer. On such occasions children did not fight back. They did not become angry and demand their right to speak, for they had no such clear rights. Indeed, to demand these might be taken by adults as a sign of psychiatric abnormality, that one was not behaving as a proper child. One eight-year-old seen at the Scottish neurological clinic was being examined precisely because of his failure to accept his subordinate status, and his parents appealed to his behaviour in the clinic as yet further evidence of this disturbance.[11]

Normally parents encountered no such difficulties. Those from professional backgrounds might give their children more scope to reply, but they too would frequently interrupt and cast doubt upon what had been said. Doctors commonly gave older children a chance to talk, but it was typically just the one chance. Even if taken it lasted only a brief while; if not, the consultation passed smoothly on to the parents.

In summary, children's incompetence and subordinate status, when coupled with their acceptance of that status and its sustained enforcement by adults, meant that they could readily be excluded from large areas of interaction and that consultations could take place principally between staff and children's adult representatives.

This, of course, does not establish that the formats used in this all-adult interaction are similar to those to be found in consultations with adult patients, merely that this is at least a possibility. The actual likelihood of this occurrence can only be established through a comparison with studies of medical work with adults. But when this is done it does seem as if something like the bureaucratic format may well be fairly uniform within the National Health Service. Such an assertion is necessarily tentative, since only a few other studies have gathered extensive observational or taped data on medical practice, while these researchers have had rather different aims from my own. Nevertheless, certain striking parallels do emerge between the principal format described in this study and that which may be glimpsed in others.

There is at present no general study of consultations in hospital outpatient departments, but there are two such studies of general practice. Since general practice might be supposed to differ far more from hospital paediatrics than the latter differs from other kinds of hospital work, such a comparison offers the thesis a severe test. Yet on inspection there are certain close and vital similarities. Byrne and Long (1976) is the most extensive study of medical practice so far undertaken, involving over 2,500 taped consultations as conducted by 71 general practitioners, 60 of them British but including 5 Dutch and 6 Irish doctors. Among their findings were these: doctors exerted almost complete control over the interaction, so much so indeed that the researchers did not think it necessary to take patient variation into account when analysing individual doctors' styles; these styles were heavily routinized, and in most cases minimized the amount of information given to patients while allowing them little opportunity to put their own point of view; at the same time, most patients seemed to be ascribed a reputable character. Character-work, or as they term it 'chastisement' or 'negative behaviour' ,was 'comparatively rare':

> They (negative behaviours) do not commonly occur in any style with any degree of frequency. With the exception of a few consultations involving patients who were trying to extract drugs from doctors, or patients trying to have bottles of proprietary substances added to a prescription (e.g. Dettol), we have not been able to discover any evidence of a consistent negative style (Byrne and Long, 1976, p.161).

Further evidence comes from the observational part of Stimson and Webb's study (1975) of general practice which, though much smaller in scope, involving only 50 consultations and 5 doctors, was more directly concerned with some of the matters dealt with here. They too note the immense interactional power of doctors, though placing some emphasis also on the patients' ability to negotiate. Similarly, as in my own study, they note the way in which appeal is made to a generalized body of medical knowledge rather than to an individual doctor's competence. They also discuss what they term the 'emotional flatness' of medical consultations as well as their impersonality, and remark upon the idealization of both medical expertise and parental ignorance. They too emphasize the politeness with which such affairs are conducted:

> There is rarely any conflict in the negotiation in the consultation. Both parties generally recognize and retain some semblance of formality and exercise restraint to prevent the encounter from completely breaking down ... verbal and non-verbal control strategies are often covert and rarely obvious or explicit. On the part of the patient particularly, they appear to operate beneath a facade of compliance and acquiescence (Stimson and Webb, 1975, pp.57-8).

Some central features of the bureaucratic format would therefore seem to be found, not only in the Scottish children's clinics which I studied, but in general practice as well. This is not to say that every study has a similar story. Research in some highly specialized settings in Britain reports very different findings on one of the most crucial dimensions of the bureaucratic format, the moral character ascribed to patients. Two recent studies of casualty departments (Jeffrey, 1974 and Gibson, 1977) and a study of the work of a drug dependency clinic (Stimson, 1978) suggest that in these settings at least, and with patients such as drunks, drug addicts and repeat drug-overdose cases, many doctors see overt character-work as a central part of the job. But these exceptions do seem to be exceptional. Elsewhere, on what we know at present, it does appear plausible to argue that the bureaucratic format, or something very like it, will prove the standard ceremonial order within the British National Health Service.

The Influence of Children upon the Bureaucratic Format

One cautionary note must be added. Even if the format is used in many adult settings it is unlikely to take precisely the form delineated here. For, although child patients can be excluded from medical encounters with considerable success, they do exert some influence upon the interaction. In comparing the bureaucratic format that I discovered in children's clinics with the descriptions of the ceremonial order in general practice consultations, I have picked out some things and omitted others. The elements shared in common would seem to be these: firm medical control; the idealization of both staff and patients'/parents' character; an emphasis on service; a combination of both politeness and impersonality; and an emphasis on collegial rather than individual medical expertise. However, there were other aspects of the format that seem less likely to be found in medical work with adults. Three things in particular need a mention, all of which follow from the very different status accorded to children and adults.

First, adults are normally responsible for their own health, and medical professionals typically have no clear rights to intervene if patients do not wish this, a position that is graphically expressed in the following quotation taken from a study of general practice (Strong, 1980):

Interviewer: Which raises another interesting question about the extent of the doctors's responsibility to patients. In that kind of case where the patient says, 'I'm happy the way I am,' there's damn all you can do about it, I suppose?

Doctor: There's damn all I *ought* to do about it.

Interviewer: If they want to kill themselves they should be free to do that.

Doctor: If he's free, white and over 21, that's my theory.

This may be an extreme statement but it expresses a fundamental truth. Those who are of an age to take care of themselves are normally allowed considerable freedom to go their own way. By contrast, not only are children not granted this right, but even those who are formally responsible for them, their parents or guardians, now have to share that responsibility with the State and its agents. Modern children are, at least in part, public property.

If this is so, why then should there be an alliance rather than any more direct form of control? The answer to this lies in the very limited exclusion of doctors' practical authority. The extra responsibility placed upon staff when they deal with children far outweighs the additional legal powers they are given. The law relating to such matters is narrowly defined. It is not the case that anything other than strict compliance with staff's instructions is either assault or alternatively neglect. Parental action has to be extreme and a child's life in some danger before staff appeal to the law. By and large staff cannot force parents to do this or stop doing that; they can merely suggest or imply. For although the state claims some right to intervene in family life it does not seek to supersede it. The ideal upbringing for a child is thought to occur in the bosom of its family and the task of the state is to support the family not destroy it. Doctors have responsibility but not power.

Thus, although there was an overt assumption in clinics of a shared responsibility for the child, in practice parents had most of it, as is clearly revealed in the following quotation. In this consultation, the only occasion on which the ultimate responsibility for a child was ever discussed, the child had presented with three previous fits of an epileptic appearance; although the hospital doctor advised that drug therapy should be started immediately the parents rejected this, citing their general practitioner's advice that this should begin only if a fourth episode occurred. He had also apparently said that it was their decision in the end; a statement with which the doctor was forced to agree:

Dr J: Well, I can only advise you on things like swimming being properly supervised. It is your personal responsibility. So be it upon your own head if you don't notify the school about swimming or if you don't observe the rules about cycling. All I can do is see her again in six months' time. Now, have you any questions?

Mother: Well, don't think we're being ungrateful.

Dr J: Well, you're quite within your rights. It's your responsibility. How you discharge it is your own decision.

This incident also brings out another factor which contributed to the making of an overt alliance between doctors and parents. Such parental defiance was most unusual and even here it was carefully warranted by appeal to other expert opinion. Since staff still had access to special legal powers, however rarely these were used, parents were under greater constraints than those faced by adult patients. Moreover, since they themselves were not the patient, the sense of responsibility for someone else was one which they shared with staff. In such circumstances it paid both parties to be accommodative.

There are, in addition, two other ways in which it seems likely that the shared responsibility for a child gave a distinctive flavour to the ceremonial order. First, the universal idealization of parents' good character and the great lengths to which doctors went in maintaining this may not be quite so strenuously followed in some other medical settings. I do not mean by this that investigative character-work with adult patients is likely to be common, merely that staff's greater responsibility for child patients, when coupled with their lack of power, is likely to have made them especially nice to parents, since they had few other resources on which to draw if they wished to bend parents to their will.

At the same time the sharing of responsibility for a child may also have lent the proceedings a rather more uniformly serious tone than is normal in consultations with adults. I have already noted the clinic's seriousness in this respect, but something more needs to be said. Since it is up to adult patients to decide how to live their own lives, they have some leeway in deciding how to treat their illnesses. They can choose when or whether they go to the doctor and, once they are there, they can still make light of their complaints if they so wish. Doctors in their turn can take their cue from their patients and adopt a light-hearted approach, at least where this seems appropriate.[12] By contrast, work of some import which is done on behalf of someone else and where that someone is small and defenceless may have a more serious air. We may make light of our own sufferings, indeed adults are normally obliged to (Goffman, 1972, pp. 406-10), but the sufferings of little children are another matter.

Finally, in considering the special qualities which the bureaucratic format seems to have when used with child patients and their parents, one should note that the consultations I witnessed do not cover the entire range of outpatient consultations. The restrictions on my data are considered more fully in the introduction; but in summary the study was limited to paediatricians and therapists and there are some grounds for arguing that such staff may be especially considerate in their dealings with parents, or at least this is what they themselves argued. Indeed, every occupation claimed a special expertise in this respect. They sustained this claim by each choosing a different group for comparison. Health visitors contrasted their approach with that of local authority doctors; local authority doctors and hospital therapists compared themselves with hospital paediatricians; and the latter distinguished their own approach from that of other hospital doctors such as surgeons. Here for instance is a paediatrician's analysis of the general orientation of paediatrics:

> Dr I: There are two kinds of medicine ... this is very much a
> simplification ... there's the caring sort of medicine and the
> organizational sort of medicine at the other extreme. And each
> speciality is an admixture of the two, and I think paediatrics is well
> towards the caring end of the scale. It attracts people who are more
> interested in the individual, more interested in families, more
> interested in the social side.

If this is so, then, although I would expect the format to be the standard mode
in outpatient clinics, it may well vary in the delicacy of its application; though
it must be said that in terms of their overt idealization of parents' character
no important differences were observed between the occupations studied here.

The Origins of the Bureaucratic Format: Medical Dominance

Having distinguished between the special features of the bureaucratic format
when used with children and those which it seems to share with other medical
consultations, at least in general practice, we may now turn to consider the
origins of the more general form and the reasons for its continued use.
Formats are transitory things which have no existence save in so far as they
are reproduced in individual encounters. What are the factors which have led
to the creation and continual re-enactment of the central features of the
bureaucratic mode across such apparently wide areas of medical practice?

The method which I shall use in my answer to this question is essentially
comparative. Just as I have described other formats besides the bureaucratic
in order to highlight its main features, so here I will draw on the rather
different circumstances in which they occurred in order to provide some
explanation of the particular form taken by the bureaucratic mode. I shall also
make use of various other historical and observational studies, for these also
may tell us something about the conditions under which particular formats
operate. The data on which my generalizations are based are rather fugitive,
but enough has already been done to enable speculation by other sociologists
and I in my turn will add to this as best I can.

In general, one can distinguish two broad strands within the bureaucratic
format which stand in need of explanation. On the one hand there is the tight
medical control of the consultation, with the closely related features of
impersonal treatment and the appeal to collegial rather than individual

expertise. On the other hand, there are the idealization of the patient's character and competence; the ideal of service; the right of patients to criticize that service, and at least the semblance of rule by reason rather than by fiat. In considering medical practice sociologists in recent years have followed Freidson (1970b) and emphasized the first of these, that is 'medical dominance'. A more balanced view must surely include the other and equally important strand, that phenomenon which I shall term 'medical gentility.'

Taking medical dominance first, its origins have already been the subject of work of some merit and, while it is pointless to repeat this at any length, it is worth providing some details of the arguments here, since elements of them will play a major part in my own analysis of gentility. Beginning then with Parsons (1951), he argues that, compared with many other occupations, medicine has certain special advantages in gaining power over its clientele. This is an area where consumer judgment is particularly ineffective, while the seeking of skilled medical help means the intrusion of outsiders into intimate areas of one's life. In such matters the patient may literally be naked and defenceless. Similarly Freidson (1970b), despite placing a far higher emphasis on medical dominance than Parsons, nevertheless concurs with his basic explanation of the phenomenon - that of the great asymmetry between medical and lay competence - although he provides far more adequate documentation of his arguments.

Other writers however, while not dismissing these as causes, have noted some further important matters. Their method has been to place current forms of medical dominance in a more detailed historical and comparative context and to contrast them, not just with medicine's past, but with the situation that obtains in quite separate professions. Such a method has its problems, since the factors cannot be held constant. One cannot really compare the kind of technical expertise which doctors now have with that which they possessed three centuries ago; while the expertise possessed by lawyers or accountants is of a quite separate order. Nevertheless, allowing for these considerable difficulties, there do appear to be several other factors which have played an important part in determining the precise form taken by medical dominance. Johnson (1972) has argued that the degree of control exerted by a profession over its clientele also depends on the following conditions: the relative numbers and financial resources of professionals and clients; the extent to which the clientele form a group with homogeneous characteristics; the extent to which the clientele are actually organized as a group; and the relative social status of professionals when compared with their clientele.

On his analysis, this explains why modern accountancy, despite its considerable technical expertise, is dominated rather than dominating. Accountants are dependent on a relatively small number of powerful clients and to stay in business must accommodate themselves to their demands. In consequence many technical matters - such as how best to introduce accounting methods which allow for inflation - are ultimately decided by the clientele and not by the profession. Jewson (1974) has pointed to a rather similar situation in medicine. The relationship between doctors and the aristocracy in eighteenth-century Britain was one of patronage. Given their relatively greater resources, such patients could enforce not just gentility but subservience; doctors were granted no monopoly of technical expertise, for aristocrats expected their own medical theories to be taken into account.

On this kind of grounds, Johnson has argued that the nineteenth century saw the creation of the modern form of medical power, not simply because there was a major growth in medical expertise at that time but because there was in addition a parallel growth in a particular kind of client. He sees the origin of the modern profession of medicine as associated with

> ... the rise to power of an urban middle class which provided an expanding market for various services based largely on individual needs, whether private or entrepreneurial (Johnson, 1972, p.52).

This expanding bourgeoisie not only gave the financial support necessary for the employment of a relatively large number of doctors in a reasonable state of affluence, but also provided the material basis for medical domination. These doctors were members of a social class that was somewhat higher in status than many of their patients; and, in addition, although they themselves had grown in number, their patients had expanded at a far greater rate, were relatively varied in nature and were organized only at a family level. Faced with this relatively weak clientele, as well as themselves possessing a growing technical expertise, doctors could exert major control over the relationship with their patients.

So far, so good. But something more is necessary if we are to explain the particular form of medical dominance exhibited in the bureaucratic format. Just what this might be is best revealed by a comparison with the private mode. As will be remembered, the special quality of the latter was a concern for product differentiation: consultations were personalized; some time was taken over the individual requirements of each patient and parent; above all, the particular excellence of the individual doctor and his hospital was emphasized. The manner in which this was done might be constrained by professional rules and organizational demands, but nevertheless, since the patients could take their money elsewhere, the need to market a distinct product subtly influenced all aspects of the consultation. Personal touches paid.

By contrast, the bureaucratic format was rather more impersonal, gave less opportunity for parents to discuss matters with the doctor, and placed its emphasis on collegial rather than individual medical expertise. These properties would seem to derive from two factors: the rather smaller resources devoted to individual patients, and the deliberate restriction of competition between doctors. I shall consider both in turn.

The Scottish clinics catered for all, and aimed at giving the same standard of service to all. Given the volume of trade relative to the resources available, the most important commodity in clinics was time. Doctors were normally in a hurry and in most settings impersonality and speed were a practical necessity. Given the pressure of events, it was impossible for staff to engage regularly in small-talk, to probe every anxiety, or to answer every question in detail. Things were no different in the American hospital. There too the normal format was the bureaucratic; and the extra touches bought by private patients were obtained only at the cost of minimizing the time and thus the service offered to others.

This is not to deny that important changes might well be possible within the brief time currently available to medical practitioners. A little more information here and there might do wonders. Nevertheless the constraints that time alone imposes cannot be over-emphasized but are rarely considered.[13] To make a comparison with teaching: most thought about how to make teaching more effective takes the size of school classes pretty much for granted. This may be realistic but it leads us to ignore the teachers' fundamental difficulty: how to control a class of thirty children. Teaching might look very different if it could be done in classes of four. The situation is much the same in medicine. The average doctor within the National Health Service is obsessed with time, and that obsession obliges him to control his consultations as tightly as possible.

The other feature which gave the bureaucratic format its distinctive shape, at least within the Scottish clinics, was the set of severe restrictions on medical competition. The general procedures here have been considered in chapter 2, but two points may need re-emphasis. First, the system was divided so as to minimize the occasions on which competition could occur. There was a careful division of labour, and the different parts tended to complement each other rather than endlessly overlapping. There was only one hospital service, and although departments had their quarrels and demarcation disputes none had a direct competitor. Since patients could not refer themselves directly to the hospital it was an adjunct to the services of the general practitioner rather than an alternative. At the same time, some of the normal motives and channels for competition were also inhibited. Since clients did not themselves pay for the service, individual staff or agencies could not boost their own income by attracting a larger or more profitable trade.[14]

The absence of such incentives and opportunities was central to the impersonal, highly controlled and relatively uninformative nature of the bureaucratic format. There was, however, one potential flaw in this strategy of containment. Although patients had to register with just one general practitioner and could only see other medical staff, apart from local authority doctors, with the permission of this practitioner, they still had rights to a second opinion. If parents were dissatisfied with the verdict at the primary care level they could ask to see a specialist. If they disliked his verdict they could ask to see another specialist, and so on. Similarly, they could register with a different general practitioner if they disliked the one they had got. In principle, parents had as much choice in the Scottish system as their private counterparts did in the United States.

Here then, apparently, was a distinct threat both to individual medical control and to the general policy of collegial expertise. A little time needs to be spent on explaining how it was circumvented. Once again, my argument here is based solely on what happened in the Scottish children's clinics but it seems unlikely that things are much different elsewhere in the British Health Service.

The first point to notice is that parents were kept in relative ignorance both as to their rights and as to the methods by which to gain a second opinion. Not only were they not routinely informed that a second opinion was available, but the general impersonality of clinics and the basic rule of collegial wisdom meant that the inner workings of medicine were never laid bare in the fashion of the private format. Not much, of course, was necessarily revealed in the latter mode, but the very mention of other doctors who had seen the child or were experts in the area indicated that there were other named alternatives.

It also indicated, and this is my second point, that there was nothing fundamentally wicked in parents' wanting a second opinion, that it was an entirely reasonable thing which any parent might want, and that the doctor would not feel offended if this is what mothers chose. Finally, since referral could come only through asking the doctor one was currently seeing, to ask to be referred was a risky business. Asking for a second opinion might prejudice one's present relationship with the doctor and give one a bad name generally, something to be avoided in a centralized medical service.

That parents might therefore be afraid to ask for another doctor is brought out clearly in the following example, one of the only two requests for a second opinion witnessed during the study. In this case the paediatrician, Dr I, had previously discharged the child, although he was still attending the surgical clinic. However, the mother had written to Dr I saying that she wanted to raise a number of matters with him; and throughout this new consultation she discussed the child's problem in a hesitant and embarrassed fashion. Finally she got round to the point:

Mother: Well, what I would like is ... (she broke off and paused) ...

Dr I: Would you like a second opinion about this?

Mother: Yes (said in a very gratified way).

Dr I: Have you spoken to Mr Blake (surgeon) about this?

Mother: No.

Dr I: (surprised tone) Why not?

Mother: Well, he seems very unapproachable. He didn't seem interested in Alistair. Although it could be as you say because it's too early to say yet (i.e. the child may be too young for proper testing), but as you think it's OK maybe we should leave it for the moment.

Dr I: Oh, no. Do have one if you want it. Shall I ask him for you? No ... (pause) ... that may not be quite such a good idea (everyone laughs). It might be best if you do it. Why not ask?

Mother: Won't he mind?

Dr I: Well ... (pause) ... No doctor *should* mind. What you've got to say is 'We're very worried, Mr Blake, and we'd be very willing to take him to anybody else as we're so worried about him. Could you please name somebody else whom we could take him to?' You see, I can't really name anyone, it's not my area.

Mother: You don't know anybody?

Dr I: Well, there are lots of doctors in Edinburgh who are very good. They're probably no better than Mr Blake but they're certainly good. But it's you who have to be satisfied, it's up to you. Mr Blake is the specialist in this area, he's the best man. I'm sorry I can't be of more help to you myself. I think it would be best if you say this yourself to Mr Blake. It would be best if it came through you.

For all her uncertainty this mother was middle-class, as was the only other parent who asked for a second opinion. What happened in this latter case shows with considerable clarity the great power that gaining such referral might give the brave. From being an impersonal affair with every doctor interchangeable for most purposes, the consultation might, in the right circumstances, be transformed into an area of personal and conflicting opinion and bear a closer resemblance to the private than to the bureaucratic format. The following quotations are from the consultation held just after the mother's return from the English hospital to which she had been referred when she asked for a second opinion:

Mother: Dr Brown (England) said that this hospital (the Scottish hospital) hadn't ruled out a hereditary cause.
Dr J: No, I'm sure he couldn't have said that. I'm sure Dr McAllister (Scottish hospital) couldn't have said that.

Dr J: Quite frankly, the report from England is a puzzle to us. What they say under the heading 'diagnosis', where they say they don't know, differs from the bottom where they say it's genetic and that there's a one in four chance of its being passed on. Both Dr McAllister and I can't understand how they can be so dogmatic that it's genetic, and yet only place it in such a vague diagnostic category.
Mother: Well, I can't understand it. At the (English) hospital, Dr Brown seemed right out on a limb. He seemed definite, but no one else paid much attention to him. Of course, when the news hit me it was like a hammer blow, so I wasn't able to take much in, but a registrar said to me not to give up hope as Dr Brown was by no means infallible. He treated me quite differently.

Having considered the particular conditions which underlay medical control in the bureaucratic format, I think it worth noting that the case I have just discussed also has something to tell us about the more general phenomenon of the medical dominance. For this apparently brave mother was by no means a typical patient. She herself was an ex-nurse while her brother-in-law was a doctor; and such behaviour, or something like this, seemed relatively common among those with medical connections.

When discussing the idealization of staff's technical authority, I noted that even those parents with some medical knowledge normally paid overt obeisance to this rule. However, the proportion who covertly attacked the doctor's authority was most striking. Apart from containing the only mother to ask for a second opinion, this group also held one of the few mothers to bring notes to a clinic, and the only parent to actually make notes during a clinic (though this latter action was merely reported of a previous occasion). Of the four mothers who made strong overt criticisms of the doctor, one was an ex-nurse and another a radiologist. In other words, although staff with medical connections or training made little direct appeal to their expertise, six out of the 19 such parents engaged in some of the most forceful action against staff's control of the consultation witnessed in the entire study.

This behaviour suggests that if the general run of parents had the knowledge that these others possessed, then the rules of the format would be quite different. Parsons and Freidson clearly have a major point when they emphasize the importance of technical expertise as a source of medical control, even if we ourselves must add to this the other factors which have been discussed in this section: relative status, relative numbers, the cohesion and uniformity of the clientele, the amount of time available, and the extent to which competition between doctors is encouraged or restricted.

The Origins of the Bureaucratic Format: Medical Gentility

For all the reasons I have just given, doctors were able to exert a powerful control over the shape and content of medical consultations; a control which was particularly marked in the case of the bureaucratic format. And yet, as we have also seen, there were clear limits to their power. The practice of medicine necessarily involves systematic moral investigation and assessment, but it was only in the charity format that these concerns were made manifest. Elsewhere doctors went to great lengths to conceal the moral basis of their work and to transform medical practice into a neutral, 'scientific' affair that dealt with purely natural happenings. What resources did staff lack or parents possess that might account for the systematic idealization of parental character and competence? I have already noted that, at least in work with children, doctors were placed in a rather special situation. They were given considerable responsibility but little power, and were therefore obliged to adopt an accommodative strategy. And yet the idealization of the clients' character does not seem to be confined solely to the children's clinic, even if perhaps it is taken to extremes here. A more general explanation is therefore needed.

One answer to this problem has already been given by Parsons (1951), who is the only writer that I know of to have treated the phenomenon of medical gentility at length. As we have already seen, he notes that patients are in a rather vulnerable position, being ignorant as well as ill. He then goes on to ask what prevents them from being systematically exploited and why is it that the doctor's relationship with the patient is characterized by 'universalism', 'functional specificity', 'affective neutrality' and 'collectivity-orientation'. These rather ugly terms cover somewhat different ground from my own, since they are addressed not just to the ceremonial order of medical consultations but to the whole doctor-patient relationship. Nevertheless the matters that I have described, the rule of reason and the idealization of character, would seem to be a part of the same package; and the answers that he provides require careful examination.

In solving his puzzle, Parsons notes two important characteristics of medical work in Western society; one that is true just of modern times and the other that is more universal. The first of these is medicine's establishment as an applied science. As a consequence he holds that it shares in the universalistic values which he sees as characteristic of science. The scientific approach, on this ideal model, ignores the particularism of status and social divisions and concentrates solely on objective truths. It is therefore irrelevant to the doctor-scientist whether he likes or dislikes his patients, or whether they are rich or poor; these characteristics are simply not at issue. More generally, the doctor, in whatever era, is faced with the difficulty that medicine often deals in highly personal matters and involves potentially shaming acts such as physical examination. Delicacy and confidentiality are therefore technically essential to the good practice of medicine; or so he suggests.

There is clearly something in these two arguments, but close inspection reveals that they alone cannot provide a full answer. This failure is principally due to Parsons's inadequate phrasing of the question. The qualities that he attributes to the doctor-patient relationship are far from being universal even within our own society - as the existence of the charity format makes clear. Thus the general properties that he ascribes to modern medicine cannot explain the major differences between one role format and another.

Even if we treat these explanations as only a partial influence, we are still faced with difficulties. Parsons argues that medicine's role as an applied science serves to guarantee the neutrality of doctor towards patient, but he fails to note that this neutrality is often a spurious construction. In other words, far from being neutral because they are scientists, doctors can appeal to the neutrality of 'natural' science in order to conceal the systematic moral investigation and judgement in which they are engaged. Finally, although he is surely correct in seeing medicine as dealing with some matters which are potentially shaming to any individual whatever his or her culture, he fails to bring out the very special emphasis on individual privacy and autonomy that is characteristic of bourgeois culture.

I shall return to these points later. For the moment, having seen that Parsons cannot offer us a fully adequate explanation of medical gentility, it is worth considering the location of the research on which his analysis was originally founded. The consultations which he observed and the doctors whom he interviewed were situated within a system of private practice. As we have already seen, such a system can enforce a highly personalized service and is likely to go further still. The idealization of patients in the private format is surely also, or at least in large part, the product of competition between doctors. Private patients might have little or no technical knowledge, but they can certainly discriminate between those doctors who are polite and attentive and those who are not. To build or maintain such a practice doctors have to establish goodwill and a good bedside manner is an essential selling point. They might well feel like moral denunciation on occasion but a sustained idealization of their patients' character is the only guarantee of a thriving business.

If anything, this tendency is likely to be reinforced by the achievement of a legal monopoly of practice and the profession's code of ethics, for these place limits on the extent to which competition is explicitly based on different theories and techniques, and tends to concentrate it instead on the smooth delivery of service.

Here then is the key to the idealization of the private patients. But why should this same phenomenon be found in a context where competition between doctors is systematically excluded? If the bureaucratic format is, as it were, robbed of the more personal touches of the private mode, why should it not also lose that heavy emphasis on the moral worth and competence of the patient?

My answer to this is that the power given to patients under a system of private practice can be replaced by another kind of resource. The power of the consumer within the British Health Service is exerted not through direct payment but through political means via the mediation of the state. As Navarro has written:

> It is impossible to explain the creation of the NHS without understanding the relationship of class forces in Britain and the war-time radicalization of the working class that had called into question the 'survival of capitalism'.... Indeed, labour movements have historically viewed social services (including health) as part of the *social wage,* to be defended and increased in the same way that *money wages* are. In fact, Wilensky has shown how the size of social wages depends, in large degree, on the level of militancy of the labour movements (Navarro, 1977, p.286).[14]

In other words, polite medical service can be the product of a trade-off between organized labour and capital and may be bought through political as well as financial muscle. In this situation doctors are still dependent upon their patients' good will, but in a somewhat different manner. Since they are not paid directly by the individual, and since medicine here is a less competitive business, doctors are not so constrained to provide a personalized service. But because the financial position, prestige and degree of self-control of the profession as a whole are under direct political management and are themselves a political issue, it pays doctors to be polite to the great mass of their patients.

In consequence there are strong collegial pressures for politeness to all, pressures that are reinforced as well as exemplified by the creation of a uniform national service.

In discussing medical dominance I noted Johnson's argument that a certain degree of heterogeneity among their patients fosters professional control. However, he goes on to note that major social and financial divisions among the clientele may fragment the profession, producing quite separate types of service in which practitioners may develop quite separate sets of interest in the struggle for resources. By contrast, where a national health service is created, doctors have a set of joint interests in common and there will be strong pressures for the development of a common culture: a culture in which gentility and service to all patients receives a heavy ideological emphasis - so long at least as working-class patients retain some political power. Crucial elements of the private format are therefore retained despite the abolition of direct payment and of most competition between doctors.[15]

The Victory of Bourgeois Medicine

One other way of putting all this is to note that the British National Health Service, despite the fairly radical shift in power on which it was based, retains a fundamentally bourgeois flavour - a proposition whose truth cannot be fully grasped unless one stands back a little to consider the rules for the entire 'doctor-patient relationship' of which the bureaucratic or private formats are merely parts:

1 Doctors serve the individual client, their duty towards him is both compelling and undivided, they should serve no other. This principle is of course modified in a number of ways, for instance as regards sick notes, research, insurance examination, and the care of the in-competent, whether children, the insane or the geriatric; nevertheless, it remains the basic orientation of medical practice.

2 Given the stress on the professional's service to his or her client, there is a central ethical emphasis on the confidentiality of the relationship. That is, not only is the relationship solely between doctor and patient and for the benefit of that patient, but the transaction is private and to be kept secret from others. Once again some practical modification may be made for students, other staff or for researchers, but the principle still holds.

3 Just as the doctor serves the individual client, so patients typically belong to individual doctors, and the relationship between different doctors and a particular patient is subject to a delicate professional etiquette. When a general practitioner refers a patient to a hospital specialist that patient is still his, and he has the right both to receive regular reports from the specialists and to reject those reports if he so wishes. Scottish local authority doctors, since they owned no patients, had no right to treat and had to refer to other professionals for this.

4 Not only is medical service given in a confidential fashion by specific

doctors to specific individuals, but individuals in many important respects also choose the service they receive. The range of choice of practitioner may be restricted in a national health service or a pre-payment plan, but the principle of consumer choice is still central. Fundamentally, it is the clients themselves and not medical personnel who normally decide when they should seek treatment and have advice. Freidson (1961, p.197) and Stimson and Webb (1975, p.155) have argued that since doctors have a monopoly of many crucial types of medical resource and a virtual monopoly of medical knowledge, this choice is necessarily limited. However, despite the state's granting of legal rights to practice, doctors have received no equivalent powers to enforce that practice on their patients. Adults cannot be brought to court for self-neglect, and when most doctors think of the law they think of their own rather than their patients' possible malpractice.

5 Patients have these rights because, like economic man in classical economics, they are overtly assumed to be rational, knowledgeable, competent and properly motivated. As such they will themselves typically recognize when they are ill and will wish to alter this state by taking or seeking appropriate care.

6 Medicine is an enterprise which deals primarily with natural phenomena. (This too has its parallels with classical economics, which gave large areas of bourgeois theorizing the status of natural laws.) This reification of illness has two consequences. First, since the state deals primarily with social matters it has little business in medicine. It may intervene to ensure that services are properly organized or that treatment is available to all, but the conduct of medicine itself is essentially a matter for those who specialize in the ways of the natural. Second, since illness is a natural affair, patients moral character is in no way questioned by it. Medical inquiry is concerned not with the investigation and rooting out of personal dereliction but with the clinical analysis and treatment of the biological sphere.

Here then, with its emphasis on the primacy of the individual and its vision of the doctor-patient relationship as essentially a private contract, is a distinctively bourgeois conception of medical encounters.[16] Yet, as we have seen, there is no necessary reason why the doctor-patient relationship should look like this. Indeed, under other conditions, keeping well, far from being a private concern, might be regarded as an essentially public duty. Instead of patients seeking treatment on their own initiative and having some right to determine whether or not they are ill, they might indeed be sought out and then treated, regardless of their own wishes. Rather than emphasizing the privacy and confidentiality of medical transactions, these might well be matters of public record and humiliation. Far from being an overtly natural and neutral phenomenon, medicine might be transformed into a thoroughly moral and judgmental activity. Such a vision has been most thoroughly captured in Samuel Butler's *Erewhon*:

> If a man falls into ill-health, or catches any disorder, or fails bodily in any way before he is seventy years old, he is tried before a jury of his countrymen, and if convicted is held up to public scorn and sentenced more or less severely as the case may be. There are sub-divisions of illness into crimes and misdemeanours — a man being punished very heavily for serious illness, while failure of eyes or hearing in one over sixty-five, who has had good health hitherto, is dealt with by fine only (Butler, 1977).

'Erewhon' may be nowhere, but elements of its laws can readily be found somewhere. Groups with little political or financial power and of a degraded social status have often been treated in very different ways from their more fortunate brethren. The degradation that this may inflict is readily compatible with the loftiest ideals of service. To take an instructive example from outside medicine, the middle-class Evangelical reformers of Victorian Britain, while equally critical of the morals of all classes of society, used quite separate means to ensure their reform. The middle and upper classes were to be persuaded by argument; the lower required laws (Bradley, 1976). Similarly, health visitors were, and in some respects still are, a kind of health police, enforcing medical 'law' upon the lowest social classes (see Dingwall, 1977).

Again this division almost exactly parallels the split between the charity format and the other model described in this study. The doctor who used the charity format was as concerned as any of her colleagues with the health and welfare of the poor, and also (Parsons might note) laid far greater overt stress in her consultations on the scientific aspects of medicine than any of them. Yet as we have seen there was little trace of gentility in most of her medical consultations and they provide a graphic example of a distinctly non-bourgeois version of medical practice. (Or rather they reveal what may happen to some patients when bourgeois norms are applied solely to the bourgeoisie.)

For her, an individual's ability to pay for medical services was based on moral characteristics; anyone who worked hard and lived sensibly could normally afford private care. The mothers at the clinic were therefore suspected to be either morally or rationally deficient, or indeed both.[17] This philosophy gave the doctor a mandate to investigate all aspects of their lives; for her task was not simply the treatment of illness but the reform of the poor so that they had no need of such charity in the future. Such investigation served a further purpose also, for it helped to distinguish the deserving from the undeserving, cases of genuine hardship from those who were lazy or evil. A charity service, in a country where medicine normally had to be paid for, not only aided those who had fallen on hard times through no fault of their own but might also, on this theory, be abused by those who were well capable of bettering themselves if they had a mind to.

We may also contrast the medical fate of those who live in total institutions or totalitarian societies with those of the freer sick elsewhere. At the height of Stalin's production drive doctors were issued with quotas for the numbers allowed to be ill; once these were filled no one else could fall sick (Waitzkin and Waterman, 1974). By contrast, it now appears that some political offences may be re-cast as psychiatric illness within the Soviet Union.[18] Armies, prisons and mental hospitals may similarly place drastic restrictions on individuals' right to be or not to be ill, choosing themselves what is to count as illness and when and how it is to be treated.

To draw a moral from all this: it is currently fashionable to see the National Health Service as representing only a partial victory for the working class. But the consideration of what a fully social system of medicine might mean shows just how partial such views are. For all our sophistication there is a strong temptation to assume that the bourgeois version of medicine, far from being the product of specific historical circumstances, is the only way in which these matters could be dealt with. Freidson (1970a, p.214) has noted how Becker, when writing of deviance, excludes biological illness as beyond the sociologists' remit. Similarly, other writers, including Freidson, take for granted the assumption that the doctor-patient relationship is and should be a private contract (using 'private' in the sense of privacy). The things which make sociological news are the exceptions to this principle: the fact that, despite the individual's right to choose or reject treatment, there is also a social duty to keep fit and co-operate with expert advice - a sick role; or the fact that although doctors claim to serve the individual patient they may sometimes in practice oppress her.

Bourgeois freedoms deserve a mention in their own right; and the fact of their continuation - in only slightly modified form and in quite different historical circumstances from those which led to their creation - needs its own analysis. Johnson (1972) has noted how the National Health Service represents merely a partial mediation by the state which now determines who should get the service, but is not directly concerned with the manner of its delivery. He himself represents this as a victory for the profession, which can continue its old dominance unchecked. Looked at in another way, the Health Service, for all its defects, is a major triumph for the patient too. He or she can now get a standard of care that before was available only to the wealthy and, at the same time, can retain many of those same rights to polite treatment, privacy and choice that were previously guaranteed only by private practice. And things might not have been so. Patient power is the only sure road to medical gentility.

Policy Considerations

I shall now conclude with some reflections on the possible implications of my analysis for the current practice of medicine. Because my comments have been fairly abstract, my remarks here will be equally general, although I do have one or two specific things to say on occasion. Since I cover a variety of topics, most of which are unconnected, I shall merely list the points I wish to make.

1. The presence of students in clinics had a major effect upon the shape and content of interaction with parents, and this was so even where no overt teaching was done. This system may produce the worst of both worlds. Not only did parents get less time, less privacy and an atmosphere which might make their lay remarks look 'silly' (at least to them), but teaching was also affected. I can make no proper assessment of the effectiveness of teaching by such a method, but the concern of staff to minimize the impact of students on patients placed major restrictions on what could be taught. Doctors were put in an impossible dilemma: those who worried a lot about teaching squeezed the parents out, while those who worried about the parents never taught, and the students just sat there, quietly bored. There were some doctors who could not cope at all with the conflicting demands and whose clinics resembled a three-ring circus run by a dazed but frantic ringmaster. Other methods of

teaching might well prove more satisfactory to both patients and students.

2. The doctors in this study overtly defined medical work as a 'natural' phenomenon. In one example with which I have dealt 'psychiatric' matters were normally avoided and doctors concentrated instead on the purely organic. That this avoidance is not an idiosyncrasy of paediatricians is shown by McDonald and Patel's (1975) study of Glaswegian psychiatrists. Even they apparently preferred organic to functional complaints. These preferences are scarcely surprising given the heavy emphasis on the organic side in medical training; the firm rule that a patient's character is to be overtly idealized; and the extremely circuitous and time-consuming work that is involved if patients are to be both criticized and idealized - whereas doctors have relatively little time for each patient.

The reification of illness that results from this avoidance has a central consequence for medical work. In our bourgeois world patients have certain rights to define themselves as physically ill, regardless of doctors' covert medical opinion. (Even parents who must share their responsibility for a child still have important powers here.) These rights are, of course, aided by the fact that many things which may be social in origin can have organic consequences. Tension at work or at home may lead to vague pains, headaches, ulcers, enuresis and so on. In other words the reification of problems within the ceremonial order of the clinic is often matched by a quite literal reification of problems within the body of the individual patient.

The challenge which this double reification presents to many branches of medicine is considerable. Although many doctors, or at least those considered here, are often content to ignore it there are some who feel that this is shirking their professional duty; the proper doctor should seek to go behind the presenting complaint and uncover the 'real' problems (Balint, M., 1964; Balint E. and Norell, 1974; Byrne and Long, 1976).

Whether doctors are the appropriate people to engage in this is a vexed question, and important objections can be raised to their doing so (Stimson, 1977). I myself will mention just one problem posed by these attempts to produce a more thoroughly social version of medicine.

To transform one's problems into illness should not, I think, always be seen as an evasion which must be faced up to. Precisely because of its natural status, illness can offer escape from difficult situations and thus soften the edges of a harsh world. To remove this freedom from individuals without having any better alternative to put in its place is a brutal act.

If doctors were always to investigate the social reasons behind the natural appearance, they might well lose half their practice. From the position of bourgeois ideology, one of the great advantages of doctors is that most of them do not normally want to poke around in the patient's psyche (though women suffer more in this respect). Going to the doctor is, on this version, a straightforward transaction. The patient presents the problem and the doctor deals with it if he or she can. But go to a psychiatrist or a social worker and who knows where you will end up?[19] If ordinary doctors ever use psychotherapy in a big way many patients might never present themselves at all. Who knows what might be 'found' behind even the most natural-seeming illness?[20]

At present this possibility seems remote. The real alternative to bourgeois medicine is more likely to come, not from the doctors themselves but from the social workers, who in Britain at least are attached in ever- increasing numbers to medical institutions and to whom such problems may increasingly be referred.[21]

3. As I have argued, patients can not only choose to be ill - within limits - they can also choose not to be ill, or at least most adult patients can. When they are not ill doctors have almost no purchase on them at all. Health is no business of doctors, only illness. It is this, coupled with medical gentility, that renders the ordinary doctor's participation in preventive medicine a rather unlikely event. To engage in systematic reform of the way we live - what we eat, drink or smoke, how we bring up our children; these are affairs beyond the doctor's normal remit, unless, that is, they result in clear illness. There may well be exceptions to this rule, but the principle at present stands firm. Doctors have not the time, the training, the inclination or the warrant to intervene routinely in patients' lives. Once again, the currently fashionable doctrines of a more thoroughly social medicine place a much greater emphasis on prevention than has been common in recent years. As things stand, however, it seems unlikely that most doctors can take much part in this movement.

4. If the causes of the impersonality, lack of choice, and relatively uninformative nature of the bureaucratic format are lack of time and an absence of competition, then the only way to amend these, if that is what is wished, is to devote far more resources to national medical services. And yet the issue has rarely been faced.

To take one example, Horobin (1978) has shown how the norm set for the size of general practitioners lists within the Health Service, perhaps the most fundamental determinant of a doctor's work, has been the subject of almost no political or academic discussion. It seems to have been derived simply by dividing the population by the number of general practitioners practising at the time the service was created. Fierce debate has occurred over the areas which are over- or under-doctored according to this norm and what might be the best policies to correct this; whether or not the norm is desirable in the first place has rarely been at issue.

I noted earlier the strong similarities with education in this respect. The way in which the norms of class or practice size are taken for granted is also illustrated by the great media scares that occur every now and again due to demographic and student change. The fuss over whether we are producing 'too many' teachers or doctors is all based on the largely unexamined assumption that our current ratios represent an ideal standard. Similarly, the efforts to produce a better service all concentrate on modifications which leave this norm untouched. Teachers discuss the pros and cons of new types of teaching and assessment, whether to abolish exams, or teach by projects instead of essays. Doctors are supposed to develop a more 'person-oriented' style or else get more paramedical assistants. Meanwhile teacher-pupil and doctor-patient ratios stay pretty much the same.

Far more research and discussion is therefore needed about the differences produced in medical consultations by simple variations in their length. Unless one is fully aware of the constraints which time imposes, any discussion of the doctor-patient relationship takes on a curiously abstract air quite remote from daily experience.

5. Having said all this, I must take care not to be misunderstood. The argument that the bureaucratic format is rather more controlled and impersonal than the private mode is quite separate from the judgment that this is a bad thing which needs an immediate remedy. Even if it can be convincingly shown that more resources do in fact produce a more personalized service, it is not clear that this should have any priority, at least as a general aim. It can be argued that many of the personal touches which seem to be added by competition are of a somewhat spurious nature.

As I have argued elsewhere (Strong, 1979), there is a distinct tendency within sociology to treat medical matters in much the same way as do soap-operas, investing them with enormous significance and turning the most routine treatment into human drama. There is clearly good reason for this on occasion, but as a general outlook it can be misleading. Many consultations are mundane affairs in which patients are willing to tolerate impersonal treatment in return for help of some kind. Besides, it is not as if this is anything unusual. To understand medical service fully we must see it as just one of a great many impersonal relationships into which consumers must enter in our society: doing the shopping; buying a house; selling a car or seeing the doctor are all, in Wenglinsky's (1973) phrase, errands (See also Strong 1977a). What customers are most interested in here is competent and efficient service, and they are quite prepared to sacrifice the more personal touches if this is the price they must pay. Few grocers have survived the supermarket era.

The crucial issue then turns around the technical quality of the service that is offered; and on this matter I am not competent to pass judgment although, as I noted in the introduction, there is no evidence that I know of that the medical care offered patients in the bureaucratic format was inferior to that found in the private format.

What I can say is that private practice certainly fostered the impression that the technical quality of care was something special. This appearance of excellence was based, ironically enough, on parents' very scepticism about medicine. Although most patients have some general distrust of doctors, they typically lack the expertise to pass correct technical judgments on the wisdom pf any one doctor. Nevertheless they still try to assess staff's competence as best they can. In a competitive market doctors can exploit this weakness by explicitly fostering the delusion of customer wisdom. The private-practice style observed in this study was one in which the doctor subtly indicated his own individual merit, flattered patients by treating them as particularly promising medical students, and congratulated them on having chosen so well. The personal charm, the lavish use of technical terms (displayed in the guise of enabling patients to make a better choice), the routine battery of impressive though often useless tests, and the casual mention of colleagues in famous hospitals, all 'prove' that you cannot get proper medicine unless you pay for it; a proof that seems to have taken in a surprising number of American sociologists. Or perhaps this is not so surprising if one remembers that thinking oneself an artful consumer is such a cherished identity in the games the middle classes play.

6. Despite the absence, as I would see it, of any general need for a highly

personal medical service, there are many instances where something rather better than the standard bureaucratic package is desirable. In particular, relatively impersonal treatment may be fine for many acute or trivial ailments, but is far less so for chronic conditions. Where a whole way of life is involved then ten, fifteen or, if the patient is lucky, thirty minutes seems rather inappropriate. The parents of the handicapped children in this study did get more time than most others and did, as we have seen, get a somewhat more personal service. Even so, it scarcely matched the complexity and scale of the problems which they faced.[22]

Securing a better service here is not just a question of devoting more resources to those most in need. It is also a question of staff's attitude. It is not simply that the bureaucratic format is best suited to acute conditions, but that doctors themselves tend to prefer acute medicine. Trained to cure and deriving great satisfaction from the speedy solution of organic problems, they are constantly faced with patients for whom they can do little and whose difficulties are as much social as natural. Their normal reaction to this dilemma is to shy away from it, one that in some respects may be no bad thing, as I have argued. There are, however, contexts in which their special skills could be put to much greater use than occurs at present, at least on the evidence presented here.

One such circumstance stood out clearly in this study, and it is with this that I shall end. Doctors believed, and there was a good deal of evidence to support their belief, that the parents of handicapped children were often racked by a feeling of personal guilt, a feeling that they themselves were responsible for their child's condition. And yet, as we have seen, doctors did very little to help such parents. The search and destroy methods used for trivial anxieties were not employed here. Parents, or so it seemed, were afraid to reveal their fears, doctors were afraid to search for them.

This mutual avoidance of the matter may be intelligible, but there is surely no necessity for things to be this way and every reason why they should be otherwise. For here at least doctors can offer some practical help. They may lack cures but they can give comfort. Moreover, it is a comfort which only they can properly provide. Social workers, where they are available, may have the training and the time to investigate the parents' world; but only doctors can pronounce with any authority on the likely aetiology of a child's condition, only they can cast things firmly within the natural sphere.[23]

9 A Methodological Appendix

The subject of this book concerns those rules which make up the bureaucratic format; but finding rules in interaction and, more especially, keeping them alive in captivity so that others may see them too, presents considerable difficulties. A brief account of these difficulties and of the various ways of tackling them may therefore be necessary, at least for the sceptical or technically-minded reader.

The method of data collection used in this study was primarily based on observation. Observation, or the systematic recording of behaviour, has several advantages over interview data in the study of social rules. First, interviews are no guide to actual behaviour (Cicourel, 1964; Phillips, 1971). Many of the studies of doctor-patient relationship, since they are based solely on interviews, are purely accounts of attitudes. As Stimson and Webb's (1975) study has shown, there is no necessary relationship between what patients do in medical consultation and what they say they do in another context. (In group interviews women recounted heroic tales of their personal combat with their doctors, but no such behaviour was actually observed in GPs' surgeries.) What people say depends very much on what questions are asked, who asks them and the general sense of the occasion. Even where rules are accurately recounted - and interview methods allow no clear check on this - it is still impossible to determine how such rules relate to actual behaviour. For no rule specifies the grounds of its own application. That is, to use a rule one also needs a further set of rules to say when, how and in what circumstances the rule is to be used. These rules of thumb are rarely spelt out formally, save in legal proceedings. Aside from these difficulties, there are good grounds for arguing that people are incapable of immediate recall of many aspects of their behaviour. It is not merely that our accounts are guided by our prejudices or immediate circumstances but that we fail to notice much of what we do, for we attend only to those things that concern us most. As Fingarette (1969) has argued, there is no need for us even to be conscious of following a rule in order to actually do so. Interview data therefore contain a strong bias against the routine and the non-eventful.

The strategy that was followed in this study was therefore to observe and record the behaviour in question systematically and then to engage in detailed analysis and exemplification. This has certain advantages for both researcher and reader. For the researcher it provides a source of data which, unlike pre-coded material, is independent of the analysis and can therefore be re-read or re-played as a check against that analysis. Similarly, in so far as examples of data are provided in the text they provide readers with the possibility of independent checking.

Certain difficulties still remain. The method is highly labour-intensive and thus, like informal interviewing, does not permit of ready generalization, though this difficulty may be surmounted if other comparable studies are available (Becker, 1969a). More crucially, there are major problems involving the accuracy of note-taking, the detection of rules in observed interaction, the quantification of such phenomena, the influence of the observer upon the recorded material and the general difficulties of analysing qualitative data. Each of these matters deserves some attention.

Recording Interaction

There is a variety of procedures for recording interaction, each with its own advantages and disadvantages. Audio or video-tape offer the possibility of highly accurate recording but are obtrusive and pose major problems for transcription. The pen and paper method used in this study is, by comparison, extremely inaccurate; much that is spoken is lost and much that is recorded is no doubt altered. At the same time however, it does enable the relatively easy study of a very large number of cases and it is this which justifies its use in the present study. To have transcribed and analysed a mechanical recording of over 1,100 consultations, some of them up to an hour long, would have been a forbidding task and yet, unless one had gathered some such large body of data, there would have been an insufficient number of 'deviant cases' for analysis - and as we have seen it is the exceptions which prove the rule.

Moreover, this rather crude method of recording seems relatively tolerable for the somewhat gross matters with which I am here concerned. To illustrate the broad components of a role format, one does not require the same degree of accuracy in recording as is necessary for those concerned with the minutiae of conversational analysis, where the precise sequence and phrasing of word and gesture is essential to the analysis.

Quantifying Qualitative Data

My central assumption here is that it is illegitimate to attempt to count social phenomena more precisely than lay persons are themselves able to.[1] An examination of everyday counting practices soon reveals that the kind of things which human beings are able to count with any ease, and in which they may reasonably expect others to arrive at a similar total, are remarkably limited. They belong solely to the world of objects. We count cars, meals or bathrooms, but counting actions or emotions seems to be a much trickier business. To say, 'I had a good day,' is a meaningful statement but to attempt to quantify its good aspects in any precise fashion is not possible.[2] Under inspection, 'good' things have their 'bad' side too; every silver lining has a cloud. In consequence it would be entirely bogus to quantify many aspects of the data which I have described here. Nevertheless, following Douglas (1971), I think there can be an important degree of certainty over people's typical meanings. Indeed, organized life would be impossible if this were not the case. A limited version of counting is thus often possible, using quantificatory statements such as 'always/typically/rarely/never'.

The reader will therefore have found a mixture of kinds of quantification within the book. On some matters, for example the number of foster-mothers or cases seen in a clinic, I feel able to be precise. For many other matters which deal with actions rather than objects and where far more judgment is therefore necessary, 'typically' or 'rarely' seem more sensible terms. For a few kinds of action I have in fact used numbers. Where these were extremely unusual and I had only a limited number of cases to study, it seemed reasonable to risk a little more quantification. Since these cases could be analysed in considerable detail, terms like 'three', 'four' or 'five' have sometimes been used. I cannot really claim to know that there were exactly three, four or five instances of X or Y. I have used numbers here because these were highly infrequent happenings for which I was specifically searching, and any possible examples of which had been given a good deal of thought. Such numbers also have, I confess, a rhetorical significance. 'Look, I could only find five!' sounds more convincing than 'I found very few exceptions'.

The Influence of the Observer

One objection that is commonly made to studies such as this is that although observation is undoubtedly a more direct way of studying action, the presence of the observer changes the action in a way that interviewing does not. Since all action is oriented in some way to the immediate social context, it is undoubtedly true that the fieldworker changes that situation. However, there are good grounds, at least in the present study, for arguing that such effects were minimal. First, as Becker has emphasized, the daily business of life has to get done, and in clinics there was no other time or place for it to be done:

> The people the fieldworker observes are ordinarily constrained to act as they would have in his absence by the very social constraints whose effects interest him; he therefore has little chance, compared to the practitioners of other methods, to influence what they do, for more potent forces are operating (Becker, 1969b, p.43).

Second, such a presence was by no means strange. The medical settings that were studied here were highly public places with nurses, students, other staff and sometimes other patients all watching the action or overhearing parts of it. Fieldwork was not uncomfortable since there were so many others engaged in somewhat similar activities. Thus, staff rapidly became used to the presence of researchers and treated them as part of the furniture. Some of them indeed, despite being told otherwise, seemed to think that only the patients were being studied.

As for the clientele, it must be remembered that all of what they said was for the record, regardless of the record made by the researchers, for doctors themselves routinely made notes on what was said by parents during the consultation. It is quite likely that had there been no audience and no note-taking at all, conversations might have taken a somewhat different turn. Parents might have found 'personal' and emotional matters somewhat easier to raise, and they could well have felt more relaxed and been more informal. However, such constraints were in the nature of the settings, they were not imposed upon them by the research.

Understanding Action

Yet another problem which plagues both the writer and the reader of sociological work is the ambiguity of human action. How can we be certain that such and such really did mean what I say it meant? This difficulty is heightened when the reader is presented with mere snippets of data, abstracted from the context in which they occurred - a procedure which is clearly essential when data are long and monographs are short. As we shall see, there are special difficulties involved in interpreting the kind of data considered here. For all of these reasons some comment is needed on the solutions that I adopted.

For some writers the difficulty of providing guaranteed interpretation of any datum has led to their rejection of all conventional sociological description. While it is certainly true that all hitherto existing sociologies have failed to provide any sure method for overcoming the ambiguities of meaning in social interaction, it would be absurd to argue that such inquiry was thereby invalid.[3] The relevant arguments could and unfortunately do fill many volumes. Two brief points may be made here.

First, although misunderstanding is commonplace in daily life, it is clear that most action is premised upon the assumption that a correct interpretation of it is both possible and likely, at least where the participants are familiar with the situation. Indeed, action is constructed very precisely so that it can be correctly interpreted by the competent insider.[4] Thus for the outsider who wishes to understand what is going on, the principal method of arriving at this is to try to become competent, to immerse oneself as fully as possible in the situation; which is, of course, the procedure adopted in this study.

One further source of help is also available. Since misunderstanding is still a common occurrence, whatever the participants' competence, they are obliged to take the possibility of failure continually into account. Indeed, in responding to one another we openly display that we have understood the previous speakers meaning in order to establish our reply as a relevant one.[5] Thus the students of interaction can be guided in their reading of these matters, not just by their familiarity with the scene but by the readings displayed by the participants. Neither procedure guarantees an objective interpretation, but the use of both may help to generate a substantial measure of confidence in the analysis.

So far, so good. It must be noted, however, that the extent and manner in which meanings and understandings are displayed varies greatly, and this may add considerably to the difficulty of the analysts' task. In any interaction a large number of different things are conveyed and some are much more liable to misinterpretation than others. The main reason for this is simple: participants typically differ in the extent to which they have shared membership in the various social worlds under discussion.

To take the example of doctor-patient consultations: it is notorious that certain messages are extremely difficult to convey. Doctors, for instance, often experience great difficulty in understanding the world in which their patients live and may operate with a set of stereotypes quite inappropriate to that world (e.g., see Macintyre, 1977).

By contrast there are other matters in which both doctors and patients typically share some competence and about which they can communicate with facility. Such would seem to be the case with the matters under consideration here. That is, with the exception of some of the Puerto Rican patients in the American hospitals, all the adult participants in these medical consultations demonstrated considerable awareness of the rules of the ceremonial order of clinics.[6]

This shared competence can present considerable analytical difficulties, greater perhaps than those found where misunderstanding is common. For where both parties are insiders, communication as to the nature of the world they share is typically indirect and allusive and, although meanings and understandings are certainly displayed, this is normally done in the most delicate of fashions. In such cases rules are spelt out only in special circumstances, as when, for example, they have been broken or when outsiders are present. Since this is done only to the deviant or the ignorant, to name a rule is to name a person and must necessarily be done with discretion if one is not to formulate oneself as incompetent or offensive.

In consequence, although I have quoted several examples in which rules were actually spelt out, these occurred but a mere handful of times. Since rules were openly formulated only in special circumstances, such occasions cannot be cited as direct evidence of normal rule use but are instead something different: acts of teaching, warning or attempted mitigation.

This general absence of relevant formulations in the interaction means that we are faced with a paradox. Interviewing generates spoken or written statements of rules, either made by or agreed with by the respondents. These can be openly displayed and sometimes even counted by the researcher. However, there is no way of knowing how these rules relate to and are used in actual behaviour. By contrast, the observation and recording of relatively trouble-free interaction provides extremely rich data on 'what happens', but few if any occasions on which we may actually see or hear the rules being followed.

Quite what the rules are is therefore unclear at first. This difficulty is compounded by two further features. For a start, the same rule may be embodied in a great variety of very different behaviour according to circumstance. I have already noted how no rule contains within it the further set of criteria for its application on particular occasions. Observation certainly permits the researcher to gather extensive data on the differing ways in which the same rule may be applied. But since rules are not normally formulated during action, still less their rules of use, seeing the same rule across a wide range of encounters presents considerable difficulties, as does the display of that rule in its various natural habitats so that others may see it too.

The other difficulty is this. Following a rule concerns the omission of certain behaviour as much as the commission of other behaviour. Here not even the acts, let alone the rules, are directly audible or visible. Absences are as important as presences; but to notice that the dog did not bark in the night is often a most difficult task and one that is even harder to prove unless one can display all of one's data.

Understanding and Formulating Rules

There are certain solutions to the problems of finding and displaying tacit social rules with the use of observational data. These procedures were used in the analysis of the material discussed here and inform the logic, such as it is, of its presentation. Apart from the special case that I have already cited where rules were already spelt out, six types of data have been presented to warrant the finding of a particular rule, though, given the limitations of time, space and enthusiasm, not all six have been listed for every rule.

First, I have given examples of typical and entirely routine uses. I hope this gives the reader some flavour of standard usage but it does not, as we have seen, necessarily display that this was indeed the rule being followed in the behaviour cited. Nor does such quotation adequately establish just what was omitted. For these purposes a second type of example is necessary. Although this book is principally concerned with the nature of the bureaucratic format in medical consultations, the rather different behaviour found in the other formats, when contrasted with that found within the bureaucratic type, gives a much clearer indication of the basic rules within the latter.

This contrast may illuminate just what is involved by the rules of the bureaucratic format, but it leaves untouched the problem of demonstrating the range of these rules and their universal application within this range. The scope of the rules has been shown first by a consideration of their outer edges, the limiting cases in which they do not apply. These form a third type of data.

One analytical strategy in these cases is to show that, although these are counter-examples, they are produced by very special circumstances and occur only within these.

To demonstrate that the rule was applied consistently, apart from these special circumstances, has required a fourth kind of data. This may be divided into two types. First, one needs a selection of examples which display a cross-section of the kinds of occasion on which the rule is necessary. Second and more importantly, one requires a detailed consideration of those situations which would seem to threaten the applicability of the rule. In other words, to establish a rule's universality one needs to examine those occasions on which it is most seriously tested. For example, in analysing the rule that the doctor is always the expert, the crucial test becomes what happens when the parents do in fact possess medical knowledge.

A fifth type of data has concerned the extent to which the rule varies systematically in use. So far I have considered only the problems of finding and displaying the most general form of a rule. But rules vary in their manner of use according to circumstances, and this too must be demonstrated. For example, all parents were treated as if they were moral, loving, intelligent and honest; but as regards their competence *vis-à-vis* the child there were important differences. Mothers' competence was totally assumed; that of fathers was openly questioned.

A final and sixth type of data has come from the discussion of these rules in interviews with doctors. Such data present considerable problems for analysis if the researcher has no other; but, taken together with the other data sources that have been outlined, they act as both a check and a useful guide.

The Generation and Testing of Hypotheses

A brief comment is necessary about the way in which the ideas in this study were produced and tested. There are various systematic methods for analysing qualitative data, and the procedure used here was a mixture of that which Glaser (1964) has termed the 'constant comparative method of qualitative analysis' and the method of 'analytic induction' as described by Robinson (1951), Cressey (1971) and Bloor (1976b). Both are alternatives to the hypothetico-deductive or 'big bang' mode of analysis that is normally used with pre-coded data. In this latter mode one systematically deduces a set of hypotheses from a body of theory and attempts to falsify them at one go. By contrast, analytic induction attempts to relate the process of generating propositions more closely to the data. Explanations are tested out all the time, trying them on one case to see if they fit, then moving on to another, and so on. Where the proposition does not cover the particular case, it may be reformulated or else the phenomenon redefined until a universal relationship is established which fits all the cases.

For its successful use the method of analytic induction requires a precise formulation of at least part of the problem. However, the research described here had initially no one focus but several overlapping ones. To begin with I had no intention of studying the doctor-patient role-relationship since I held 'role' to be an old-fashioned and exploded concept. It was only at a late stage in the project and as a result of writing on various other themes that I became convinced that there were clear structures here. Making up one's mind as late as this has important disadvantages. If I had discovered this earlier on I could have designed the study far more systematically to test my propositions. Since I did not, I was faced with a dilemma. On the one hand, I needed a method that would enable the generation of a coherent set of ideas but that would also, at least initially, leave matters somewhat open and offer scope for modification. On the other hand, once I had a series of propositions, I required a method that would enable me to test them in some relatively adequate form.

In consequence, I began the analysis with a method that had a strong resemblance to the 'constant comparative method' proposed by Glaser. He argues that

> ... in contrast to analytic induction the method is concerned with generating and plausibly suggesting (not provisionally testing) many properties and hypotheses about a *general* phenomenon (Glaser, 1964, p.438).

As its name implies, this method consists of comparing each datum with a given selection of categories and seeing whether or not it fits. Once one has coded for a category several times and developed a more sophisticated version of it, one then codes only if the datum that is being examined points to a new aspect of the category. The only exception to this are categories of great theoretical interest but of which there are very few examples. If the datum fits under none of them, then the categories are modified or an entirely new one produced. The aim is to bring whatever initial ideas one has systematically to the data, and in the process of this to see what new ideas can be generated. Once all the data have been examined, the material relating to each is systematically scrutinized and further sub-divisions or re-groupings made, as items are found to differ or cluster together.

In my use of this method I made one important modification. This process of hypothesis generation was carried out on only one half of the data, with most of the material from the American hospital and most of that from the Scottish neurological clinic being excluded. Having completed the initial analysis of the first half of the data, I then re-organized my basic categories according to my current ideas, re-analysed the coded data and wrote a first, though only partial, draft. This provided me with a systematic set of propositions which I was then able to test by analysing the further half of my data. Where these did not fit the argument was amended. This latter step rendered my analysis, in this instance, more akin to the method of analytic induction.

Notes

Chapter 1   Introduction

1   For a definition of the ritual order see Goffman (1975a). As he points out, we seem to lack a word which captures the full meaning of this order. 'Ritual' is not quite right because it does not convey the fact that matters of considerable substantive import are involved. None of the alternatives in sociological use are any better: 'ceremony', 'politeness', 'expressive' - all fail in this respect. Our secularized culture makes such a sharp division between the practical world and that of ceremony that we have no terms left with which to grasp the intensely moral and ritual nature of the way in which we frame our practical concerns.

2   This distinction cannot be pushed too far as there are also resemblances between the forms of different kinds of service relationship (Wenglinsky, 1973; Strong, 1977a).

3   For a more extended critique of Parsons's model see Bloor and Horobin (1975), and Strong and Davis (1977).

4   This model is considered in more detail in chapter 8. Perhaps the best introduction to it is contained in Goffman (1961).

5   A more systematic if far less detailed comparison of these formats is contained in Strong and Davis (1977). Note also that the analysis of Goffman presented in this article is somewhat different from that given in this book. This change is due principally to my reading the paper by Gonos (1977) on Goffman.

6   This article is concerned solely with the use of the game format in therapists' work with children. However, the same mode was also used by doctors in the developmental assessment of young children. Indeed, it would seem to be a standard format available to any adult in our culture for use with the very young.

7   This is not entirely fair to Goffman, since one of his central themes has been the micropolitics of encounters; that is, how people use frames to suit their own particular ends (Goffman, 1970, 1971a). Indeed, for many readers Goffman presents too cynical a view of interaction. His very concern with the relationship of individuals to frames leads him to treat frames themselves as given, a tendency that is reinforced by his failure to consider either the range

of frames in use within any one activity-system, or their historical origins, or their current uses. These matters are discussed more fully in chapter 8.

8   See Bittner's (1965) formulation of how official plans are used in this fashion in organizations.

9   The attempt to make one set of standards apply to each and every action and encounter is, of course, the definition of radicalism. As Bittner (1963) has shown, such attempts necessarily fail and indeed those radical movements that survive do so only by creating elaborate procedures for enabling their members to ignore those large areas of reality that do not fit their creed.

Chapter 2   Medical Systems and Settings

1   For most practical purposes there is no difference between the NHS in Scotland and the NHS in England and Wales. For other general sociological comparisons between the British and American systems, see Freidson (1970a) and Mechanic (1971). For a more personal account of the NHS see Roth (1977), as well as a view by an American doctor (Fisher, 1974). All these comparisons are by American authors.

2   It should be noted that the Scottish city was famed for the degree to which such services were planned, centralized and to some extent imposed upon the population. Although these features are characteristic of the British health services as a whole when compared with American health services, the Scottish city displayed them to an unusual degree.

3   Interestingly, there was one medical institution in the Scottish city that did promote itself somewhat in the American fashion. This was a hospital for the long-term care of severely retarded children. These institutions have been starved of public funds, and such promotion is one way of redeeming the balance. An assessment and nursery centre for handicapped children which opened at the end of the study also began to promote itself along the same lines.

4   One must not over-emphasize the extent to which records were linked. The GP and hospital record systems were not themselves linked, nor were the local authority records linked to the hospital, or vice versa.

5   Given the importance of medical conditions as a source of variation in the nature of consultations, it would be useful to quantify these. However, although large numbers of different kinds of condition were seen in the course of the research, to give precise figures here would be merely guesswork. This would make sense only if it were based on a detailed analysis of the patient records; and although this was attempted for a selection of 60 cases for the Scottish neurological clinic it proved immensely problematic. The three

researchers spent a month each on this task, and to have studied them all would have been impossible. Moreover, one is not comparing like with like. The term 'diagnosis' covers very different types of entity. 'Headaches' for example are symptoms, while others such as 'fall' are assertions about cause, and yet others, such as 'spina bifida', are simply descriptions (Blaxter, 1978). Finally, the process of diagnosis is a phenomenon of varying method and accuracy. Different doctors may produce different diagnoses, and any one diagnosis may have a differing degree of certainty from case to case and consultation to consultation.

Chapter 3   Natural Parenthood

1   Macintyre (1976) has commented on a rather similar reification of character in medical work with pregnant women, though two important differences from this should be noted. Reification in children's clinics was a matter of surface ceremony; it did not necessarily reflect what staff actually thought of mothers. The same character was ascribed to mothers whatever their marital or other status; whereas, as Macintyre shows, 'maternal instincts' were presumed to occur only in married women while the single but pregnant woman 'naturally' wished to be rid of her child.

2   For an analysis of the reconstitution of character, see Garfinkel (1956b). Note also that face-work is not tied to the preservation of the good, nor is character-work to the denunciation of the bad. Where a player is cast as a villain, then face-work may be essential to preserve this image of evil; conversely, even the worst sinners may be redeemed.

3   The charity mode has the least empirical foundation of any format considered in this study. Although it is based on the work of only one doctor and there are likely to be some idiosyncratic elements within this particular usage, there is some evidence from other studies that its central feature - explicit moral investigation - can be found in a rather similar form elsewhere. Recent studies of British casualty departments have described the open denunciation of certain disreputable cases such as repeat suicide attempts and drunks (Jeffrey, 1974; Gibson, 1977); and Byrne and Long (1976, pp.57-8) give a detailed illustration of the lengths to which character-work may go in general practice - if very rarely. Thus, although such behaviour seems most unusual, it clearly does exist in places. There was also a hint in the Scottish hospital that such scenes had not been unknown in the past. Here, for instance, are a doctor's comments to his students after seeing a case of severe nappy rash and asking the mother to come in to the mother and baby unit:

Dr G: She doesn't seem very well cared for, but then it is her first baby.

He says that the nurses will teach her how to look after a baby properly.

Dr G: They do it much better than in the old days. The old nurses were very dictatorial. They snatched babies away from mothers as soon as they came in if they suspected they weren't well looked after. Now they teach them much more surreptitiously ... (pause) ... I hope ... (laughter).

4   This division is similar to that found in other studies of judgmental work (Emerson, 1969; Macintyre, 1977).

5   Of the 18 occasions on which fathers alone brought the child, 11 consultations took place in the Scottish neurological clinic; one in the Scottish general medical clinic; 4 in the Scottish occupational therapy department, in so far as those can be called consultations; and on two occasions in the American clinics. Since one father attended several times and in two different settings the total number of fathers seen on their own was 13.

6   One other point should be noted about the treatment that fathers received when present with their spouses. Although I have argued that they had a subordinate position in clinics, it was more common for wives to check their remarks with their partner than for husbands to do this. Many wives looked towards their husbands for their assent; their husbands only rarely reciprocated when they themselves spoke. This, coupled with the fact that it was fathers who often asked the more awkward questions - a point which I shall raise later, suggests that although mothers were given some priority in medical consultations, their authority as regards their children was not as absolute as might be gathered just from this account.

Chapter 4   Collegial Authority

1   Since no check was made on patient records, this analysis is based only on the cases in which I was informed that the cases were private.

2   'From the point of view of the authority, the important issue about any act becomes, not whether it is performed in accordance with a particular rule, but whether it is performed in accordance with the rule establishing authority itself' (Werthmann, 1969, p.620).

3   I have not considered the fourth case here, since it was so complex. Even though the dispute was left unresolved, its main elements did seem to conform to the general picture I have drawn in this chapter. What appears to have

happened is that the mother, who was extremely dubious about the usefulness of treatment offered by the doctor, was afraid to say so directly but instead gave a whole series of seemingly absurd excuses for not being able to fix a definite time for the next appointment, each of which provoked the doctor into yet more detailed investigation of these reasons. As the doctor's grumpiness increased so did the mother's, until she gave an angry denunciation of the treatment her child had had at the clinic. Both parties then cooled down; but the mother left without having fixed a definite time for a new appointment and did not in fact return.

4 It could, however, be argued that extreme non-verbal dissent is partly designed to enforce an investigation by the superior party, thus drawing some of the sting from a subordinate's challenge by making it a requested item. (This may well have been part of the reasoning behind the bizarre excuses given by the mother described in note 3, above). Perhaps it is better to leave intentions out of this altogether and merely state that such behaviour is a typical response by the weak, and that, whatever its motivation on any particular occasion, it can produce the above effects.

5 These 20 cases were seen in 7 different settings, 5 in Scotland and 2 in America, and involved 10 different staff members, all but one a doctor. Since no check was made on patient records this total is based on what was mentioned in clinics. It may well have some accuracy, for staff routinely inquired about parents' occupations for the records, while a visit from a parent with medical connections was a matter for warning by nurses and general comment between staff. They were well aware of the threat posed by such parents. Note also that there was no difference between the private and bureaucratic formats in respect of the problems that such parents presented or the treatment they received. Thus I have included, within this total of 20 cases, 2 private patients from the American hospital.

6 This does not mean that these parents presented no threat to staff's authority, merely that they obeyed the surface ceremony. Beneath that ceremony, some of these parents in fact mounted very severe challenges (see chapter 8).

Chapter 5   A Joint Venture

1 Goffman (1971a) contains a very detailed treatment of a whole range of 'illegitimate' motives and interests that the providers of services may have, and of the ways in which these are concealed. Doctors are not alone in their problems.

2 *Dr Finlay's Casebook* was a long-running 1970's television series, revived briefly in the 1990s, based on characters created by the novelist, A.J. Cronin

(1896-1981). Cronin had qualified as a doctor in Glasgow and practised medicine for some years before becoming a full-time writer. The series depicted general practice in a small community on the border of the Scottish Highlands in the late 1920s and early 1930s. [*Footnote expanded for 2001 edition*].

Chapter 6   Medical Control

1   The past neglect in medical sociology of the influence of patients upon medical consultations has led in recompense to some exaggeration of that influence. The interactionist tradition is famous for demonstrating that the lower orders in organizations have more power than they have been conventionally ascribed. It is equally famous, or perhaps notorious, for the neglect of the way in which those normally thought to be powerful do in fact exercise their control. The irony which is one of the main strengths of the tradition is always in danger of degenerating into whimsy.

2   There is one important exception to this. Parents did not attempt any direct manipulation of the audience, but they did have one powerful source of indirect manipulation. There seemed to be a general rule that absolutely all adults, no matter what the situation, were obliged to smile and wonder at a young child if called upon to do so by mothers. Those parents of handicapped children who resisted the doctors' diagnosis commonly appealed to this rule to divert the conversation on to other matters. By calling for shared wonderment they seemed to hope that others would be forced to agree that their child was normal (see Davis and Strong, 1976b).

3   Heath (1978) gives a detailed analysis of the centrality of records to general practice consultation and the way doctors are able to conjure elaborate performances out of just a few fragments of notes.

4   Doctors could also use official form-filling to indicate that nothing very serious was at issue. The questions on the developmental assessment forms in the local authority clinics were not normally differentiated from each other. All were asked with the same light and routine air, even though some doctors asked for more precision than others. It should also be noted that some of the junior American doctors who did the work-up, which was also a highly standardized affair, did so in a heavily bureaucratic manner as if to display their subordinate status. They were filling in a form for the Chief and not for themselves.

5   One of the parents seen at the developmental clinic in the American hospital was however reported to have made notes on a previous visit. He had apparently already visited numerous hospitals across the United States in an

attempt to have his son defined as normal rather than retarded. The staff suspected that the notes were to aid him in legal action against the hospital; they turned out to be notes on the test procedures, made so that he could coach his son for the next visit.

6   For an analysis of small talk and the concepts of pre- and post-activity talk see Turner (1972).

7   In this study I have not attempted to analyse systematically the specific routines used by individual doctors. That such routines existed was obvious, for note-taking became far more rapid and accurate once a doctor's particular style had been 'learnt'. The best evidence for the distinct but highly routinized nature of diagnostic practice is Bloor's (1976a, 1976b) detailed study of adeno-tonsillectomy decision-making by eleven ENT surgeons. Note also that although the routinization of practice was more immediately obvious when staff worked to an official form, this should not be taken to mean that such forms imposed a common set of routines on all who used them. Different doctors used the form in different ways. The crucial point is that individually those ways were heavily routinized.

8   The only exception to this rule was the developmental clinic in the American hospital, where the doctors worked together with a social worker. The latter watched the child being assessed through a one-way screen, and afterwards the two staff members went into emotional matters with parents. Although several assessment sessions were observed, the researchers were excluded from the later proceedings. The clinic was seen as a special venture by the hospital and saw very few patients compared with the Scottish neurological clinic. The introduction of strong emotions into medical work seems likely to represent a major break with the bureaucratic format.

9   This analysis is based solely on cases observed in the Scottish clinics, since the only American children seen with serious conditions who had attended the hospital over a long period were seen in the amphitheatre clinic. This setting, as will be seen in the next chapter, was not typical of other clinics within the hospital. Such children were certainly patients of these latter clinics, but unfortunately none were observed in the brief American visit.

Chapter 7   Ease and Tension in the Alliance

1   Although staff shared, at least at this basic level, a common set of categories for classifying parents, I do not mean to suggest that there was any necessary agreement about who was and who was not dim, sensible, bright, and so on. Just as they differed over their right to moralize, so too different staff applied these categories in different ways, something which on a few, rare occasions

    led to fierce internal disputes.

2   This rule did not apply with such force in the more regular and less formal therapy sessions. In consequence, therapists felt themselves better able to judge the normal level of care which children received.

3   The amphitheatre clinic gave even greater prominence to the clinical format than the Scottish clinic. Indeed, where the parents could not speak competent English or where a child was unaccompanied by parents, the clinical format was almost totally dominant, a fact which resulted in tears in some younger children and great offence in adolescents.

4   The difficulties that such problems caused for the overall promise of medicine are similar to those that they also cause for religious faith. Religion, like medicine, both distinguishes between a natural and a social world and yet invests the natural world with moral meaning. Fatal or handicapping conditions have thus always presented religions with difficulties in accounting for their existence. Voysey (1975) discusses some of the 'theodicies', or justifications of the existence of God in the face of evil, that have been developed to explain handicap. Modern medical theodicy rests on the promise that disease will be overcome by scientific research and manipulation - a programme which has recently come in for considerable criticism. Many have challenged humankind's right and ability to master 'nature' in this way. The most famous critique of medical aspirations is that of Illich (1975), whose own theodicy is fundamentally religious: pain and suffering are not things to be overcome but to be accepted as teaching us about life.

5   Davis and Strong (1976b) contains a more detailed analysis of the conditions for ease in such circumstances.

6   These 26 consultations took place in 6 different settings and involved 9 doctors; no foster-mother was seen in a therapy department. Of the 17 foster-mothers, three were seen in the general paediatric clinics in the American hospital and at least one was seen in each of the types of Scottish clinic, although all the repeat cases were seen in the neurological clinic.

7   There were, however, some similarities with the position that natural mothers found themselves in. A foster-mother might well lose her job if a doctor complained, while she was often accompanied to the clinic by a social worker from her employing agency. Her professional competence was therefore on the line on such occasions.

8   A total of 12 Scottish local-authority social workers were seen in clinics. None accompanied a child by themselves but most were present with foster-mothers, unlike the 11 house-mothers who in all but one case were a child's sole representative in a clinic. Neither of these kinds of professional was observed in the American consultations. It should be noted that part of the praise which foster-mothers were so openly given might well be due to the tensions

between doctors and social workers from outside agencies. To compliment a foster-mother might be a subtle way of putting down the social worker who, by implication, knew less and was doing less good. Such battles were normally fought indirectly, but some indication of the major challenge which social workers represented may be gained from the following excerpt, where the doctor is attacked in a fashion never dared by any parent:

SW: The parents adopting the child do have the right to know its background.
Dr I: Yes. (They briefly discuss another topic.)
SW: So much depends on the medical side.
Dr I: What do you mean?
SW: Well, on this examination.
Dr I: Well, I'll write and say that I think there is a very small risk and no more and that he's OK for adoption, with this proviso.
SW: Well (significantly). There is a problem of course.

The foster-mother left the room and the social worker then repeated at length what she had said about their duty to adopting parents and how they would have to tell them everything about the child. The doctor repeated his remarks. This did not seem to satisfy the social worker, who repeated her arguments several more times. Eventually she broke off with a sigh and stood up to leave. But then she added:

SW: We had a lot of trouble with that last child we had from you.
Dr I: Well, you didn't have it from me. You've never had a child from me.
SW: No ... (pause, then adding significantly) But it was from *here*, wasn't it? (Doctor looks blank and does not reply.) Ah, well, doctor, goodbye.
Dr I: Goodbye.

Chapter 8   Conclusions and Generalizations

1   See in particular 'Fun in Games' (Goffman, 1961).
2   The originality and importance of this model is well brought out in Helmer (1970).
3   See 'Role Distance' (Goffman, 1961) and, in particular, his recent critique of the over-deterministic use of framing in conversational analysis (Goffman, 1975b). Here Goffman argues that the whole concept of frame is no more than

a useful fiction, a heuristic pretence that action is so determined when in fact it is not:

> Thus the whole framework of conversational constraints - both system and ritual - can become something to honor, to invert, or to disregard, depending as the mood strikes. It's not that the lid can't be closed; there is no box (Goffman, 1975b, p.35).

4   Note that this is the only study in which Goffman systematically observed and recorded the workings of a particular activity-system. Yet, having done so, he concentrated not so much on the frame itself but on the ways in which members distanced themselves from it.

5   The two instances of this phenomenon were: first, the two knowledgeable parents who were granted a semi-collegial status; and second, all those occasions when teaching was carried out. It may be objected that this latter activity forms a quite separate system of its own. Although this is true, the clinical format which partly informed this activity represented an alternative mode which could have been used to frame the interaction with parents.

6   This passage is cited in the first chapter of this volume.

7   These metaphors are more fully developed in the work of Weinstein (1964,1966,1969), though he too is concerned only with the genesis of particular encounters and not with the generation of formats.

8   Once again it is slightly unfair to accuse Goffman of not being aware of the reification of formats. He typically has most things covered in an aside or a footnote somewhere:

> I can only suggest that he who would combat false consciousness and awaken people to their true interests has much to do, because the sleep is very deep. And I do not intend here to provide a lullaby but merely to sneak in and watch the way the people snore (Goffman, 1975a, p.12).

Nevertheless, one may legitimately argue that the political and historical aspect of formats is neglected in Goffman's work and constitutes perhaps its major omission (Annett and Collins, 1975). See also the excellent political analysis of a format in Barth (1966).

9   This analysis suggests that it is part of the human condition to move continually back and forth between reified and instrumental versions of social form. The belief that we can create a de-reified world is therefore as illusory as the closely-related search for guaranteed knowledge. Illusions can, however, be most important. The fact that we shall never arrive at the truth should not prevent us from seeking it out as best we can; our inability to

construct a fully rational world need not deter us from trying.

10 A much fuller account of some of these properties is given in Davis and Strong (1976b).

11 For an excellent description of sustained childish defiance see Werthman (1969).

12 This seems to be borne out by a study of interaction in an outpatient clinic at an adult hospital in which I am currently engaged.

13 The direct financial interest in gaining extra trade that exists in a private practice system may weaken professional standards, for doctors may end up selling services that the client wants rather than those in which they themselves believe. Private clients can shop around until they find a doctor to certify that they have the disease they think they have, but in non-competitive systems people have to make do with the doctor's version. There was a distinct tendency for the American hospital to validate new diseases promoted by parental pressure-groups in a more wholehearted fashion than their Scottish colleagues. Middle-class American parents could more readily choose whether their child had 'learning disability' or was 'autistic'. See also Freidson's (1970b, pp. 91-3) distinction between client- and colleague-dependent practice.

14 Note that this analysis also explains the standard use of the bureaucratic format in the American hospital in all but private patients. The Welfare State has come rather later to the United States and is still far less developed. Nevertheless, since federal and state governments now intervene on a large scale in medicine, poor patients carry some political weight; for hospitals are heavily dependent on such funding, even the private foundations such as the one studied here.

15 A certain element of competition for patients does exist within the NHS: between highly specialized units which take referrals from all over the country, and also, if to a lesser extent, between general practitioners whose patients are free to register elsewhere (though this is not the easiest of moves) and who are paid directly in accordance with the number of patients on their register. This competitive pressure will therefore reinforce the pressure exerted by political power.

16 For a systematic treatment of the theories of Victorian burgesses on the rights of the individual and the role of the state see Poggi (1977).

17 By contrast, whereas any mother who attended the 'charity' clinic was an object of suspicion to the doctor, and simply to be there was to cast her character in doubt, the reverse assumption operated in the Scottish clinics. That parents, or at least most of them, were naturally loving and competent was not just for public consumption but was a deeply held belief. Their attendance at the hospital was prima facie evidence not of their incompetence but of their

good character.

> Dr I: (to students) It's important to check on family circumstances because with a child showing delay you've always got to be on the look-out for emotional and social deprivation, but there's never been any hint of this here. *They've always kept appointments* [my emphasis] and so on, and Therapist F hasn't mentioned it, and this is one of the things she's on the look-out for.

18 These remarks should not be taken to mean that Soviet doctors and patients are normally subject to heavy political constraints. The typical doctor-patient relationship would seem to be of a heavily bourgeois kind. Freidson (1970a) ascribes this to the independent power which experts attain. I would see it also as a product of working-class power. Its establishment in a Communist state has exactly the same functions as it does in a capitalist state: it legitimates the government and helps to buy off the opposition. For both kinds of society are of the distinctly modern type in which, whether or not there are genuine elections, there is nevertheless a mass participation in politics — what Barraclough (1967) calls the *party-state* or what Bauman (1976), following Bendix, calls *plebiscitarianism.*

19 See Scheff (1968) for an instructive analysis of the way a psychiatrist can totally transform a presenting problem. Such games may be fun to play and even helpful at times. Whether they should interfere with the business of ordinary doctoring is another matter.

20 Modern psychotherapy has of course a distinctly bourgeois flavour, with its emphasis on 'non-directive' techniques and its goal of 'self-realization'. Nevertheless, while still connected with the doctrine of individualism, such beliefs seem highly destructive of its core - and more readily compatible with a collectivist vision of the world. It can be argued that techniques like encounter groups are devices by which investigative character-work may be carried out while leaving the therapists' hands clean - one simply gets the patients to do character- work on each other. It is precisely because of its bourgeois trimmings that psychotherapy is so much more saleable a commodity than Samuel Butler's vision of a fully social version of medicine. It should also be noted that in some full-blown psychotherapeutic doctrines even diseases like cancer are transformed into personal rather than bodily malignancies. For a fervent modern statement of the bourgeois position on the naturalness of illness see Sontag (1978).

21 The trends are contradictory here. The United States has a far more self-obsessed culture than that of Britain, and is the principal home of psychotherapy. The increasingly popular 'family medicine' (Janeway, 1974)

(a medical training which is half organic medicine and half psychiatry) has no equivalent in British medical schools, despite the popularity of Balint in some departments of general practice. On the other hand, the relative lack of choice between practitioners under the NHS means that it would be less easy for the British patient to escape if a more social version of medicine was introduced. An instructive account of how the system can already operate, with a child patient deemed to need psychiatric treatment by doctors but not by parents, can be found in Roth (1977).

22 The special assessment and treatment unit for handicapped children which opened at the end of this study seems to have provided a more personal service than was previously available in outpatient clinics. At any rate, parents who had experience of both services drew a sharp distinction between them (Gibson, 1977).

23 Of course there may be some occasions when doctors too believe that parents were at least partly responsible. Even here however it is normally kinder to place these things firmly in a natural frame.

Chapter 9   A Methodological Appendix

1 My stress here is upon capacities, not upon actual counting practices, for clearly there may be some things which people could count if they so chose but which only social scientists have any interest in. Moreover, there are some tribes where arithmetic is so under-developed that the precise counting of anything stops at a handful.

2 See the marvellous critique of 'quantophrenia' and the rise of the accountants in social science in Sorokin (1956).

3 Some authors have been so disturbed by the failure to generate foolproof interpretive methods that they have abandoned all interest in conventional subject-matters and concentrated solely on analysing the methods that are used in everyday life to this end; their hope being that here at least some certainty is to be found. The more optimistic of them have an essentially Cartesian strategy. They have deliberately suspended belief in all the things that sociologists normally claim to know, hoping that if some small area of life can be found about which knowledge can be truly guaranteed, then a proper sociology might eventually be constructed on this firm basis. While this quest for certainty has produced some brilliant studies of lay methodology and the structuring of talk, the larger programme is surely a delusion and is likely, for all its rigour, to go the way of the many previous attempts to find epistemological bedrock. The best we can hope for in this world, even if we study practical reasoning, is a plausible story.

4   Paradoxically, if competent insiders could not normally grasp the meaning of events, deceit would prove a most difficult matter. Its ready accomplishment depends on others both continuing to operate with the premise that things are as they seem and possessing the skills to interpret things in the normal fashion. Sudnow (1972) gives a nice example of this in his paper on glancing. As he shows, it is a central property of social scenes that they can be understood at a glance, at least by those familiar with them. They are indeed skilfully constructed in order that insiders can so read them, and dissimulation merely uses the same procedures to different ends.

5   See Goffman (1975b, pp.13-15) for an elaboration of this point. Some may object that, although this is true, one cannot have any proper confidence in the readings one makes until the procedures by which meaning and understanding are displayed have been fully analysed and are available to the sociological researcher. The weakness in this argument is that there are no good grounds for restricting it to sociologists; and applied generally it becomes ridiculous. If this were in fact the case, no one could become competent in any social sphere without formal instruction in ethnomethodology. If the laity can acquire a working competence in these matters, one sufficient for their purposes, I see no reason why constructive sociologists cannot do the same.

6   Quite why this is so is beyond the scope of this monograph. It is not surprising that doctors and therapists should have this facility, since this is their daily task, but parents' ability here poses more of a problem. The competence shown by the great majority of parents in this study would seem to derive from three main sources. First, certain of the rules relate to identities which are in standard use in our culture, e.g., our images of mothers, fathers and childhood. Second, as I suggest in chapter 8, it seems likely that the bureaucratic role format is, with minor modifications, in standard use across large areas of medical practice. Most parents will therefore have had considerable experience of the form. Finally, it is also likely that the bureaucratic format found in medical consultations has a good deal in common with those used in many other types of service relationship, though so far no detailed comparison has been made between these (But see Bigus, 1972; Wenglinsky, 1973).

Bibliography

Annett, J. and Collins, R. (1975), 'A Short History of Deference and Demeanour', in R. Collins (ed), *Conflict Sociology*, Academic Press, New York.

Atkinson, P. (1976), 'The Clinical Experience', PhD thesis, University of Edinburgh [Published as *The Clinical Experience: The Construction and Reconstruction of Medical Reality*, Gower, Farnborough, 1981. Second edition published by Ashgate, Aldershot, 1997].

Balint, E. and Norell, J.S. (1973), *Six Minutes for the Patient*, Tavistock, London.

Balint, M. (1957), *The Doctor, His Patient and The Illness*, Pitman Medical, London.

Barraclough, G. (1967), *An Introduction to Contemporary History*, Penguin Books, Harmondsworth, Middlesex.

Barth, F. (1966), *Occasional Paper No.23: Models of Social Organization*, Royal Anthropological Institute, London.

Bauman, Z. (1976), *Socialism: the Active Utopia*, Allen & Unwin, London.

Becker, H.S. (1969a), 'Social Observation and Case Studies', in H.S. Becker, *Sociological Work*, Aldine, Chicago.

Becker, H.S. (1969b), 'Fieldwork Evidence', in H.S. Becker, *Sociological Work*, Aldine, Chicago.

Bennett, A.E. (1976), *Communication Between Doctors and Patients*, Oxford University Press, Oxford.

Bigus, O. (1972), 'The Milkman and His Customer: A Cultivated Relationship', *Urban Life and Culture*, vol.1, pp.131-65.

Bittner, E. (1963), 'Radicalism and the Organization of Radical Movements', *American Sociological Review*, vol.28, pp.928-40.

Bittner, E. (1965), 'The Concept of Organization', *Social Research*, vol.32, pp. 239-55.

Blaxter, M. (1978), 'Diagnosis As Category and Process, the Case of Alcoholism', *Social Science and Medicine*, vol.12a, pp.9-18.

Bloor, M. (1976a), 'Decision-making in ENT Outpatient Clinics and Variations in the Hospitalization of Children for Adeno-Tonsillectomy', PhD thesis, University of Aberdeen.

Bloor, M. (1976b), 'Bishop Berkeley and the Adeno-Tonsillectomy Enigma', *Sociology*, vol.10, pp.43-61.

Bloor, M. and Horobin, G. (1975), Conflict and Conflict Resolutions in Doctor-patient Interactions, in C.Cox and A.Mead (eds), *A Sociology of Medical Practice*, Collier-Macmillan, London, pp. 271-84.

Blum, A. (1970), 'The Sociology of Mental Illness', in J.Douglas (ed.), *Deviance and*

Respectability: the Social Construction of Moral Meanings, Basic Books, New York, pp.36-60.

Bradley, I. (1976), *The Call to Seriousness: The Evangelical Impact on the Victorians*, Jonathan Cape, London.

Butler, S. (1977), *Erewhon.* [The edition cited cannot be identified but the book was first published in 1872 and has been widely reprinted ever since].

Byrne, P.S. and Long, B.E.L. (1976), *Doctors Talking to Patients*, HMSO, London.

Cicourel, A. (1964), *Method and Measurement in Sociology*, Free Press, New York.

Cressey, D. (1971), *Other People's Money: A Study in the Social Psychology of Embezzlement*, Wadsworth, Belmont, CA.

Davis, A.G. (1978), 'Children and Medical Work', Draft Ms. [Published as *Children in Clinics: A Sociological Analysis of Medical Work with Children*, Tavistock, London, 1982].

Davis, A.G. and Strong, P.M. (1976a), 'The Management of A Therapeutic Encounter', in M. Wadsworth and D. Robinson (eds), *Studies in Everyday Medical Life*, Martin Robertson, London, pp.123-37.

Davis, A.G. and Strong, P.M. (1976b), 'Aren't Children Wonderful? - A Study of the Allocation of Identity in Developmental Assessment', in M. Stacey (ed), *The Sociology of the National Health Service*, Sociological Review Monograph No.22, Keele, Staffs., pp.156-75.

Davis, F. (1963), *Passage Through Crisis: Polio Victims and Their Families*, Bobbs-Merrill, Indianapolis.

Dingwall, R.W.J. (1977), 'Collectivism, Regionalism and Feminism: Health Visiting and British Social Policy 1850-1975', *Journal of Social Policy*, vol. 6, pp.291-315.

Douglas, J.D. (1971), 'Introduction', in J.D. Douglas (ed), *Understanding Everyday Life*, Routledge & Kegan Paul, London, pp.3-44.

Emerson, R. (1969), *Judging Delinquents*, Aldine, Chicago.

Fingarette, H. (1969), *Self-deception*, Routledge & Kegan Paul, London.

Fisher, R.L. (1974), 'A Connecticut Yankee in Great Britain: Report of A Travelling Fellowship', *Hartford Hospital Bulletin* , vol. 29, pp.349-54.

Fletcher, C.M. (1973), *Communication in Medicine*, Nuffield Provincial Hospitals Trust, London.

Freidson, E. (1961), *Patients' Views of Medical Practice*, Russell Sage, New York.

Freidson, E. (1970a), *Profession of Medicine*, Dodd, Mead, New York.

Freidson, E. (1970b), *Professional Dominance*, Atherton, New York.

Garfinkel, H. (1956a), 'Some Sociological Concepts and Methods for Psychiatrists', *Psychiatric Research Reports*, vol.6, pp.181-95.

Garfinkel, H. (1956b), 'Conditions of Successful Degradation Ceremonies', *American Journal of Sociology*, vol.61, pp.420-4.

Gibson, H. (1977), 'Rules, Routines and Records: the Work of an Accident and

Emergency Department', PhD thesis, University of Aberdeen.

Glaser, B. (1964), 'The Constant Comparative Method of Qualitative Analysis', *Social Problems*, vol.12, pp.436-45.

Goffman, E. (1961), *Encounters*, Bobbs-Merrill, Indianapolis.

Goffman, E. (1963), *Behaviour in Public Places*, Free Press, New York.

Goffman, E. (1968a), *Asylums*, Penguin, Harmondsworth, Middlesex.

Goffman, E. (1968b), *Stigma: Notes on the Management of Spoiled Identity*, Penguin, Harmondsworth, Middlesex.

Goffman, E. (1970), *Strategic Interaction*, Basil Blackwell, Oxford.

Goffman, E. (1971a), *The Presentation of Self in Everyday Life*, Penguin, Harmondsworth, Middlesex.

Goffman, E. (1971b), *Relations in Public*, Penguin, Harmondsworth, Middlesex.

Goffman, E. (1972), *Interaction Ritual*, Penguin, Harmondsworth, Middlesex.

Goffman, E. (1975a), *Frame Analysis*, Penguin, Harmondsworth, Middlesex.

Goffman, E. (1975b), 'Replies and Responses', 'Working Papers and Pre-publications', Centro Internazionale Di Semiotica E Di Linguistica, Urbino [Published in *Forms of Talk*, Blackwell, Oxford, 1981].

Gonos, G. (1977), ' "Situation" Versus "Frame": the "Interactionist" and the "Structuralist" Analyses of Everyday Life', *American Sociological Review*, vol. 42, pp. 854-67.

Heath, C.C. (1978), 'Some Interactional Features of Doctor-Patient Consultations: the Social Organization of Medical Record Cards and Non-Spoken Activity Episodes', PhD thesis, University of Manchester.

Helmer, J. (1970), 'The Face of the Man Without Qualities', *Social Research*, vol. 37, pp.547-79.

Hilliard, R., Rayner, C. and Silverman, D. (1977), 'The "Patient-Centred" Model in a Hospital Setting: A Pilot Study of a Paediatric Cardiology Unit', Mimeo, Goldsmiths' College, London [See special issue of *Sociology of Health and Illness*, vol. 3 (1981), pp. 251-336].

Horobin, G. (1978), 'The Impossibility of General Practice', paper given at Scottish Branch Meeting of BSA Medical Sociology Group, Dundee.

Illich, I. (1975), *Medical Nemesis: The Expropriation of Health*, Calder and Boyars, London.

Janeway, C.A. (1974), 'Family Medicine - Fad or for Real', *New England Journal of Medicine*, vol. 291 (7, 15 August), pp. 337-43.

Jeffrey, R. (1974), 'Natural Rubbish: Deviant Patients in Casualty Departments', Paper Given At National Deviancy Conference on Medical Ideologies, Bath. [Published as '"Normal Rubbish": Deviant Patients in Casualty Departments', *Sociology of Health and Illness*, vol. 1(1979), pp.90-107].

Jewson, N.D. (1974), 'Medical Knowledge and the Patronage System in 18th Century England', *Sociology*, vol. 8, pp.369-85.

Johnson, T. (1972), *Professions and Power*, Macmillan, London.

Ley, P. and Spelman, M.S. (1967), *Communication with the Patient*, Staples Press, London.

Lofland, J. (1976), *Doing Social Life: The Qualitative Study of Human Interaction in Natural Settings*, Wiley, London.

McDonald, E.B. and Patel, A.R. (1975), 'Attitudes Towards Alcoholism', *British Medical Journal*, 2 May, pp.430-1.

Macintyre, S. (1976), 'Who Wants Babies? - the Social Construction of Instincts', in D.L .Barker and S. Allen (eds), *Sexual Divisions and Society: Process and Change*, Tavistock, London, pp.150-73.

Macintyre, S. (1977), *Single and Pregnant*, Croom Helm, London.

Mechanic, D. (1971), 'The English National Health Service: Some Comparisons with the United States', *Journal of Health and Social Behaviour*, vol. 12, pp.18-29.

Navarro, V. (1977), 'Social Class, Political Power, and the State; Their Implications in Medicine', *International Journal of Health Services*, vol.7, pp.254-92.

Parsons, T. (1951), *The Social System*, Routledge & Kegan Paul, London.

Phillips, D.L. (1971), *Knowledge From What - Methods in Social Research*, Rand McNally, Chicago.

Piliavin, I. and Briar, S. (1964), 'Police Encounters with Juveniles', *American Journal of Sociology*, vol. 69, pp.206-14.

Poggi, G. (1977), 'The Constitutional State of the 19th Century: An Elementary Conceptual Portrait', *Sociology*, vol. 11, pp.311-32.

Robinson, W. (1951), The Logical Structure of Analytical Induction, *American Sociological Review*, vol. 16, pp.812-18.

Roth, J. A. (1963), *Timetables - Structuring the Passage of Time in Hospital Treatment and Other Careers*, Bobbs-Merrill, Indianapolis.

Roth, J.A. (1975), 'The Treatment of the Sick', in J. Kosa and I.K. Zola (eds), *Poverty and Health: A Sociological Analysis*, Harvard University Press, Cambridge, MA, pp.214-43.

Roth, J.A. (1977), 'A Yank in the NHS', in A.G. Davis and G. Horobin (eds), *Medical Encounters*, Croom Helm, London, pp.191-205.

Scheff, T. (1968), 'Negotiating Reality: Notes on Power in the Assessment of Responsibility', *Social Problems*, vol. 16, pp.3-17.

Sontag, S. (1978), *Illness As Metaphor*, Farrar, Strauss and Giroux, New York.

Sorokin, P. (1956), *Fads and Foibles in Modern Sociology*, Henry Regnery, Chicago.

Stimson, G.V. (1977), 'Social Care and the Role of the General Practitioner', *Social Science and Medicine*, vol. 11, pp.485-90.

Stimson, G.V. (1978), 'Treatment Or Control? Dilemmas for Staff in Drug Dependency Clinics', in D.J. West (ed.), *Problems of Drug Abuse in Britain*, Cambridge University Press, Cambridge, UK.

Stimson, G.V. and Webb, B. (1975), *Going to See the Doctor*, Routledge & Kegan

Paul, London.

Strong, P.M. (1977a), 'Medical Errands', in A.G. Davis and G. Horobin (eds), *Medical Encounters*, Croom Helm, London. pp.38-54.

Strong, P.M. (1977b), 'Alcoholics, the Sick Role and Bourgeois Medicine', Mimeo.

Strong, P.M. (1979), 'Sociological Imperialism and the Profession of Medicine: A Critical Examination of the Thesis of Medical Imperialism', *Social Science and Medicine*, vol.13a, pp.199-215.

Strong, P.M. (1980), Doctors and Dirty Work: the Case of Alcoholism, *Sociology of Health and Illness*, vol. 2, pp.24-47.

Strong, P.M. and Davis, A.G. (1977), 'Roles, Role Formats and Medical Encounters: A Cross-cultural Analysis of Staff-Patient Relationships in Children's Clinics', *Sociological Review*, vol. 25, pp.775-800.

Strong, P.M. and Davis, A.G. (1978), 'Who's Who in Paediatric Encounters: Morality, Expertise and the Generation of Identity and Action in Medical Settings', in A.G. Davis (ed.), *Relations Between Doctors and Patients*, Saxon House, London, pp.48-75.

Strong, P.M. and May, D.R. (1980), 'Sociological Concepts of Childhood', in R.G. Mitchell (ed.), *Child Health in the Community*, Second Edition, Churchill Livingstone, London.

Sudnow, D. (1967), *Passing On: the Social Organization of Dying*, Prentice-hall, New Jersey.

Sudnow, D. (1972), 'Temporal Parameters of Interpersonal Observation', in D. Sudnow (ed), *Studies in Social Interaction*, Free Press, New York, pp.259-79.

Turner, R. (1972), 'Some Formal Properties of Therapy Talk', in D. Sudnow (ed), *Studies in Social Interaction*, Free Press, New York, pp.367-96.

Voysey, M. (1975), *A Constant Burden*, Routledge & Kegan Paul, London.

Waitzkin, H.K. and Waterman, B. (1974), *The Exploitation of Illness in Capitalist Society*, Bobbs-Merrill, Indianapolis.

Weinstein, E. (1966), 'Towards A Theory of Interpersonal Tactics', in C. Backman and P.Secord (eds), *Problems in Social Psychology*, McGraw-Hill, New York, pp.394-5.

Weinstein, E. (1969), 'The Development of Interpersonal Competence', in D. Goslin (ed.), *A Handbook of Socialization Theory and Research*, Rand McNally, Chicago, pp.753-75.

Weinstein, E. and Deutschberger, P. (1964), 'Tasks, Bargains and Identities in Social Interaction', *Social Forces*, vol.42, pp.451-6.

Wenglinsky, M. (1973), 'Errands', in A. Birenbaum and E. Sagarin (eds), *People in Places: the Sociology of the Familiar*, Nelson, London, pp.83-100.

Werthman, C. (1969), 'Delinquency and Moral Character', in D. Cressey and D. Ward (eds), *Delinquency, Crime and Social Process*, Harper and Row, New York, pp.613-22.

Additional References to 2001 Foreword

Goffman, E. (1983) 'Felicity's Condition', *American Journal of Sociology*, vol. 89, pp. 1-53.

Maynard, D. W. (1996) 'On"realization" in everyday life: The forecasting of bad news as a social relation', *American Sociological Review*, vol. 61, pp. 109-31.

Strong, P.M. (1988) 'Minor Courtesies and Macro Structures', in P. Drew and A. Wootton (eds), *Erving Goffman: Exploring the Interaction Order*, Polity Press, Cambridge.

Strong, P.M. and Robinson, J. (1990). *The NHS Under New Management*, Open University Press, Milton Keynes.

Index